Multidimensional Ranking

HIGHER EDUCATION DYNAMICS

VOLUME 37

Series Editor
Peter Maassen, *University of Oslo, Norway, and University of Twente, Enschede, The Netherlands*
Johan Müller, *Graduate School of Humanities, University of Cape Town, Rondebosch, South Africa*

Editorial Board
Alberto Amaral, *CIPES and Universidade do Porto, Portugal*
Akira Arimoto, *Hiroshima University, Japan*
Nico Cloete, *CHET, Pretoria, South Africa*
David Dill, *University of North Carolina at Chapel Hill, USA*
Jürgen Enders, *University of Twente, Enschede, The Netherlands*
Patricia Gumport, *Stanford University, USA*
Mary Henkel, *Brunel University, Uxbridge, United Kingdom*
Glen Jones, *University of Toronto, Canada*

SCOPE OF THE SERIES

Higher Education Dynamics is a bookseries intending to study adaptation processes and their outcomes in higher education at all relevant levels. In addition it wants to examine the way interactions between these levels affect adaptation processes. It aims at applying general social science concepts and theories as well as testing theories in the field of higher education research. It wants to do so in a manner that is of relevance to all those professionally involved in higher education, be it as ministers, policy-makers, politicians, institutional leaders or administrators, higher education researchers, members of the academic staff of universities and colleges, or students. It will include both mature and developing systems of higher education, covering public as well as private institutions.

For further volumes:
http://www.springer.com/series/6037

Frans A. van Vught • Frank Ziegele
Editors

Multidimensional Ranking

The Design and Development of U-Multirank

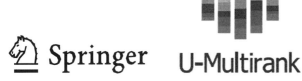

Editors
Frans A. van Vught　　　　　　　Frank Ziegele
University of Twente　　　　　　Centre for Higher Education (CHE)
Enschede, The Netherlands　　　Gütersloh, Germany

ISSN 1571-0378
ISBN 978-94-007-3004-5　　　e-ISBN 978-94-007-3005-2
DOI 10.1007/978-94-007-3005-2
Springer Dordrecht Heidelberg London New York

Library of Congress Control Number: 2012933115

© Springer Science+Business Media B.V. 2012
No part of this work may be reproduced, stored in a retrieval system, or transmitted in any form or by any means, electronic, mechanical, photocopying, microfilming, recording or otherwise, without written permission from the Publisher, with the exception of any material supplied specifically for the purpose of being entered and executed on a computer system, for exclusive use by the purchaser of the work.

Printed on acid-free paper

Springer is part of Springer Science+Business Media (www.springer.com)

Preface

This book is the result of an intensive two-year research project focused on the design and testing of a new, globally applicable ranking tool for higher education and research. This project was initiated by the European Commission and undertaken by an international consortium of research groups working together as the Consortium for Higher Education and Research Performance Assessment (CHERPA): Centre for Higher Education (CHE, Germany), Center for Higher Education Policy Studies (CHEPS, The Netherlands), International Centre for Studies in Entrepreneurship and Innovation Management (INCENTIM, Belgium), Centre for Science and Technology Studies (CWTS, The Netherlands) and l'Observatoire des Sciences et Techniques (OST, France). The project resulted in a final report to the European Commission on the feasibility of a new ranking instrument called U-Multirank. This report *'U-Multirank: Designing and Testing the Feasibility of a Multidimensional Global University Ranking'* is available on the website of the European Commission: http://ec.europa.eu/education/higher-education/doc/multirank_en.pdf

As the international debate on rankings in higher education and research continues, we thought it worthwhile to also publish a volume that addresses the major issues concerning ranking in higher education and research, and that sets the new multidimensional ranking tool (U-Multirank) within a broader context. This book (in Part I) discusses and analyzes the many current ranking practices and methodologies and introduces (in Part II) our own approach: a multidimensional and user-driven ranking methodology.

This book has been written by a team of authors all of whom participated in the U-Multirank project. The full project team was Maarja Beerkens (CHEPS), Sonja Berghoff (CHE), Uwe Brandenburg (CHE), Julie Callaert (INCENTIM), Koenraad Debackere (INCENTIM), Elisabeth Epping (CHEPS), Gero Federkeil (CHE), Jon File (CHEPS), Ghislaine Filliatreau (OST), Wolfgang Glänzel (INCENTIM), Ben Jongbloed (CHEPS), Frans Kaiser (CHEPS), Bart van Looy (INCENTIM), Suzy Ramanana-Rahary (OST), Isabel Roessler (CHE), Françoise Rojouan (OST), Robert Tijssen (CWTS), Philippe Vidal (OST), Martijn Visser (CWTS), Frans A. van Vught (CHEPS, project leader), Don F. Westerheijden (CHEPS), Erik van Wijk (CWTS), Frank Ziegele (CHE, project leader), and Michel Zitt (OST).

In addition the project team was greatly assisted by an Advisory Board and an international expert panel. The members of the Advisory Board constituted by the European Commission were: Kurt Deketelaere, League of European Research Universities (LERU); Henning Detleff, Business Europe; Christian Hemmestad Bjerke, European Students' Union (ESU); Marlies Leegwater, Bologna Secretariat; Howard Newby, University of Liverpool/European University Association (EUA); Viorel Proteasa, Bologna Follow up Group (BFUG); Dragan Stojanovski, European Students Forum (AEGEE); Richard Thorn, European Association of Institutions in Higher Education (EURASHE); Karine Tremblay, Organisation for Economic Cooperation and Development, (OECD); Isabel Turmaine, International Association of Universities (IAU); Noel Vercruysse, BFUG; Henrik Wolff, European Network for Universities of Applied Science (UASNET); Richard Yelland, OECD; Adam Tyson, Robin van IJperen, Richard Deiss, Sophia Eriksson, Endika Bengoetxea, Barbara Nolan, Margaret Waters (all European Commission/Education and Culture); and Peter Whitten, European Commission/Research and Innovation.

The international expert panel consisted of: Nian Cai Liu, Shanghai Jiao Tong University; Simon Marginson, Melbourne University; Jamil Salmi, World Bank; Alex Usher, International Observatory on Academic Ranking and Excellence (IREG); Marijk van der Wende, OECD/Institutional Management in Higher Education (IMHE); Cun-Mei Zhao, Carnegie Foundation.

Interested and committed stakeholder representatives were crucial to the processes of designing and testing the new transparency tool. Over the life of the project the project team met regularly with stakeholders, who provided vital input on the relevance of potential performance indicators and dimensions, on methods of presenting the ranking outcomes and on different models for implementing the new ranking tool. The CHERPA project team is grateful to all of these stakeholders, both individuals and organizations, for investing their time and energy in the development of U-Multirank.

The U-Multirank project was undertaken by CHERPA under contract for the European Commission. The intellectual property rights to the material relating to this project belong to the European Commission and are used in this book with its express permission. This book reflects the views of its authors and the European Commission cannot be held responsible for any use made of the information contained herein.

The authors would like to take this opportunity to thank those involved in the language editing and layout of this book, in particular Karin van der Tuin-Wagenvoort, Ingrid van der Schoor and Rose-Marie Barbeau, without whose commitment and hard work this book would not have been produced.

For more information on U-Multirank, please see: www.u-multirank.eu

Frans A. van Vught
Frank Ziegele

Contents

1 **Introduction: Towards a New Ranking Approach in Higher Education and Research** 1
Frans A. van Vught, Don F. Westerheijden, and Frank Ziegele

Part I Multidimensional Ranking

2 **Transparency, Quality and Accountability** 11
Frans A. van Vught and Don F. Westerheijden

3 **Classifications and Rankings** 25
Gero Federkeil, Frans A. van Vught, and Don F. Westerheijden

4 **An Evaluation and Critique of Current Rankings** 39
Gero Federkeil, Frans A. van Vught, and Don F. Westerheijden

5 **Impact of Rankings** 71
Frans A. van Vught and Don F. Westerheijden

Part II U-Multirank

6 **Background and Design** 85
Gero Federkeil, Frans Kaiser, Frans A. van Vught,
and Don F. Westerheijden

7 **Dimensions and Indicators** 97
Gero Federkeil, Ben Jongbloed, Frans Kaiser,
and Don F. Westerheijden

8 **Data Collection** 125
Julie Callaert, Elisabeth Epping, Gero Federkeil, Ben Jongbloed,
Frans Kaiser, and Robert Tijssen

9	**The Pilot Test and Its Outcomes**	135
	Julie Callaert, Elisabeth Epping, Gero Federkeil, Jon File,	
	Ben Jongbloed, Frans Kaiser, Isabel Roessler, Robert Tijssen,	
	Frans A. van Vught, and Frank Ziegele	
10	**An Interactive Multidimensional Ranking Web Tool**	167
	Gero Federkeil, Jon File, Frans Kaiser, Frans A. van Vught,	
	and Frank Ziegele	
11	**Concluding Remarks**	179
	Frans A. van Vught and Frank Ziegele	

Index 191

Contributors

Julie Callaert is a senior researcher at the Center for Research & Development Monitoring (ECOOM) at the Catholic University of Leuven (Belgium) where she studies innovation, science and technology indicators with a focus on patent-related indicators and technometrics. After receiving her degree in Industrial Psychology from the Catholic University of Leuven in 2001, she began working as a researcher in the university's Department of Applied Economics. In this role, she participated in a European framework project on the identification of centres of scientific excellence. In 2009, Julie Callaert completed her Ph.D. studies, for which she was awarded a grant from the Intercollegiate Centre for Management Science, Belgium. For her doctoral thesis, she examined the complexity of combining scientific and technology development activities in academic environments. She spent one year as a visiting Ph.D. student at the Ecole Polytechnique Fédérale de Lausanne, where she studied mechanisms for combining the production and valorisation of academic research.

Elisabeth Epping holds a Master's degree from the University of Twente, where she studied Public Administration. She graduated in 2010, writing her Master's thesis on the internationalization processes of higher education. She joined the Center for Higher Education Policy Studies in autumn 2010. Her research activities include the U-Multirank project of which Elisabeth was project secretary. In addition she is part of a research team studying the impact of quality assurance in cross-border quality and on a project identifying barriers to promoting European standards and guidelines for quality assurance at institutional levels.

Gero Federkeil is Project Manager at the Centre for Higher Education (CHE) in Gütersloh, Germany. He is responsible for ranking and international ranking activities at CHE, including U-Multirank. In Germany he is a member of the Association of Evaluation. In October 2009, he was elected Vice-President of IREG Observatory on Academic Ranking and Excellence. Gero Federkeil is an internationally recognized expert in the field of rankings. His main fields of work and publication include rankings, performance indicators, benchmarking, quality assurance and issues of employability/university-labor market relations. Before joining the CHE in 2000, he worked for the German Council of Science and Humanities for seven years in the fields of higher education policy, the labor market and higher education, investments in higher education, evaluation and university medicine. He holds a Master's Degree in Sociology (1989) from Bielefeld University.

Jon File holds a first-class Honours degree in Sociology from the University of Cape Town. He was Academic Secretary at the University of Cape Town between 1987 and 1997 and a member of the 13-person National Commission on Higher Education (1995/1996) appointed by the new South African government to put forward proposals for the transformation of higher education. He joined CHEPS as Director of Development and Consultancy in 1998 and served as Executive Director from 2004 to 2009. Jon File's major project involvement is in policy-oriented and development projects. He has been project leader on ten extensive capacity development projects, at institutional and system levels, in South Africa, Ethiopia, Uganda and Mozambique. He has also been co-manager for six European Commission projects in higher education policy, including U-Multirank, and served as a member of the OECD review teams for higher education in the Czech Republic and Portugal. Since 2009 he has been a (Visiting) Senior Fellow of the L.H. Martin Institute for Higher Education Leadership and Management at the University of Melbourne, Australia. His current interests are comparative perspectives on the effects of government policies on higher education institutions; planning at institutional and system levels; higher education reform in the context of major socio-political transformation; and the development of higher education leaders and managers through education and training programmes.

Ben Jongbloed holds a Master's degree in Econometrics from the University of Groningen and a Ph.D. in Public Administration (Public Finance) from the University of Twente. Since starting to work for CHEPS at the University of Twente in 1992, his research and scholarly publications have focused in particular on governance and resource allocation issues in higher education. His work addresses topics such as funding methodologies for higher education, performance measurement in higher education, and university-industry collaboration. In 2004, he was one of the authors of the Kluwer publication *Markets in Higher Education: Rhetoric or Reality?* He has worked on several international research projects funded by the European Commission, including a recent (2010) study of governance and funding reforms in European higher education.

Frans Kaiser is senior research associate at CHEPS. His background is in public administration and he has two decades of experience in comparative studies in higher education, both from a qualitative and a quantitative perspective. Frans Kaiser is an expert in comparison of international higher education systems and policies as well as in the design and use of indicators for international comparison and has conducted several studies and projects on comparative issues and indicators in higher education, including the U-Map project.

Isabel Roessler is project manager at the Centre for Higher Education (CHE) in Germany. She studied social sciences with a main focus on business and political science and has been working for more than 5 years in the area of higher education research. At CHE Isabel Roessler works on the university ranking project and supports the faculties during data collection and analysis. She is responsible for designing a ranking of Master's programs within the CHE University Ranking. In addition she also works on international projects at CHE within a broader ranking context.

Robert Tijssen has a professorial chair in Science and Innovation Studies at Leiden University. He is also Visiting Professor at Stellenbosch University (South Africa) and associate adjunct professor at the University of Queensland (Australia). He is a Board member of the European Network of Indicators Designers (ENID) and a member of the Netherlands Graduate School on Science, Technology and Modern Culture (WTMC). A large part of his current research is devoted to quantitative empirical studies of structures and dynamics within science and innovation systems, focusing on institutional and geographical dimensions. Robert has more than 20 years of experience in consultancy work and commissioned studies for clients in the public and private sector worldwide, mainly on the measurement, assessment, monitoring and evaluation of scientific research performance – either the level of individual organizations, or at the meta-level of science systems, higher education systems or innovation systems.

Frans A. van Vught is a high-level expert and advisor at the European Commission. In addition he is president of the European Center for Strategic Management of Universities (Esmu), president of the Netherlands House for Education and Research (Nether), and member of the board of the European Institute of Technology Foundation (EITF), all in Brussels. He was president and Rector of the University of Twente, the Netherlands (1997–2005). He was the founding director of the Center for Higher Education Policy Studies (CHEPS) and has been a higher education researcher for most of his life. He has published widely in this field and in various languages. His many international functions include the memberships of the University Grants Committee of Hong Kong, the board of the European University Association (EUA) (2005–2009), the German 'Akkreditierungsrat' (2005–2009) and of the L.H. Martin Institute for Higher Education Leadership and Management in Australia. van Vught is a sought-after international speaker, a member of the editorial board of several international journals and has been a consultant to many international organizations, national governments and higher education institutions all over the world. He was one of the leaders of the U-Multirank pilot project. He is Honorary Professor at the University of Twente and at the University of Melbourne and holds several honorary doctorates.

Don F. Westerheijden graduated from the Faculty of Public Administration and Public Policy at the University of Twente in 1984 and subsequently completed his dissertation there, on political and bureaucratic decision-making, in 1988. Since then he has worked at CHEPS, where he coordinates research related to Quality Management. He is also involved in supervision of Ph.D. candidates at CHEPS. He has edited and contributed to books on quality assessment in higher education, and produced a number of articles on the topic. In addition, he is a member of the editorial boards of several journals which address quality in higher education. Don has been involved in self-evaluation and external quality assessment processes in many countries, from Holland to Hong Kong. He also advises on, formulates and evaluates quality assurance policies for higher education institutions, national governments and international agencies.

Frank Ziegele is director of the CHE (Centre for Higher Education) in Gütersloh, Germany, and professor of higher education and research management at the University of Applied Sciences Osnabrück, leading an MBA programme in higher education management. He trained as an economist and his research and publications focus on higher education finance, governance, strategic management, contract management and ranking. He has contributed some 100 publications to the field of higher education policy and management and delivered more than 80 projects in higher education reform and research. He is an editorial board member of the journals *Wissenschaftsmanagement* and *Higher Education Management and Policy* and was member of the executive board of the Gesellschaft für Hochschulforschung (the German society for higher education research). He was one of the leaders of the U-Multirank project.

Chapter 1
Introduction: Towards a New Ranking Approach in Higher Education and Research

Frans A. van Vught, Don F. Westerheijden, and Frank Ziegele

1.1 Introduction

League tables are all around us. In sports, for instance, there are seasonal league tables for baseball or football competition and lists ranking the number of times cyclists have won the Tour de France or the fastest runners in marathons, etc. Since the early twenty-first century we have also had league tables in higher education and research, global university rankings usually showing Harvard as the best university in the world, followed by the names of a number of other globally renowned universities. But while sporting league tables are well-accepted, university rankings remain hotly debated. Later in this book we will go into greater detail about the methodological critique of university league tables. This chapter briefly introduces three basic ideas that we will elaborate in more detail in the rest of this volume and which together define our 'new' approach to ranking in higher education and research:

- 'user-driven' rankings
- multidimensionality and multileveledness
- a participative approach to ranking

We start with our epistemological position. The more we engaged in the ranking debate, the more we realized that there is a deep, epistemological reason why the

F.A. van Vught (✉)
University of Twente, Enschede, The Netherlands

D.F. Westerheijden
Center for Higher Education Policy Studies, University of Twente,
Enschede, The Netherlands

F. Ziegele
Centre for Higher Education, Gütersloh, Germany

whole idea of league tables is wrong, and why transparency tools or rankings of higher education and research institutions can only be user-driven, adaptable to users' needs.

1.2 An Epistemological Argument

Each and every observation of reality is theory-driven: every observation of a slice of reality is driven by the conceptual framework that we use. In the scientific debate, this statement has been accepted at least since Popper's work (Popper, 1980): he showed abundantly that theories are 'searchlights' that cannot encompass all of reality, but necessarily highlight only certain aspects of it. He also showed that scientific knowledge is 'common sense writ large' (Popper, 1980, p. 22), meaning that the demarcation between common sense and scientific knowledge is that the latter has to be justified rationally: scientific theories are logically coherent sets of statements, which moreover are testable to show if they are consistent with the facts.

Failing scientific theories, sports have been organized with (democratic) forums that have been accepted as the bodies authorized to set rules. The conceptual frameworks behind sports league tables are well-established: the rules of the game define the winners and create leagues table from the results. Yet those rules have been designed by humans and may be subject to change: in the 1980s–1990s football associations went from awarding two points for winning a match to three points, changing the tactics in the game (more attacks late in a drawn match), changing the league table outcomes to some extent, and sparking off debates among commentators of the sport for and against the new rule.[1] Commentators also debate the meaning of Tour de France winners' lists: the route of the Tour changes from year to year, so is winning the Tour in year x an achievement equal to that of winning in year y? Similarly, marathons are run on different courses which offer different chances of scoring a world record time—some courses (ironically including the original Marathon-to-Athens route) do not even qualify according to the rules for official marathon record times and fast times run on these courses are not recognized.[2]

This disquisition into sports illustrates the lighter side of our epistemological point about university rankings. All rankings are made up of selected 'indicators' that imply the conceptual framework through which reality is addressed. There is a body in charge of choosing those 'indicators'. In sports, such bodies are recognized organizations and it is accepted that they design and redefine the rules of the game, including the indicators. It is equally understood that rules and indicators are not derived scientifically but are artificial: rugby and football are different and it is impossible to say whether the number one rugby team is a better sports team than

---

[1] http://en.wikipedia.org/wiki/Three_points_for_a_win
[2] http://www.nytimes.com/2011/04/19/sports/19marathon.html

1 Introduction: Towards a New Ranking Approach in Higher Education and Research

the number one football team. Because there is no such thing as a theory of sports *per se*. There are theories about sport psychology, sports training or sports fans' behavior, but not a scientific theory of 'best' sport.

In university rankings, the rules of the ranking game are equally arbitrary, because there is no scientific theory of 'the best university', nor even of quality of higher education. But unlike sports, there are no officially recognized bodies that are accepted as having the authority to define the rules of the game, nor is there an explicit understanding that different conceptual frameworks (hence different indicators) define different competitions and hence validly different but incomparable rankings. There is no understanding, in other words, that e.g. the Shanghai ranking is simply a game that is as different from the *Times Higher* ranking game as rugby is from football. Equally, there is no understanding that the organization making up one set of rules and indicators has no more authority than any other to define a particular set of rules and indicators.

The issue with the usual university rankings is that they tend to be presented as if their collection of indicators reflects *the* definitive quality of the institution; they have the pretension, in that sense, of being guided by what is in reality a nonexistent theory of the quality of higher education.

We do not accept that position. Rather than assume an unwarranted position of authority we want to reflect critically on the different roles of higher education and research institutions vis-à-vis different groups of stakeholders, to define explicitly our conceptual frameworks regarding the differing functions of higher education institutions, and to derive sets of indicators from the conceptual framework together with input from the relevant stakeholders. Finally, we would present the information encapsulated in those indicators in such a transparent way that the end-users of rankings can make their own decisions about what is best for their purpose(s), resulting in individually tailored and time-dependent rankings.

In this sense, we want to 'democratize' rankings in higher education and research. Based on the epistemological position that any choice of sets of indicators is driven by their makers' conceptual frameworks, we suggest a user-driven approach to rankings. Users and stakeholders themselves should be able to decide which indicators they want to select to create rankings that are relevant to their purposes.

1.3 Multiple Dimensions and Multiple Levels

A second basic principle behind our departure from current practices in international rankings of higher education and research institutions concerns multidimensionality. It is only a slight overstatement to say that current international rankings are focused on a single dimension of the activities of the institutions, viz. research. The bulk of indicators used in those rankings, as we will show in Chaps. 3 and 4, concern research output (publications), research impact (citations) and research reception by the academic community (citations, Nobel prizes). We will also argue that reputation of higher education institutions as measured in international surveys also measures research renown—if it measures anything specific. The main reason the majority of current international rankings focus on research indicators lies in their availability: publication and citation databases already exist and are relatively easily transformed into league tables.

The two main shortcomings of that approach are interconnected. The first and main point is that higher education and research institutions engage in activities other than just research, and see their mission resting partly in those other activities as well (meaning that these other activities are not accidental or unimportant). Historically, going back to their medieval beginnings, education was the first mission of universities. Science and research became a central mission of universities only with the rise of the German research university in the nineteenth century. Since around that time, other categories of higher education institution were introduced to maintain a special focus on education, such as the *Grandes Écoles* in France and the subsequent rise of *polytechniques*/polytechnics in other countries. At the same time, the learned societies or academies expanded into specialized research institutions. More recently, explicit attention is also given to the 'third mission' of higher education and research institutions, variously defined as knowledge transfer and as engagement with the regional community of the institution. A good ranking must take those different missions into account, and must reflect the different portfolios of individual institutions in those areas. The way to do this would seem to be to offer a wide selection of indicators, covering the different mission elements: research, education and third mission. This differs from the way in which some current global rankings have adapted their methodology, i.e. to allow users to choose one indicator out of their research-oriented composite indicator. That amounts to 'subdimensionality' rather than multidimensionality.

The other, associated shortcoming is that different stakeholders (students, parents, employers, policy makers, institutional leaders etc.) are interested in, and need to take decisions about, different activities. Prospective students are the most pertinent example, as many rankings publicly claim to be aimed at assisting students and prospective students to find the best place to study. Future students would be interested in information about 'what they will get' if they invest considerable amounts of time, money and intellectual effort in a certain study program, so clearly information about the education offered by specific study programs. The link between research and education has been debated for a long time in the higher education literature, but whatever the answer, it is clear that there is not an automatic, deterministic and positive relationship between indicators of research output and the student learning experience. Good rankings must include education indicators for prospective students. Similar lines of arguments can be developed for other groups of stakeholders: each needs specific information on one or more of the mission elements of higher education and research institutions and is not served well by a standard set of research-oriented indicators only.

More or less hidden in the statement that prospective students want information 'about education in a certain study program' is the issue of multiple levels. Students will experience certain study programs, not the whole institution—especially in large, comprehensive higher education institutions and if study programs are offered as specialized paths. Similarly, other stakeholders may be interested in the performances of specific research groups or specific training programs rather than in the performance of an institution as a whole. There is a need, accordingly, for rankings focused at this level of (disciplinary or multidisciplinary) 'fields'. There is a need for field-based rankings alongside the institutional rankings that appear to be of prime interest to institutional management, political decision-making, etc.

1.4 A Participative Approach

Discussions about the quality and effects of rankings often focus on the selection and operationalization of indicators and their weights. The choice and construction of indicators is a crucial issue, but it is not the only one. Each ranking's quality is also determined by its underlying processes of data collection, data quality control, etc. For these processes, the interaction of ranking institution with their stakeholders and higher education and research institutions is crucial, we argue. Let us define as 'stakeholders' all the different groups interested in a ranking: students, parents, university leaders and management, academics, employers, policy makers, and the general public.

Looking at existing rankings we find that the depth of stakeholder involvement varies considerably. We intend to contrast our approach with the current global rankings, which are the archetypal object of public discussions. We will show in detail in Chaps. 3 and 4 that those international rankings are mainly based on publicly available, often bibliometric, data, and use indicator weights determined by the rankers themselves. The institutions that produce such rankings apparently do not need intensive stakeholder input to do so.[3] In our concept of user-driven, multidimensional rankings, stakeholder involvement plays a crucial role in the whole process from conceptualization to presentation of the ranking. In this sense our ranking methodology implies a participative approach.

Three arguments highlight the important role of stakeholder involvement. First, let us assume that a specific ranking tool uses indicators which are perfectly designed; they are reliable, valid, comparable and available in the international context. However, it is still not guaranteed that this hypothetical methodologically correct ranking really is useful for potential users. The risk is that the resulting ranking

---

[3] It should be acknowledged, however, that the *THE* went through an extensive process of (online) user consultation when revising its methodology in 2010.

would not be relevant for its users, because it is not related to the decisions and choices users intend to support by use of the ranking. A fundamental principle in formulating a ranking and indicator system should be to test its relevance against stakeholder needs from the initial design phase. In a user-driven ranking the purpose of its design should be to identify a broad set of indicators related to the needs of the relevant stakeholder groups, through stakeholder workshops or online surveys. Moreover, stakeholders can also be offered the opportunity in later phases to assess the usefulness of the resulting ranking system, which can influence amendments in the design.

A second argument concerns the difference between the customary unidimensional rankings and our multidimensional approach. Multidimensional rankings are more complex than a single composite ranking. More effort is needed to explain to the users how multidimensional rankings can be used in a meaningful manner. User-friendliness thus becomes an important feature of a good multidimensional ranking. But user-friendliness cannot be achieved without stakeholder consultation to indicate what makes a ranking understandable and relevant to users. User-friendliness will mean different things to different stakeholder groups; a 'lay' user such as a prospective student, confronted with the intricacies of higher education for the first time, may need more and other explanations than a university president. In an intensive dialogue process adequate ranking presentation modes will have to be discussed with the stakeholders.

A third important argument in favor of stakeholder involvement is the consultation of field experts in the case of a field-based ranking (i.e. a ranking of a specific field of knowledge rather than of the whole institution). The challenge of field-based rankings is to adapt data collection instruments and indicators to the specific situation of the respective field. Since the development of most fields in the knowledge society is highly dynamic, one can only benefit from the virtues of field-based ranking if the model and indicators are regularly discussed with field experts. Rankings, and not only those that are field-based, need a continuous advisory structure to adapt the ranking methodology to ongoing developments in the higher education and research system. Good rankings have to implement a continuous process of stakeholder consultation, not only in the design phase but in the implementation phase as well.

These arguments demonstrate that stakeholder consultation should not be regarded as merely a formal element of legitimization. Stakeholders' input is needed, must be taken seriously and must be integrated systematically in the processes of designing, producing and implementing rankings. Of course the responsibility for the methodology and results of a ranking cannot be shifted to stakeholders; responsibility always rests with those producing a ranking.

The points outlined in the previous sections require further explanation, which we will present extensively in Part I of this book. We simply wanted to establish from the outset our position concerning rankings, and the reasons for developing our user-driven and multidimensional ranking approach.

In Part II we will report on the design and development of a new global ranking tool, based on the basic principles just described. This new ranking tool, called

U-Multirank, was developed and tested during a two-year international project funded by the European Commission. The full report on this project is available, free of charge, on: http://ec.europa.eu/education/higher-education/doc/multirank_en.pdf

Reference

Popper, K. R. (1980). *The logic of scientific discovery* (Rev. ed.). London: Hutchinson.

Part I
Multidimensional Ranking

Chapter 2
Transparency, Quality and Accountability

Frans A. van Vught and Don F. Westerheijden

2.1 Introduction

Major considerations underlying the general interest in international higher education and research rankings are that on the one hand there is an increasing need to obtain valid information on higher education across national borders while on the other hand higher education and research systems are becoming more complex and—at first sight—less intelligible for stakeholders. Ashby's Law of Requisite Variety makes us realize that as higher education systems become more complex so too must our ways of looking at these systems. In other words: if for a simple higher education system all we need to know may be contained in a simple league table, with today's international views on higher education more sophisticated instruments are required to render this complex world more transparent (cf. van Vught, 1993). This is even more the case as the role of higher education in society expands and institutions perform along more dimensions. Consequently, more categories of stakeholders in society come into contact with higher education and research without the 'social capital' of knowing the higher education and research system intimately. Transparency becomes a major issue and it is becoming obvious that the needs for transparency among different stakeholders in higher education are increasingly diverse. In this and the following chapters we intend to develop a 'transparency perspective' on higher education and research. Reinforcing the epistemological reasoning mentioned in Chap. 1, we will argue that transparency tools must be designed to cater for different stakeholders' needs.

F.A. van Vught (✉)
Center for Higher Education Policy Studies, University of Twente, Enschede, The Netherlands

D.F. Westerheijden
Center for Higher Education Policy Studies, University of Twente,
Enschede, The Netherlands

It is widely recognized now that although the current transparency tools—especially university league tables—are controversial, they seem to be here to stay, and that especially global university league tables have a great impact on decision-makers at all levels in all countries, including in universities. They reflect a growing international competition among universities for talent and resources; at the same time they reinforce competition by their very results. On the positive side they urge decision-makers to think bigger and set the bar higher, especially in the research universities that are the main subjects of current global league tables. Yet major concerns remain as to league tables' methodological underpinnings and to their policy impact on stratification rather than on diversification of mission. Governments try to build 'world-class' universities through special funding, stimulating mergers or taking other measures for those universities; some fear that this concentration of effort leads to loss of interest and resources for other parts of higher education systems.

Several target groups (stakeholders) for transparency tools have already been mentioned or implied: policy-makers and leaders of higher education institutions. Quite often, public statements will mention another target group i.e. students and potential students. We will come back later to the issue of target groups.

Besides the epistemological arguments for a user-driven ranking mentioned earlier, there are theoretically-grounded reasons why transparency tools such as rankings are simultaneously more necessary and more debatable in higher education than in an 'average' sector of society. In economic terms, higher education is an *experience good* or maybe even a *credence good*. An experience good is one the quality of which can only be judged after consumption; this is in contrast to the textbook case of 'search goods', i.e. a good whose quality can be judged by consumers in advance. With credence goods, even after consumption consumers do not know the quality of the good (Bonroy & Constantatos, 2008; Dulleck & Kerschbamer, 2006): doctors' consults, computer repairs and education are given as standard examples. Whether or not students really know how good the teaching has been in enhancing their knowledge, skills and other competencies (we may need to distinguish initial from post-initial higher education, in this respect, cf. Westerheijden, 2003), we may safely assume that they cannot know the quality beforehand. Similar arguments can be built for other stakeholders in higher education such as companies, professions and governments. This implies that a principal-agent like asymmetry of information exists, and that is what transparency tools such as quality assurance, classifications, league tables and rankings ought to alleviate in order to maximize the social benefit of higher education.

The objective of this and the following chapters is to develop an overview of existing transparency tools and to study the international literature on classification and ranking to work out implications for the design of the transparency tool that we will present in Part II of this volume. Since '… indicators and league tables are enough to start a discussion … [but] are not sufficient to conclude it' (Saisana & D'Hombres, 2008, p. 8), we will also discuss 'lessons learned' in the area of transparency tools and the standards to be observed in the selection of dimensions/indicators and databases for worldwide institutional classification and focused rankings on the one hand and for field-based rankings on the other.

2.2 Working Definitions

Globalization leads to increasing competitive pressures on higher education institutions, in particular related to their position in global university league tables, i.e. the so-called 'reputation race' (van Vught, 2008), for which their research performance currently is almost exclusively the measure. As we will explain below, existing global league tables implicitly suggest that there is in fact only one model that can have global standing: the large comprehensive research university. This has an adverse effect on diversity since academic and mission drift (isomorphism) can be expected to intensify as a result. Such one-sided competition also jeopardizes the status of universities' activities in other areas, such as undergraduate teaching, knowledge exchange, contributions to regional development, to lifelong learning, etc. and of institutions with different missions and profiles. As a result more *vertical stratification* ('better' or 'worse' prestige or performance) rather than *horizontal diversification* (differences in institutional missions and profiles) can be expected to result from the current league tables (Teichler, 2007). In other words, hierarchy rather than diversity will be enhanced, as specialization and diversification are not generated unless the incentive structure favors this (Marginson & van der Wende, 2007). The creation of transparency tools that make (vertical *and* horizontal) diversity and different forms of excellence transparent rather than obscured, may be a first step towards creating a more diversified incentive structure and thus contributing to maintenance of the—highly valued!—diversity in higher education worldwide.

A number of terms have been introduced now that require at least working definitions. For us, *transparency tool* is the most encompassing term, including all the others; it denotes all manner of providing insight into the diversity of higher education. Transparency tools are instruments that aim to provide information to stakeholders about the efforts and performance of higher education and research institutions.

A *classification* is a systematic, nominal distribution among a number of classes or characteristics without any (intended) order of preference. Classifications give descriptive categorizations of characteristics intending to focus on the efforts and activities of higher education and research institutions, according to the criterion of similarity. They are eminently suited to address horizontal diversity.

Rankings are instruments to display vertical diversity in terms of performance by using quantitative indicators. In general terms rankings are hierarchical categorizations intended to render the outputs of the higher education and research institutions according to criterion of best performance. Most existing rankings in higher education take the form of a league table. A *league table* is a single-dimensional, ordinal list going from 'best' to 'worst', assigning to the entities unique, discrete positions seemingly equidistant from each other (from 1 to, e.g., 500). There are other approaches to ranking using a multidimensional framework and sorting institutions in groups instead of league tables. We want to distinguish such rankings from league tables as being the better, more sophisticated instruments.

Our point here is that readers need not see a ranking as inherently bad, although bad ones do exist.[1]

Quality assurance is mentioned in this context because evaluation or accreditation processes also produce some information to stakeholders (review reports, accreditation status) and in that sense help to achieve transparency. As the information function of quality assurance is not very extended (more in Sects. 2.3 and 2.3.2, below) and as quality assurance is too ubiquitous to allow for an overview on a global scale in this book, in the following we will focus on classifications and rankings. Let us underline here, however, that rankings and classifications on the one hand and quality assurance on the other play complementary roles.

2.3 Quality Assurance

For historical reasons we begin our overview of the types of information delivered by transparency instruments with quality assurance. In the following chapters we will more specifically focus on classifications and rankings.

Internal and external quality assurance as introduced in many countries in the 1980s and 1990s was, seen from our perspective of transparency, the first major effort to publish information on the quality of higher education. But this transparency perspective differs from the usual contemporary policy debates on quality assurance, which emphasize the contrasting pair of accountability and quality enhancement. The transparency function of quality assurance has so far been an additional or secondary aim at best. Let us nevertheless investigate what the different quality assurance instruments can contribute to transparency instruments, because they are well established in many higher education and research systems.

2.3.1 Information Offered by Quality Assurance in Research: Peer Review, Bibliometrics and Practical Research Assessment

2.3.1.1 Peer Review and Performance Indicators

Peer review has grown out of networks of correspondence by letters among gentlemen-scientists in the middle of the seventeenth century. Henry Oldenburg, secretary of the British Royal Society, has been credited with the innovation, made in order to

---

[1] A complication is that 'ranking' may be a noun or a verb, while there is no corresponding verb for 'league table'; some confusion in our use of verbs may be unavoidable.

ensure the quality (i.e. truthfulness and originality) of the Royal Society's *Proceedings* (Boas Hall, 2002). It began, then, as gentlemen-scientists reading other gentlemen-scientists' manuscripts for contributions to the *Proceedings*, a publication read by the same and other gentlemen-scientists.

When performing science became a matter for competitive grants from the public purse, the same method was applied: colleagues would read and judge others scientists' proposals, and rate (or rank) them to decide who would win part of the limited amount of grant money. The scarce good changed from journal space to grant money; the reading changed from scientific results, observations and methods to research plans; the audience changed from fellow-scientists to decision-makers (Rip, 1994). Evaluating research proposals became a standard peer review practice in many countries for many decades, as national or disciplinary research councils distributed their funds (e.g. the NIH in the US, Sweden's Vetenskapsrådet or the British ESRC). The peer review method itself remained mainly accepted (Zuckerman & Merton, 1971), because the peers kept to judging individual written pieces (manuscripts or proposals) against the background of the discipline as a body of accepted knowledge. It is also important to realize that at any one time, only a minority of researchers would apply in a round of research fund competitions: these research evaluations were (and are) piecemeal exercises, from the point of view of their method.

Next, peer review made a dimensional jump to judging the state of large chunks of research fields or even discipline in their entirety, as happened in all kinds of smaller and larger foresight exercises, especially since the 1970s (e.g., Irvine & Martin, 1984; van der Meulen, Westerheijden, Rip, & van Vught, 1991). These exercises most often aimed to inform decision-makers about strategic funding of large research efforts or research programs, e.g. on the establishment of a national supercomputer center. Their method changed peer review from an individual reviewer's exercise to ad hoc committee work.

The final step was to extend the method of peer committee review into countrywide research assessment exercises. These were first introduced in Europe in British higher education and research in the early 1980s (Leisyte, Enders, & de Boer, 2008; Westerheijden, 2008), but other forms appeared as well, as in the Netherlands. The contrast between the British and Dutch approaches merits some attention.

In the 'hard' New Public Management approach characterizing the UK (Paradise Bleiklie et al., 2009) the Research Assessment Exercise (RAE) was meant to determine funding, not of selected individual research projects or programs but for all public research funding in the 'normal' recurrent funding of higher education. In essence, its method was that ad hoc committees of peers were given publications and information by university departments, which they had to process to come to a single, semi-numerical judgment about the quality of the department's research. The best outcome was the judgment that a department's research was leading in the world (in different RAE exercises, this could be expressed as '5', '5*' or something similar). More than 25% of all the quality-related research funding went to four higher education institutions (Cambridge, Oxford, University College London and Imperial

College), which were also among the institutions for which more than 50% of their total recurrent governmental grant resulted from the research funding (Westerheijden, 2008). Obviously, then, the British RAE first of all was meant to inform the funding authorities, and judging by the recurrence of RAEs ever since the 1980s the funding councils were on the whole satisfied with this type of information.

In the much softer approach in the Netherlands, after some initial controversial ad hoc budget reduction exercises in the first half of the 1980s (de Groot & van der Sluis, 1986; Grondsma, 1987), research evaluations were introduced that in fact were *not* used to redistribute governmental research funding (Spaapen, van Suyt, Prins, & Blume, 1988). After two rounds, the government even relinquished control of the research evaluations to the umbrella organization of the universities, for the sole purpose of informing research management decisions by institutional leadership (VSNU, 1994). Accordingly, since the early 1990s the Dutch research evaluations had institutional leaders as their intended audience. And those leaders were happy to use the information for all kinds of decisions from bonuses for research groups performing well to the reorganization of those performing poorly (Jongbloed & van der Meulen, 2006; Westerheijden, 1997). The information they were given consisted mostly of four numerical indicators about a research group's productivity, quality of products, relevance of research and the vitality and feasibility of the group and its program (Vereniging van Universiteiten, Nederlandse Organisatie voor Wetenschappelijk Onderzoek, & Koninklijke Nederlandse Akademie van Wetenschappen, 2003). Additionally, a short accompanying text provided qualitative support for the performance indicators for each research program which could inform more detailed management decisions.

In some Central European countries too, after the fall of communism around 1990, countrywide research evaluations were introduced in order to inform public funding of university research. In their effort to do away with the corrupting effects of the *nomenklatura*, these regularly recurring evaluations were strongly based on objective performance indicators: publication figures played an important role in e.g. Poland and Slovakia. It is interesting to observe that the British research assessment exercise after 2008 also relies much more on objective indicators.

2.3.1.2 Fundamental Research Assessments

The types of indicators used in research assessment in recent decades have evolved from crude counting of publications to sophisticated measures of impact. That development may help to explain why in the UK nowadays the indicators for the new type of RAE are called 'metrics' rather than 'performance indicators'. Since this is not the place to give a detailed account of bibliometrics, let us just summarize them as measurements of research outputs, in particular publications, and their impacts. They can be used for different purposes (e.g. for mapping newly emerging areas of research), but they are best-known as indicators of research quality—note that quality is equated not with productivity (numbers of publications), but with *impact* of the products (number of citations as signs of use by fellow scientists) (Cozzens, 1981; Leydesdorff & van der Schaar, 1987; Moed, 2005; Moed et al., 1985). As such they have given much new insight and are among the mainstays of 'informed peer review' (Rinia, van Leeuwen, van Vuren, & van Raan, 1998). However, their use is not without problems: the standard model of research from which bibliometric indices proceed, i.e. that the large majority of knowledge claims are published in international (English-language) peer-reviewed journals, applies only to a small portion of disciplines and—as far as the English language is concerned—to only part of the world (van Raan, 2005). Alternative measures are being developed for knowledge areas where this standard communication model does not apply, e.g. focusing more on conference proceedings or book publications. Besides, pros and cons of alternative indicators remain under debate, e.g. the superiority of the 'crown indicator' of the Leiden rankings over the 'Hirsh index' (Bornmann, Wallon, & Ledin, 2008; Hirsch, 2005; van Raan, 2006).

As a byproduct, all these research evaluations can be used to inform stakeholders and the general public by rating or ranking higher education institutions according to the 'points' earned in the assessment exercises. In the UK, results of existing national peer-review based schemes on research quality (RAE) are used as indicators in some rankings (e.g. *The Times* Good University Guide) together with information derived from the teaching quality (TQA) exercises. Peer-review based assessments enrich rankings with a widely accepted perspective on the performance of institutions. However, we must consider that national peer reviews differ very much in purpose, concept and measures or ratings; their results cannot be standardized or normalized for international comparison. Up to now there are neither regular nor systematic international peer reviews that could be used to inform international rankings.

What the points awarded in research evaluation exercises actually mean, or how those meanings shifted over the years, appears to have been less important to some users than the fact that they could be ranked and rated: so many '5-stars' etc. In the UK, the RAEs were given ample public attention through the press. In the Netherlands this was much less the case, possibly because there was not a single major news event in the form of publication of all national ratings at the same time. Rather each discipline, and more recently each (small cluster of) research groups in a single university was evaluated separately, leading to minor news attention—if any. Nevertheless, institutional leaders in the Netherlands often used the absolute amount of points gained by research groups as a criterion for internal financial reallocation (Jongbloed & van der Meulen, 2006; Westerheijden, 1997), even though the evaluating agencies kept warning against adding up the scores on the different dimensions.

2.3.1.3 Practical Research Assessments

Much of the knowledge-generating activity in higher education institutions can be called applied research—this applies (in varying degrees) both to higher education institutions called 'universities' but also to, e.g., the 'universities of applied sciences' (*Fachhochschulen*) in Germany or the 'institutes of technology' in Ireland. The archetype of peer review, still so influential in the quality assurance schemes for research just mentioned, was developed in the context of fundamental research; what does that mean for the evaluation of applied research?

We have to acknowledge that the term 'applied research' is contested, if not downright old-fashioned. This indicates that the characteristics of knowledge-creating activities can be manifold and that, therefore, it is difficult to come up with a single name for everything that is not the purest form of basic research: Mode-2 research is one of the more popular ones (Gibbons et al., 1984). In line with that, evaluation of these other forms of knowledge-creating activities must be manifold as well. The route from fundamental research to product innovation may lead through patents and co-authored papers—indicators have been developed on patents, income from licenses, co-authored papers, etc.[2] (Debackere, Verbeek, Luwel, & Zimmermann, 2002). Indeed, 'practice-oriented research' in universities of applied science may have a range of outputs; the Dutch Council of the Universities of Applied Science, the HBO Council, mentions 'publications, presentations and other products' (HBO-raad, 2008).

It may be warranted to mention the Dutch situation here as it is one of the few places in the world where systematic approaches to evaluating other forms of research are being developed; their main thrust is 'evaluation of research in context' (ERIC is therefore the acronym of what was previously known as the sci-Quest method), i.e. seeing research as more than just (international, peer-reviewed) publications for fellow-researchers, but rather as knowledge processes and products for use by non-academic or non-scientific stakeholders. This implied that (Spaapen, Dijstelbloem, & Wamelink, 2007, p. 57):

> we are not looking for an instrument to evaluate a specific research group or program, but a process of interaction. And we are not so much looking for indicators that can tell us how good or bad the 'quality' of the research is, but we are looking for indicators that tell us whether the group succeeds in fulfilling its mission in a relevant context.

We call this evaluation of 'other' knowledge production 'practical research assessments'. The core of the ensuing evaluation method is called the 'Research Embedment and Performance Profile (REPP)', including, in one of the pilots, several indicators in each of the following dimensions: science & certified knowledge; education & training; innovation & professionals; public policy & societal issues; and collaboration & visibility.

---

[2] A worldwide scoreboard of University-Industry Co-publications (UICs), as identified within the international peer-reviewed research literature indexed by Thomson Reuters' Web of Science (WoS) database, covering more or less the same higher education institutions as appear in the ARWU, may be found on www.socialsciences.leiden.edu/cwts/hot-topics/scoreboard. This scoreboard is primarily designed for international benchmarking and strategic analysis of higher education institutions' (applied) research performance.

In its quality assurance scheme for such practice-oriented research, the Dutch HBO council mentions a wide range of products and further refers to impact on, and satisfaction of, development of the field, the profession and society, and education and training (HBO-raad, 2008). In addition, the HBO council's quality assurance scheme looks at the relevance and sustainability of networks with stakeholders (true to the characteristics of Mode-2 research).

As is the case with the national research evaluations in the Netherlands, these alternative evaluations are meant to inform research management within the higher education institutions; institutional leadership therefore remains the main audience. These methods have been developed recently; it is too early to look at their impact or to expect their having been used in communication with wider audiences.

2.3.2 Information Offered by Quality Assurance in Higher Education: Peer Review, Performance Indicators, Accreditation and Audits

Quality assurance schemes for the educational function of higher education institutions have been designed since the 1970s but mostly since the 1990s in many countries around the world (Brennan, El-Khawas, & Shah, 1994; Dill, 1992; Goedegebuure, Maassen, & Westerheijden, 1990; Neave, 1994; van Vught & Westerheijden, 1994; Westerheijden, Brennan, & Maassen, 1994; Woodhouse, 1996). This simple statement is the clue to much of the answer to the question regarding the information provided by quality assurance in higher education. First, the statement implies that the current quality assurance schemes still bear the markings of their perhaps 15- to 40-year history: they were designed to answer questions relevant at the time (Jeliazkova & Westerheijden, 2002; Westerheijden, Stensaker, & Rosa, 2007). Second, quality assurance was designed as a national issue, answering to national agendas—although those agendas themselves were partly inspired by international policy developments, such as the spread of variants of New Public Management (Paradeise, Reale, Bleiklie, & Ferlie, 2009).

The national agendas were mainly influenced by the dominant stakeholders, which in many countries meant that the public authorities played an important role, and their perspective through the eyes of public higher education generally is in the legal context. The latter addition means that nationally existing classifications of higher education institutions were taken for granted from the very beginning: there was no calling into question of what makes up a 'university', a 'polytechnic', a *Fachhochschule* or whatever names were used for different categories of higher education institutions. Similarly, nationally defined degrees were taken for granted as well (Schwarz & Westerheijden, 2004). Comparability across jurisdictions was hardly ever an issue in the initial design of quality assurance schemes.

Quality assurance schemes, depending on their design, produce different types of information, some of them tending towards 'hard data' in (performance) indicators, others tending towards 'soft' judgments by external reviewers. The externally available data are a core product of quality assurance from the accountability viewpoint: through giving objective and comparable information governmental (or other public) funding bodies and taxpayers could see that their money was well spent. Accountability is a major aim of quality assurance in the governance perspective, stimulated by New Public Management approaches which focus on proving performance across all public services. The other main aim of quality assurance, quality improvement or quality enhancement, is served more by judgmental information and specific recommendations from knowledgeable peers to the individual study program or higher education institution that has been evaluated; in other words, by focusing on peer review. The judgmental type of information resulting from peer review processes may benefit from not being too public; otherwise the open discussion among peers could be negatively influenced by considerations of what the public (the press!) may make of statements about weaknesses and problems (van Vught & Westerheijden, 1994). The line between helpful recommendations and 'naming and shaming' is no thicker than a sheet of newspaper.

Another type of problem surfaces when basing quality assurance solely on performance indicators. The natural tendency then is to give most attention to their being *measurable*. In research terms, reliability is prioritized over validity of the indicators.

At least a partial way out of the paradox that performance indicators tend to produce comparable but irrelevant information and peer review does not produce much public information (or if it does it is not of a comparative nature) is that in the practice of quality assurance the two are complementing each other: indicators are used for reporting and as a basis for more holistic judgmental statements by knowledgeable peers ('informed peer review').

Quality assurance, inserted as it is in the governance discourse, is almost invariably about ensuring that provision of higher education does not fall under a threshold level of quality; public authorities want to protect students against 'rogue providers', 'degree mills' and the like. Accordingly, the public information provided by quality assurance schemes in the large majority of cases is limited to statements that program X or institution Y is of 'basic quality', 'sufficient', 'trustworthy', and that these programs or institutions can be 'accredited'. Sometimes differentiations are made between 'confidence' and 'broad confidence', or between 'conditional accreditation' and 'accreditation', suggesting that some remain closer to the threshold than others, but the differences are not easily understood by outsiders such as potential students.

The main point for us is that quality assurance of this type does not differentiate among study programs or institutions very clearly: all higher education seems to be lumped together as 'generally OK' (except the few that do not pass the test). In this way, the academic concept of quality as *excellence* (Harvey & Green, 1993) is not evidently supported by most quality assurance schemes, whatever may be the rhetoric of decision-makers when justifying these policy instruments.

In quality assurance schemes focusing on the program level, the information produced in the form of indicators is mainly about the educational process, its inputs, throughput and outputs, and about the services supporting the educational process, including services such as ICT, libraries etc. In quality assurance schemes focusing on the institutional level, the balance of information tends to be different, with descriptions of the institutional organization, processes and administration being prevalent, and more summary information on the education function. When these institutional evaluations focus on the organization and implementation of institutional quality assurance systems, they are usually called 'audits'. Audits address quality assurance at a meta-level, evaluating the mechanisms and processes that institutions have in place to assess their internal education quality.

References

Boas Hall, M. (2002). *Henry Oldenburg: Shaping the Royal Society*. Oxford: Oxford University Press.
Bonroy, O., & Constantatos, C. (2008). On the use of labels in credence goods markets. *Journal of Regulatory Economics, 33*(3), 237–252.
Bornmann, L., Wallon, G., & Ledin, A. (2008). Is the h index related to (standard) bibliometric measures and to the assessments by peers? An investigation of the h index by using molecular life sciences data. *Research Evaluation, 17*(2), 149–156.
Brennan, J., El-Khawas, E. H., & Shah, T. (1994). *Peer review and the assessment of higher education quality: An international perspective*. London: QSC, Open University.
Cozzens, S. E. (1981). Taking the measure of science: A review of citation theories. *Newsletter International Society for Sociology of Knowledge, 7*, 16–21.
de Groot, H., & van der Sluis, J. (1986). *Bestuurlijke reacties op bezuinigingen: een economisch model*. Rotterdam: Erasmus Universiteit Rotterdam.
Debackere, K., Verbeek, A., Luwel, M., & Zimmermann, E. (2002). Measuring progress and evolution in science and technology – II: The multiple uses of technometric indicators. *International Journal of Management Reviews, 4*(3), 213–231.
Dill, D. D. (1992). Quality by design: Towards a framework for academic quality management. In J. C. Smart (Ed.), *Higher education: Handbook of theory and research* (Vol. VIII). New York: Agathon Press.
Dulleck, U., & Kerschbamer, R. (2006). On doctors, mechanics, and computer specialists: The economics of credence goods. *Journal of Economic Literature, 44*(1), 5–42.
Gibbons, M., Limoges, C., Nowotny, H., Schartzman, S., Scott, P., & Trow, M. (1984). *The new production of knowledge*. London: Sage.
Goedegebuure, L. C. J., Maassen, P. A. M., & Westerheijden, D. F. (Eds.). (1990). *Peer review and performance indicators: Quality assessment in British and Dutch higher education*. Utrecht: Lemma.
Grondsma, T. (1987). *Spelbenadering en contractie*. Rotterdam: Erasmus Universiteit Rotterdam.
Harvey, L., & Green, D. (1993). Defining quality. *Assessment & Evaluation in Higher Education, 18*(1), 9–34.
HBO-raad. (2008). *Basisdocument kwaliteitszorgstelsel ten aanzien van het onderzoek aan hogescholen 2009-2015: Nadere uitwerking van het brancheprotocol kwaliteitszorg onderzoek (BKO) in een kwaliteitszorgstelsel*. Den Haag: HBO-raad.
Hirsch, J. E. (2005). An index to quantify an individual's scientific research output. *Proceedings of the National Academy of Sciences of the United States of America, 102*(46), 16569–16572.
Irvine, J., & Martin, B. R. (1984). *Foresight in science*. Oxford: Frances Pinter.

Jeliazkova, M., & Westerheijden, D. F. (2002). Systemic adaptation to a changing environment: Towards a next generation of quality assurance models. *Higher Education, 44*(3–4), 433–448.

Jongbloed, B., & van der Meulen, B. R. (2006). *Investeren in Dynamiek – Eindrapport Commissie Dynamisering – Deel 2: De follow-up van onderzoeksvisitaties: Onderzoek in opdracht van de Commissie Dynamisering, Eindrapportage.* s. l. Den Haag: Ministerie van Onderwijs & Wetenschappen.

Leisyte, L., Enders, J., & de Boer, H. (2008). The freedom to set research agendas – Illusion and reality of the research units in the Dutch universities. *Higher Education Policy, 21*, 377–391.

Leydesdorff, L., & van der Schaar, P. (1987). The use of scientometric methods for evaluating national research programmes. *Science & Technology Studies, 5*, 22–31.

Marginson, S., & van der Wende, M. (2007). *Globalization and higher education.* Paris: OECD.

Moed, H. F. (2005). *Citation analysis in research evaluation.* Dordrecht: Springer.

Moed, H. F., Burger, W. J. M., Francfort, J. G., & van Raan, A. F. J. (1985). The use of bibliometric data as tools for university research policy. *International Journal Institutional Management in Higher Education, 9*, 185–194.

Neave, G. (1994). The politics of quality: Developments in higher education in Western Europe 1992–1994. *European Journal of Education, 29*(2), 115–133.

Paradeise, C., Bleiklie, I., Enders, J., Goastellec, G., Michelsen, S., Reale, E., et al. (2009). Reform policies and change processes in Europe. In J. Huisman (Ed.), *International perspectives on the governance of higher education: Alternative frameworks for coordination* (pp. 88–106). New York/London: Routledge.

Paradeise, C., Reale, E., Bleiklie, I., & Ferlie, E. (Eds.). (2009). *University governance: Western European comparative perspectives.* Dordrecht: Springer.

Rinia, E. J., van Leeuwen, T. N., van Vuren, H. G., & van Raan, A. F. J. (1998). Comparative analysis of a set of bibliometric indicators and central peer review criteria. Evaluation of condensed matter physics in the Netherlands. *Research Policy, 27*(1), 95–107.

Rip, A. (1994). The republic of science in the 1990s. *Higher Education, 28*, 3–23.

Saisana, M., & D'Hombres, B. (2008). *Higher education rankings: Robustness issues and critical assessment. How much confidence can we have in higher education rankings?* Luxembourg: Office for Official Publications of the European Communities.

Schwarz, S., & Westerheijden, D. F. (Eds.). (2004). *Accreditation and evaluation in the European higher education area.* Dordrecht: Kluwer Academic.

Spaapen, J., Dijstelbloem, H., & Wamelink, F. (2007). *Evaluating research in context: A method for comprehensive assessment* (Vol. 2). The Hague: Consultative Committee of Sector Councils for Research and Development (COS).

Spaapen, J., van Suyt, C. A. M., Prins, A. A. M., & Blume, S. S. (1988). *De moeizame relatie tussen beleid en onderzoek: Evaluatie van vijf jaar Voorwaardelijke Financiering.* Zoetermeer: Ministerie van Onderwijs & Wetenschappen.

Teichler, U. (2007). *Higher education systems. Conceptual frameworks, comparative perspectives, empirical findings.* Rotterdam: Sense Publishers.

van der Meulen, B. R., Westerheijden, D. F., Rip, A., & van Vught, F. A. (1991). *Verkenningscommissies tussen veld en overheid.* Zoetermeer: Ministerie van Onderwijs & Wetenschappen.

van Raan, A. F. J. (2005). Fatal attraction: Conceptual and methodological problems in the ranking of universities by bibliometric methods. *Scientometrics, 62*(1), 133–143.

van Raan, A. F. J. (2006). Comparison of the Hirsch-index with standard bibliometric indicators and with peer judgment for 147 chemistry research groups. *Scientometrics, 67*(3), 491–502.

van Vught, F. A. (Ed.). (1993). *Governmental strategies and innovation in higher education* (2nd ed.). London: Jessica Kingsley.

van Vught, F. A. (2008). Mission diversity and reputation in higher education. *Higher Education Policy, 21*(2), 151–174.

van Vught, F. A., & Westerheijden, D. F. (1994). Towards a general model of quality assessment in higher education. *Higher Education, 28*, 355–371.

Vereniging van Universiteiten, Nederlandse Organisatie voor Wetenschappelijk Onderzoek, & Koninklijke Nederlandse Akademie van Wetenschappen. (2003). *Standard evaluation protocol*

2003–2009 for public research organizations. Utrecht/Den Haag/Amsterdam: VSNU/NWO/KNAW.

VSNU. (1994). *Quality assessment of research: Protocol 1994.* Utrecht: VSNU.

Westerheijden, D. F. (1997). A solid base for decisions: Use of the VSNU research evaluations in Dutch universities. *Higher Education, 33*(4), 397–413.

Westerheijden, D. F. (2003). Movements towards a European Dimension in Quality Assurance and Accreditation. In D. F. Westerheijden & M. Leegwater (Eds.), *Working on the European Dimension of Quality: Report of the conference on quality assurance in higher education as part of the Bologna process, Amsterdam, 12–13 March 2002* (pp. 16–41). Zoetermeer: Ministerie van Onderwijs, Cultuur en Wetenschappen.

Westerheijden, D. F. (2008). Who rules research commands the university: A comparison of research assessment schemes in the United Kingdom and in the Netherlands. *Evaluation in Higher Education, 2*(1), 1–34.

Westerheijden, D. F., Brennan, J., & Maassen, P. A. M. (Eds.). (1994). *Changing contexts of quality assessment: Recent trends in West European higher education.* Utrecht: Lemma.

Westerheijden, D. F., Stensaker, B., & Rosa, M. J. (2007, April 2–5). *Is there a logic in the development of quality assurance schemes? From comparative history to theory.* Paper presented at the INQAAHE conference, Toronto.

Woodhouse, D. (1996). Quality assurance: International trends, preoccupations and features. *Assessment and evaluation in higher education, 21*(4), 347–356.

Zuckerman, H., & Merton, R. K. (1971). Patterns of evaluation in science: Institutionalization, structure and functions of the referee system. *Minerva, 9,* 66–100.

Chapter 3
Classifications and Rankings

Gero Federkeil, Frans A. van Vught, and Don F. Westerheijden

3.1 Introduction

In this chapter, an overview will be given of the existing classifications and rankings in higher education and research. The examples of rankings and classifications that will appear most often are listed in Table 3.1 and include the following (for a longer list of rankings around the world, see e.g. www.arwu.org/Resources.jsp, last accessed April 28, 2011).

3.2 Higher Education Classifications

Attempts to get to grips with the diversity of higher education and research institutions have been increasing ever since these systems became too large for stakeholders to know all institutions individually. In the centrally steered systems of Europe's nation-states, bureaucratic categorizations fulfilled an important function in this respect, distinguishing academies, institutes, universities, polytechnic schools, national research centers, colleges, etc. More sophisticated classification instruments became necessary when finer distinctions within such broad categories were needed, or when comparisons were made across state boundaries. Another need for more differentiated distinctions arises from the increasing importance of institutional strategies, which lead to a heterogeneous picture of institutional goals, missions and task

---

G. Federkeil (✉)
Centre for Higher Education (CHE), Gütersloh, Germany

F.A. van Vught • D.F. Westerheijden
Center for Higher Education Policy Studies, University of Twente,
Enschede, The Netherlands

Table 3.1 Major classifications and rankings

Type	Name
Classifications	Carnegie classification (USA)
	U-Map (Europe)
Global league tables and rankings	Shanghai Jiao Tong University's (SJTU) Academic Ranking of World Universities (ARWU)
	Times Higher Education (Supplement) (THE)
	QS (Quacquarelli Symonds Ltd) Top Universities
	Leiden Ranking
National league tables and rankings	*US News & World Report* (USN&WR; USA)
	National Research Council (USA) PhD programs
	Times Good Education Guide (UK)
	Guardian ranking (UK)
	Forbes (USA)
	CHE Das Ranking/University Ranking (CHE; Germany)
	Studychoice123 (SK123; the Netherlands)
Specialized league tables and rankings	*Financial Times* ranking of business schools and programs (FT; global)
	BusinessWeek (business schools, USA + global)
	The Economist (business schools; global)

priorities. Two classifications stand out internationally: the US Carnegie classification and the European U-Map classification tool.

The major classification in higher education was developed in the USA, where the Carnegie Foundation first published its classification in 1973 as a tool for researchers; it turned into a major, authoritative concept for all of the USA and beyond (McCormick & Zhao, 2005):

> Clark Kerr headed the Carnegie Commission when it created the classification system, so it is not surprising that the scheme bore marked similarities to another element of the Kerr legacy, the mission differentiation embedded in the 1960 California Master Plan for Higher Education. Indeed, one goal of the new system was to call attention to—and emphasize the importance of—the considerable institutional diversity of US higher education. The classification provided a way to represent that diversity by grouping roughly comparable institutions into meaningful, analytically manageable categories.

The Carnegie classification is entirely run and funded by the Carnegie Foundation. The success of the Carnegie classification is due to the fact that the Carnegie Foundation has the generally accepted authority as the implementing organization of the US classification. Over the years, the Carnegie classification turned into a league table instrument in popular use: it was seen as more prestigious to be a 'research university' than an associate degree-granting college, in fact taking the nominal length of the highest degree awarded at an institution as a proxy for its overall quality. Whether the prestige acquired in public view was connected with actual differences in quality of performance was doubtful (Kuh, 2011). In the latest version, published in 2005, a multidimensional classification has been developed, counteracting this tendency to simplified ranking. 'These classifications provide different lenses through which to view US colleges and universities, offering researchers greater analytic flexibility' (www.carnegiefoundation.org/classifications, accessed April 28, 2011). They are organized around three fundamental questions: *what* is taught (Undergraduate and Graduate Instructional Program classifications), *who* the students are (Enrolment Profile and Undergraduate Profile), and what the *setting* is (Size & Setting). The original Carnegie Classification framework—now called the Basic classification—has also been substantially revised.

The European U-Map classification has been developed since 2005. U-Map is a user-driven, multidimensional European classification instrument that allows all higher education (and research) institutions to be characterized along six dimensions. By doing so, U-Map allows creation and analysis of specific activity 'institutional profiles', offering 'pictures' of the activities of an institution on the various indicators of all six dimensions. U-Map can be accessed through two online tools (a Profile Finder and a Profile Viewer) that allow stakeholders to analyze the institutional profiles (e.g. for benchmarking), comparative analysis or institutional strategic profiling.

U-Map has been developed in close cooperation with the designers of the most recent Carnegie classification. It is a major new transparency tool in European higher education and in the U-Multirank project aimed at developing a multidimensional global ranking tool; it has been an important source of experience and inspiration (see www.u-map.eu).

3.3 Higher Education Rankings and League Tables

In this section, we give an overview of some of the most influential rankings and league tables. In Chaps. 4 and 5 we will present our critique of these rankings and league tables, which will set the stage for the design principles that form the groundwork for our multidimensional ranking tool, called U-Multirank, to be discussed in Part II of this volume.

Since the early part of the twentieth century, rankings and league tables of higher education have existed, starting in the USA (Dill, 2006; Kuh, 2011). Overviews—almost necessarily incomplete—on existing ranking systems by the Institute for Higher Education Policy (IHEP, dating from 2006)[1] and by the Shanghai ranking group (updated until 2010)[2] list altogether almost 40 countries on all continents with a number of countries producing competing rankings, totaling at least 50 national ranking systems and 10 global ones 'of varying significance' (Hazelkorn, 2011, p. 5).

---

[1] See http://www.ihep.org/Research/nationalrankingsystems.cfm (accessed April 28, 2011).
[2] See http://www.arwu.org/resources.jsp (accessed April 28, 2011).

Generally speaking, rankings and league tables compare higher education institutions by ordering them one after the other according to the degree to which they fulfill certain criteria. An important characteristic of rankings and league tables is that they allow users to see at a glance which institution occupies which rank order position in the 'top-n' of something.

The major dimensions to analyze and classify rankings and league tables would seem to be:

- Level: e.g. institutional vs. field-based
- Scope: e.g. national vs. international
- Focus: e.g. education vs. research
- Primary target group: e.g. students vs. institutional leaders vs. policy-makers
- Methodology and producers: what sources of data are used and by whom?

With five dimensions, a summary overview in the form of a table of all rankings' characteristics per dimension may be unattainable; we will however mention some examples in each of the following subsections.

3.3.1 Institutional and Field-Based Rankings

In broad terms, interests of users of rankings can focus at institutional or field levels of higher education and research. By *fields*, we may mean smaller organizational units like faculties, schools or departments focusing on a single area of knowledge (e.g. academic disciplines like economics or physics, or interdisciplinary areas like business studies or nanotechnology) or single programs of either study or research in such an area. Most global league tables (ARWU, THE, QS, Leiden, HEEACT, Webometrics) rank higher education and research institutions, and it is this institutional focus which most easily connects them with the reputation race. For several years now, ARWU, THE, QS and HEEACT rankings have published results for broad fields, too, but with the exception of the ARWU the selections of institutions in those broad field rankings are based on their institutional rankings, i. e. only fields in institutions selected as top-n are considered, overlooking specialized institutions with only one or a few fields like business schools. Some global rankings fill the gap left by the major global rankings, as they focus on one specific field, e.g. the *Financial Times*' ranking of business studies programs. In a way, the latter straddles the field vs. institution divide to the extent that some of the business schools included in its rankings may be independent institutions rather than schools or faculties of larger universities.

Many national rankings also pertain to higher education and research institutions as a whole, such as those by *USN&WR* and Perspektywy. Again, these are closely connected to institutional prestige and reputation. More typically though, national rankings such as the CHE Ranking and SK123 are geared to helping prospective students make an informed choice of study programs matching their individual wants and needs, rather than about organizational units of higher education and research institutions.

Interest in the field level is understandable in students or individual researchers looking for a place to study or to do research: programs across institutions may deliver quite different qualities (we will return to the information needs of target groups below). Showing the average value of indicators for entire higher education and research institutions obscures local strengths and weaknesses, while it is argued that for all but the very best and richest institutions it is neither possible nor desired to be equally prominent in all fields (see also Chap. 4, where we approach this issue from the standpoint of methodological critique).

On the other hand, decision-makers in government or leaders of higher education and research institutions have a legitimate interest in the overall characteristics of institutions: some characteristics only apply at the level of an institution as a whole, going across or beyond field levels (e.g. mission, participation policies), and the institutional level is a useful first-order approximation for in-depth characteristics (e.g. for finding partners in benchmarking exercises). Policy-makers often limit themselves to the institutional level because it is at that level that they may make policy decisions, while field-level decisions are the prerogative of institutional management and academic experts (institutional autonomy and academic freedom might otherwise be jeopardized).

3.3.2 National or International Scope

The earliest league tables were published to compare colleges (higher education institutions) across the 50 US states—a national level in a technical sense, but as a higher education system about as large as the European Higher Education Area (EHEA), which eminently is an international higher education system of 47 countries. In character though, the USN&WR league tables are more like national league tables and rankings in other countries, though: they aim to inform US students about the 'best' study options available anywhere in the country at the institutional level. Similarly, but then at the field or study program level, the CHE Ranking started with the aim to inform students looking for undergraduate study across all 16 federal states in Germany as well as students in Austria and (German-speaking parts of) Switzerland. We can fairly safely say that national-level rankings and league tables tend to be designed for a clearer purpose and with a more focused target group in mind than global ones. With growing higher education and research systems in many countries, national actors increasingly see a need for national rankings or league tables to restore transparency; the number of countries where they can be found continually increases.

International league tables are more often aimed at ranking entire higher education institutions. They are the most controversial and most talked-about league tables at the moment, at least as far as they have the aura of establishing quality or reputation of the universities as a whole. The most prominent examples include the ARWU and the THE rankings. Some other international league tables such as the Leiden Ranking or Webometrics are more explicit about their limited scope and limited claims: they wish to inform about research performance and impact (Leiden ranking) or about web presence and activity (Webometrics). In that way, they seem to evoke less vehement debate than the former two. With regard to the growing demand for more international transparency in the context of international mobility of students, on the one hand we see national rankings expanding to neighboring areas (the CHE Ranking now includes German higher education institutions as well as institutions from, among others, Austria, Switzerland and the Netherlands). On the other hand, the Europe-wide CHE Excellence Ranking focuses on the market for Master and PhD students in an as yet small number of fields in international, research-oriented universities throughout Europe. It was first piloted in 2007 and has begun to cover major areas in sciences as well as in humanities and social sciences.

3.3.3 Focus on Education or on Research

The issue of focus has a double meaning. First, rankings and league tables may be *intended* to inform about education or about research. For instance, the professed aim of the USN&WR, CHE Rankings and SK123 is to inform students about the best institutions where they can study, an obvious focus on education. The Leiden ranking is explicit in its focus on informing about the research performance of higher education institutions.

The second meaning of the dimension has to do with the *actual indicators* used to compose the ranking. One of the criticisms we will examine in Chap. 4 is that there is not always a clear correlation between the indicators used to establish the ranking (often research-based, especially when we look at the international league tables) and the focus they claim to have (e.g. to inform students). Most national rankings with their focus on information for (prospective) students show indicators on teaching or they use a mix of teaching and research indicators (plus some context variables). The majority of indicators used in global rankings measure research performance, or institutional reputation which is believed to be dependent on research performance or on context variables rather than on the education function.

3.3.4 Primary Target Groups

Most national rankings began with the professed aim of informing (prospective) students and their parents about universities and programs of their country. The 2001 edition of 'America's Best Colleges' edited by *US News & World Report* (USN&WR) announced to those target groups that it would 'provide a detailed map to improve your odds of ending up in the right place'.[3] It is a challenge for those

---

[3] *US News & World Report: America's Best Colleges.* 2001 edition, p. 8.

rankings in particular to find a balance between the need to reduce in a valid manner the complexity of information for the core target group, prospective students, who are among the groups least informed about higher education on the one hand, and, on the other hand, the need to deliver sophisticated and elaborate information for the higher education sector itself, which is important for the acceptance of rankings within higher education (Federkeil, 2006).

A similar situation pertains for international field-based rankings, e.g. rankings of business schools as published by, among many others, (for a long list of MBA rankings, see www.find-mba.com/mba-rankings) the *Financial Times* (FT; http://rankings.ft.com/businessschoolrankings): they intend to assist prospective students to find the best short course or MBA degree program for them. It is worth noting that international field-based rankings have first appeared in professional fields that are internationally integrated, such as business studies. In recent years, more rankings have begun to address specific academic fields in a differentiated manner, e.g. the Excellence Ranking of the Centre for Higher Education (CHE) in Europe and the field rankings in the Shanghai, Taiwanese and Times Higher league tables.

It should be recognized that not all students are alike: the USN&WR ranking or the student information websites such as Studychoice123.nl (SK123) or that of the CHE are in the first instance aimed at informing prospective students entering higher education for the first time, typically adolescents in their final year of secondary education. The *Financial Times* (FT) ranking is aimed at more mature persons with several years of professional experience who wish to upgrade or extend their knowledge through gaining specific skills. And the Aspen Institute's 'Beyond Grey Pinstripes' ranking of MBAs (www.beyondgreypinstripes.org) is aimed at students interested in curricula emphasizing green values and ethical business models. These are completely different groups of students with different cost/benefit calculations about studying, with different knowledge about higher education institutions and with different information needs as a result. Consumption motives (living on campus for 3–5 years, broad academic learning to form one's personality, etc.) will be more important to first-time students, while investment motives may more readily characterize the returning students (e.g. which competencies and how much additional income could be gained with 2 years of part-time study with this particular school or program?).

By contrast, international/global league tables of higher education institutions as a rule do not refer explicitly to a defined target group but address a broader public inside and outside higher education and around the world. The most prominent global league table, the Academic Ranking of World Universities (ARWU) was intended originally as an instrument to compare Chinese universities' research performance in science and technology fields, and of the Chinese national higher education system with the rest of the world, particularly with universities in the US. Hence it was intended mainly as a national steering instrument for research policy and planning; the implicit target group of such league tables then is the set of policy-makers within public authorities (ministries of education and science & technology).

More detailed rankings such as the Leiden Ranking seem to target management decision-support, to find out which universities are comparable to one's own, or which might be interesting partners for a benchmarking exercise in the research dimension. Such questions and decisions indicate that institutional leaders and their support staff would be the prime target group for this ranking. Similarly, the Webometrics league table informs institutional leaders about the relative web presence of their higher education or research institution, which might lead to decisions regarding e.g. open access publishing. These and comparable rankings are designed to answer specific information needs of staff members (different ones, depending on the individual ranking being focused) in higher education and research institutions closely associated with the strategic decision-making level.

3.3.5 *Organizational and Methodological Overview*

The previous sections focused on what rankings do and for whom. Here we would like to go into some more technical considerations regarding how rankings are produced. Together, these determinants on the production side of rankings may help to establish the credibility of a ranking, besides being of interest to the methodological development of U-Multirank (see Part II). Regarding data collection methods, broadly, we distinguish the use of existing statistics, objective data obtained from the participating higher education and research institutions and, finally, surveys.

3.3.5.1 Producers of League Tables

The majority of national league tables are produced by media companies. Again this trend started with *US News & World Report*. Other examples of media league tables are *The Times* Good University Guide, league tables by the newspapers *Guardian* and *Independent* in the UK, national league tables in France (*Nouvel Observateur*) and Italy (*Sole 24 Ore*). A minority of rankings is published by independent, national non-profit organizations, such as the CHE Ranking in Germany (with media partner *Die Zeit*), Studychoice123 in the Netherlands. Organizations earning their keep through education fairs and the like, such as the Polish Perspektywy Foundation (www.perspektywy.org) also produce rankings. Furthermore, there are a few examples of national rankings published by public institutions, e.g. the Higher Education Evaluation and Accreditation Council of Taiwan (HEEACT) or the Nigerian Rectors' Conference. In the UK, the government-sponsored Commission for Employment and Skills (UKCES) had a review published in 2009 advocating a publicly-run ranking of study programs in further and higher education focusing especially on student retention and earning (www.guardian.co.uk/education/2009/oct/22/league-table-plan-for-universities; accessed November 04, 2009).

In contrast to national rankings, the majority of global league tables (three out of five) are compiled by academic institutions (CWTS/Leiden University, Ecôle des

Mines, Consejo Superior de Investigaciones Científicas (CSIC) in Spain). Similarly, the ARWU used to be compiled by the Shanghai Jiao Tong University (SJTU), but since 2009 it has been published by ShanghaiRanking Consultancy, an independent organization. The international, primarily Asia-oriented organization of QS links its ranking to its education fairs and similar activities. The THE ranking is the outlier among the global rankings, being organized by a major newspaper.

The Taiwanese HEEACT and the Dutch SK123 consortium (a consortium including all stakeholders, with governmental subsidy) would seem to be the rankers most closely related to public authorities, yet they are not in any way connected with governmental policy-making regarding higher education and research institutions, although the HEEACT in its evaluation and accreditation roles is associated with implementation of existing policies. Also the academic institutions producing global league tables are mainly public actors. Both CHE and the Polish foundation Perspektywy are public-private partnerships, being independent non-profit organizations with close relationships to national rectors' conferences.

3.3.5.2 Data Collection Methods

The three main ways of collecting the information used in quality assurance, classifications, rankings and league tables seem to be the use of statistics from existing databases, data collected on purpose from within participating higher education and research institutions, and surveys among stakeholders such as staff members, students, alumni or employers. We will briefly look at the strengths and weaknesses of these methods from the standpoint of creating a credible transparency instrument.[4]

National and International Statistics

Availability and comparability are the two issues concerning national statistics on higher education and research. Availability depends on the capacity and resources of governments (or other higher education authorities, but let us call them governments, for short) for collecting information, and on their needs. Different steering models require and produce different information; for instance, only if governmental funding of higher education institutions depends on student numbers, must statistics on students be collected by the government's statistical office. Going deeper, what happens with part-time students, students from migrant backgrounds, students in non-degree programs, disabled students, etc. may depend on the peculiarities of the funding model. For example, are they counted at the beginning or the end of the academic year, as 'heads' or as 'full-time equivalents'? As a consequence,

---

[4] Other perspectives might include the one dominant in quality assurance, namely that collecting data within the institution is crucial to a self-evaluation, which among other things is needed for creating ownership of the evaluation within the institution. Such perspectives do not concern us here.

it becomes understandable that nationally-collected statistics are not necessarily available and are not comparable for cross-national transparency tools. National statistics may be used in national rankings, but are not used in international rankings due to the lack of comparability.

Due to this lack of cross-national comparability, international publications on higher education and research statistics, e.g. OECD's annual *Education at a Glance*, are riddled with footnotes in almost every table or indicator. Prohibiting for global rankings is also that international databases with statistics on higher education, research and innovation systems such as those of UNESCO, OECD and Eurostat are collected at the national level, not at the level of individual higher education and research institutions, or units/programs within higher education and research institutions. Of course, then, these databases are not used in rankings.

International databases with information at the institutional level or lower aggregation levels are currently available for specific subfields: research output and impact, and knowledge transfer and innovation.

Regarding research output and impact, there are worldwide databases on journal publications and citations (the well-known Thomson Reuters and Scopus databases). These databases, after thorough checking and adaptation, are used in the research-based global rankings. Their strengths and weaknesses are treated elsewhere (especially in Sect. 4.2.6) and their application in our own approach to ranking is discussed in Part II of this volume.

Regarding knowledge transfer and innovation, a worldwide database of patents has been compiled by the European Patent Office (EPO). This database, called PATSTAT, includes patents from many countries, including among others American, Japanese and European patents. As it also contains names and affiliations of applicants, it might be used to gain insight into the innovativeness of higher education and research institutions, or into co-patents indicating university-industry relationships. This database is so far not being used in current global rankings. In Part II we will describe how we have developed a way to include this database in our new ranking tool.

At national level, there may exist databases made up of time series surveys of student satisfaction, alumni and first destination surveys, etc. Examples include CHE and Studychoice123 (or SK123), as well as student and alumni surveys in other major countries around the world, e.g. the National Survey of Student Engagement (NSSE) in the USA, and also there are longstanding surveys in the UK, Australia or Japan. All of these target a few broad themes that are quite similar: students' satisfaction with their current studies, alumni satisfaction with their completed studies mostly from the point of view of the studies' contribution to their early career, and early career (first destination) data. However, the ways in which these themes are addressed in the surveys, as well as the terms and categories of higher education and labor market, are so specific to the separate countries and survey methodologies (fact-based or opinion-oriented questions; online, telephone or mail questionnaires, etc.), that such databases cannot be used immediately for cross-national ranking purposes. They are an important source for many national rankings, however.

Institutional Self-Reported Data

Many rankings and league tables ask participating higher education and research institutions to produce data themselves, due to the lack of externally available and verified statistics (Thibaud, 2009). This is paradoxical, remembering that Hazelkorn portrayed the rise of rankings as 'reflect[ing] a lack of public trust in institutional-based quality assurance' (Hazelkorn, 2011, p. 101). Many types of data are most efficiently gathered from higher education and research institutions, e.g. about staff composition, institutional facilities, budget reallocation, or license income. However, monopolies on data create a 'principal-agent' problem and invite 'gaming the rankings' through manipulation of data (see Chap. 5). Less sinister but also problematic for creating comparable rankings, individual institutions' definitions of terms may differ—certainly across countries but sometimes even within countries. Normalization to a single, globally-used definition may not always be straightforward.

For these reasons, self-reported data ought to be externally validated or verified. Measures for verification include statistical methods of checking plausibility (e.g. analysis of extreme cases and time series analysis), triangulation with other data-sources (e.g. on research funds) including official national higher education statistics and using the expertise and knowledge of an advisory board.

In the USA, the Integrated Postsecondary Education Data System (IPEDS) has long been established as a publicly available, verified source of data on higher education institutions (http://nces.ed.gov/ipeds). It is based on a system of interrelated surveys conducted annually by the US Department of Education's National Center for Education Statistics (NCES). IPEDS is the major data-provider for the Carnegie Classification (see Sect. 4.4.1). A European bridge between institutional data and regular collections of statistics has been studied in the EC-supported EUMIDA project. EUMIDA explored the feasibility of publishing detailed data at the level of all individual higher education institutions as part of a future European Observatory on Universities. The final report of the project concluded that 'regular data collection is feasible because data is available, the legal obstacles are not overwhelming, the perimeters of institutions are largely agreed, and the overall effort is within the scope of the current activities of most statistical authorities' (Bonaccorsi et al., 2010). In the framework of the Observatory, regular data collection is intended, in cooperation with EU member states' representatives in Eurostat. Also, the Expert Group AUBR recommended setting up a regular observatory on institutional research information (AUBR Expert Group, 2009).

Until IPEDS and higher education and research institution observatories become worldwide phenomena, ad hoc data collection by asking higher education and research institutions directly will remain a necessity.

Surveys

A number of rankings use survey-data to get information on institutions' reputations especially, through peer surveys (e.g. THE, QS, USN&WR, CHE), as well as information from satisfaction surveys of students and graduates (e.g. CHE, SK123). We disregard here website 'surveys' that do not live up to standards of methodology, such as ratemyprofessors.com: to begin with, there is no information about the sample of respondents or even control of who responds beyond the simple setting up of a web account. Nor is there control of whether respondents took classes with the professor they are rating.

The survey method is in general strong in eliciting respondents' opinions rather than facts. This may reflect the adage that 'quality is in the eye of the beholder', but that is only relevant to other users of rankings if the beholders have fact-based opinions, which is questionable on a worldwide scale—even on the smaller scale of the USA as a whole, where sometimes supposedly informed people blunder in speaking about Princeton Law School (http://en.wikipedia.org/wiki/Princeton_Law_School), or the German-speaking part of Europe (Berghoff & Federkeil, 2006) where opinions of academics on higher education institutions in other countries than their own regularly proved to be far from fact-based.

Evidence shows (Federkeil, 2009) that the reputation of universities as an attribution of quality among particular groups is strongly affected by the structure of the sample in terms of regional distribution, fields and the types of persons being asked. This is particularly challenging for international surveys on reputation. Unfortunately the rankings that rely heavily (34–40%) on peer surveys do not give much information about the samples, response rates, etc. A major problem of the worldwide QS survey among academics, for instance, used to be the extremely low response rate of 2%. Academic reputation is known to be rather stable (Federkeil); the fact that there are large changes in the results of some universities from 1 year to the next suggests that surveys face problems of reliability. The quality of results heavily depends on the quality of the sample. In 2009, a discussion broke out in the USA about the trustworthiness of peer reports as used in the USN&WR (and the same might apply to the QS and THE league tables): respondents to the ranking survey were accused of valuing other higher education institutions lowly to make their own institution stand out better (see e.g. www.insidehighered.com/news/2009/08/19/rankings).

Student (or graduate) satisfaction with their higher education experience is particularly relevant for those rankings that address prospective students. Experience from e.g. the CHE and SK123 rankings and national student surveys in Northern America,[5] the UK[6] and Australia[7] shows that national student and graduate surveys produce fairly robust comparative information about higher education institutions.

---

[5] The National Survey of Student Engagement (NSSE) is an annual survey among students in the United States and Canada, which focuses on time and effort that students expend on their studies and about how institutions encourage students to participate in their learning.

[6] The National Student Survey (NSS) is an annual, national survey in higher (and further) education in the United Kingdom of final-year undergraduate students to ask feedback on the student learning experience.

[7] The Course Experience Questionnaire (CEQ) is an annual, national survey among recent graduates of Australian higher education institutions about their experience regarding teaching, generic skills and overall satisfaction.

Until recently however there was little experience with international comparability of this type of survey data. The outcomes of the international student satisfaction survey developed in the context in U-Multirank (see Part II) show that such data can indeed be created.

References

AUBR Expert Group. (2009). *Assessing Europe's University-Based Research – Draft.* s. l. Brussels: European Commission – DG Research.

Berghoff, S., & Federkeil, G. (2006). *Reputation indicators in university rankings.* Paper presented at the CHER 19th Annual Conference, Kassel, Germany.

Bonaccorsi, A., Brandt, T., De Filippo, D., Lepori, B., Molinari, F., Niederl, A., et al. (2010). *Feasibility study for creating a European University Data Collection: Final study report.* Brussels: European Commission, Directorate-General Research.

Dill, D. D. (2006, September 7–9). *Convergence and diversity: The role and influence of university rankings.* Paper presented at the CHER 19th annual research conference, Kassel, Germany.

Federkeil, G. (2006). Rankings and quality assurance in higher education. *Higher Education in Europe, 33*, 209–218.

Federkeil, G. (2009). Reputation indicators in rankings of higher education institutions. In B. M. Kehm & B. Stensaker (Eds.), *University rankings, diversity and the new landscape of higher education* (pp. 19–34). Rotterdam: Sense Publishers.

Hazelkorn, E. (2011). *Rankings and the reshaping of higher education: The battle for world-class excellence.* London: Palgrave Macmillan.

Kuh, G. D. (2011). Rehabbing the rankings: Fool's errand or the Lord's work. *College & University, 86*(4), 8–19.

McCormick, A. C., & Zhao, C.-M. (2005, September/October). Rethinking and reframing the Carnegie classification. *Change, 37*, 51–57.

Thibaud, A. (2009). *Vers quel classement européen des universités? Etude comparative du classement de Shanghai et des autres classements internationaux* (No. Note de Benchmarking 4). Brussels/Paris: Institut Thomas More.

Chapter 4
An Evaluation and Critique of Current Rankings

Gero Federkeil, Frans A. van Vught, and Don F. Westerheijden

4.1 Introduction

This chapter gives an overview of the state of the art concerning the research on rankings along two aspects: a critique of ranking methodology, and identification of good practices. Rankings and league tables have been criticized on methodological grounds by many commentators (among many others: Brown, 2006; Dill & Soo, 2005; Enserink, 2007; Gottlieb, 1999; Högskolverket, 2009; King et al. 2008; Klein & Hamilton, 1998; Leeuw, 2002; Marginson, 2006, 2008, 2009; Merisotis, 2003; Saisana & D'Hombres, 2008; Usher & Savino, 2006; van der Wende, 2008; van der Wende & Westerheijden, 2009; Van Dyke, 2005; van Raan, 2005; Yorke, 1998); in the following, we will build on their (and others') works to summarize the main methodological criticisms of rankings and league tables. In addition, we shall look at the current rankings. We have three purposes for doing that. First, we want to update and extend this kind of critique. Second, we want to identify and highlight good practices. And third, a detailed overview of some major transparency tools offers suggestions that may be useful for developing the indicators for the new multidimensional ranking instrument (U-Multirank) in Part II of this volume.

G. Federkeil (✉)
Centre for Higher Education (CHE), Gütersloh, Germany

F.A. van Vught • D.F. Westerheijden
Center for Higher Education Policy Studies, University of Twente,
Enschede, The Netherlands

4.2 Methodological Evaluation and Critique

4.2.1 The Problem of Unspecified Target Groups

Rankings are often said to be for informing students, so that students may make a more rational choice of the higher education institution they are going to attend. Rapp called this 'The common 'politically correct' purpose' (Presentation at EUA, The role of evaluation and ranking of universities in the quality culture, July 02, 2009). But do league tables give students the information they want? It is one of the principles of 'good ranking' in the Berlin Principles (which will be discussed in Sect. 6.2) that rankings should be geared towards their target group. Until recently, too little attention was paid to this aspect: it was simply assumed implicitly that whatever indicators were available must be relevant, and would apply to all groups of readers of rankings (King et al., 2008).

In the simplest models of communication, three elements are distinguished: the sender, the message and the receiver. To understand information needs, we should start with the receivers and the decision situation they are in. What do they want to do and what information do they need in order to do this well? 'Receivers' can be 'clients', institutions or funders. Clients can be further specified into current students, prospective students (sometimes their parents are also seen as clients) and employers or professionals for whom and with whom graduates will work after finishing their studies. When it comes to 'what to do?' interesting choices include: what to study, which candidate to hire, which higher education institution to choose as a partner in a project, which projects to fund, etc. Obviously, for such different decisions, different actors need different information on different objects—the case for a multidimensional transparency tool is obvious once this is realized.

Besides, for some of these decisions, more than just the characteristics ('qualities') of higher education institutions play a role in practice. The college choice process of students may be the best-known example of that statement: prospective students may have very different motivations in choosing to study a certain program in a certain location. They may be investment-motivated or focusing on consumption motives (Westerheijden, 2009), in addition to being constrained in their choice of options through social factors. Rankings should give information on investment (e.g. future job chances) *and* consumption motives (e.g. the sports facilities available at the higher education institution) and in that way alleviate social constraints. Therefore, multidimensionality is required even for a single target group and a single function of the higher education institutions.

It is contested, however, to what extent existing transparency tools reach the groups among students most constrained by social factors (briefly addressed in e.g.: Cremonini, Westerheijden, & Enders, 2008). Rankings might thus continue and even strengthen social stratification of students rather than help widen access.

Such sociological worries may apply less to choices by e.g. institutional leaders; for them, the lack of credible and comparable information on other higher education institutions is the main reason for their interest in transparency tools. Research universities especially have begun to reference themselves worldwide (Marginson, 2008), urging decision-makers in these higher education institutions to think bigger and set the bar higher. A consequence of this worldwide phenomenon may be the aforementioned global 'reputation race' (Hazelkorn, 2011; van Vught, 2008) among research-oriented higher education institutions. Reputation is an efficient and therefore attractive indicator of 'quality' for actors who do not have the time, need or other resources to delve deeply for detailed information (Stigler, 1961), or to worry about what makes up 'quality'. Hence also the remark that: 'Rankings enjoy a high level of acceptance among stakeholders and the wider public because of their simplicity and consumer-type information' (AUBR Expert Group, 2009). One might question if institutional managers *should* not be interested in the detailed information rather than in reputation, but if we can surmise that institutional managers may expect that stakeholders are mainly interested in reputation, it is in their interest to 'keep up appearances' in the eyes of stakeholders. Reputation is 'good' for institutional managers (van Vught), because a high reputation is what their stakeholders act upon. A good reputation gives better access to funds, highly-performing staff members, well-prepared first-year students, etc., all of which will result in measurably better performance in later years.

A deplorable side effect of the information efficiency argument is that there may be a tendency among users of rankings and league tables to simplify them to a one-dimensional league table anyway. We will come back to such effects in Sect. 4.3.3.

4.2.2 The Problem of Ignoring Diversity Within Higher Education and Research Institutions

World university league tables are the type of transparency tools that catch most public attention. They are primarily rankings of *whole* institutions, i.e. they compare whole institutions across all fields, ignoring internal variance in qualities of specific academic fields within an institution. For some purposes, it may be desirable to have institution-wide information, but in many, especially global, league tables treating the institution as a whole seems to be an unquestioned assumption. We would like to call that assumption into question, because evidence shows that performance in different departments/fields can vary widely within one institution. Only a very small number of 'world class' universities perform highly in (almost) all of their departments. The most appropriate and realistic strategy for most universities around the world is to focus their efforts on being outstanding in a limited number of fields. The majority of higher education institutions thus have both high and low(er) performing departments.

In order to underline this point, we compared the engineering and humanities field rankings of the 2008 THE Ranking; it showed that only 22% of the universities ranked among the top 100 in one of the two broad areas of engineering and humanities & arts were also among the top 100 in the other field. Ranking whole institutions blurs those differences, which in many cases are deliberate profiles based on strategic decisions taken by universities.

In addition, many stakeholders, e.g. (prospective) students and teachers/researchers, are mainly interested in information about specific fields. Prospective students want to be informed about the programs in the field they want to study (with some contextual information about the institution as a whole); researchers want to compare with colleagues in their field. Also, for university leaders who are interested in managing the competitive position of their whole university, institutional rankings are not sufficiently informative: they need to know which fields/departments are performing well and which are not. For the strategic management of a university it makes a decisive difference if performance is average across all fields or if top performers and poor performers can be identified. However, with only institutional-level information, in both cases this university ends up in the middle of a league table. With regard to these primary knowledge needs of target groups, institutional league tables produce misleading averages of the performance of fields/departments.

In global league tables that include (broad) field-based rankings (ARWU, THE, HEEACT) the selection of universities that are included is based on institutional league tables. This means that only institutions that are included in the overall institutional league table (e.g. the 200 or 500 'world class' universities overall) can enter the field-based rankings. Some specialized institutions therefore may have no chance to enter the ranking in their particular field of strength. For example, the Institut d'études politiques de Paris (SciencePo) has a high reputation in its field but did not make it on the social science list of the THE ranking because it does not offer enough 'mass' by including other fields as part of the set of institutions considered by the Times Higher Education.

As *national* rankings usually include all higher education institutions within a national system this selection problem does not occur. Hence their sample of universities in field-based rankings is not dependent on any pre-selection based on institutional indicators. The *Times Good University Guide* e.g. calculates a national institutional ranking but the field-based rankings (which occupy the most pages in the print edition) list all British universities offering degree programs in those fields.

4.2.3 The Problem of Narrow Range of Dimensions

Global league tables tend to concentrate on the few dimensions for which measurable data are publicly available, e.g. bibliometric databases, or lists of Nobel Prize winners. Global league tables create the impression among readers, however, that they address the institutions' *overall quality*. The ARWU and the HEEACT league tables are prime examples of rankings based on research (productivity and impact); Webometrics looks at the web presence and impact of higher education institutions; the Ecole des Mines ranking is even narrower, being explicitly based on a single indicator of elite labor market success (the number of alumni holding a post of chief executive officer in one of the *Fortune* Global 500 companies). A problem arises once this narrow range of information is regarded as overall institutional quality, because of course institutional quality is a much more encompassing concept. Even if a number of rankings seem to correlate, this may be a measurement artifact (for instance, many rankers use the same database for publications and quotations[1]) rather than an indication of an underlying 'true' quality across different dimensions of performance.

As mentioned above, sometimes the tendency to ascribe overall quality to a narrow ranking is a deplorable side-effect of the natural tendency to strive for information efficiency by users of league tables. Some rankers stimulate that tendency by overtly suggesting that their league tables show the 'best' universities in the world. Others are more reticent in this respect.

All existing global league tables emphasize the research function of higher education institutions, because that is where they can define measurable indicators. The other functions of higher education institutions—education, the 'third mission'—and other characteristics making up the quality of higher education institutions—e.g. international orientation—are not valued in the conceptual frameworks that in fact underpin the indicators used in current global rankings.

4.2.4 The Problem of Composite Overall Indicators

The 'classical' league table model is based on a single composite indicator calculated out of weighted indicators used in the ranking. The Shanghai ARWU, the THE, and HEEACT as well as most national rankings (e.g. USN&WR, Perspektywy) aggregate their diverse indicators into a composite overall score by giving particular weights to the single indicators. Composite indicators are used in many performance indicators systems and rankings (OECD 2008). In the course of growing complexity of many social systems they can be seen as an instrument of 'distilling reality into a manageable form'. But at the same time they carry the danger of oversimplifying complex social realities and calculating misleading averages out of opposite indicators. Presenting results in the form of one composite overall indicator, although very common, at the same time is one of the 'main courses for the institutional unease' with league tables in higher education (Usher & Savino, 2006). It leads to the impression that whatever limited set of indicators is used, they depict overall quality, and in a further step this intensifies the reputation race.

There are several aspects to a critical assessment of composite indicators. First, assigning weights to individual indicators requires a conceptual model with a set of arguments about the relative importance and priorities of the indicators for the construct of quality. An older study on the US News & World Report Rankings delivered by the National Opinion Research Center (1997) confirmed 'that the

---

[1] The THE bases its rankings on the same source, Thomson Reuters, as the ARWU and Leiden Rankings.

weights used to combine the various measures into an overall rating lack any defensible empirical or theoretical basis'.[2] Assigning weights to indicators is necessarily arbitrary, as there are neither generally accepted theoretical nor definite empirical arguments for assigning particular weights to individual indicators (Dill & Soo, 2005). At the same time, the chosen arbitrary weights define the model of higher education institutions actually supported by the league table. In ARWU as well as THE, this is a research-oriented, large institution, because that is the type of institution producing large numbers of publications and citations (Filliatreau & Zitt, s. a.), and by doing so, setting its reputation. Reputation is further enhanced by the higher education institution being located in a (for tourists or newspapers) major, well-known city—and by establishing a university brand (Marginson, 2008).

Second, as we argued before, different target groups of rankings and individual users have different priorities and preferences in comparing universities and in making choices. Even more, as mentioned above, prospective students have heterogeneous preferences with regard to their criteria for selecting a university. Rankings that aim to be relevant for users' decision-making processes should take into account this heterogeneity and leave the decision about the relevance—hence weights—of indicators to the users. A composite indicator with fixed weights inevitably means patronizing users of rankings by deciding about the importance and relevance of different indicators. Eccles (Eccles & Gootman, 2002) pointed to an additional aspect: the approach of giving fixed weights usually fails to cater to the interests of non-traditional students who may have priorities and interests in finding an institution different from 'mainstream' weighting systems. In recent years some rankings introduced (in web-based rankings) an interactive tool to leave the decision about the relevance of indicators to the users. Some rankings (e.g. the Guardian Ranking) are doing this by allowing the user to assign their own weights to a number of individual indicators as the basis for the calculation of a composite indicator. Others like SK123, the CHE University Ranking and the interactive ranking of Taiwan universities HEEACT allow users to give priority to a number of indicators and having a personalized ranking of universities fulfilling those user-set criteria.

Third, the methodology of the then THE/QS and Shanghai rankings to construct their composite indicator appears to be statistically problematic. It has been demonstrated (Saisana & D'Hombres, 2008) that the results of the composite indicator used by both rankings are anything but robust. Based on a sensitivity analysis and simulations using a multitude of possible weighting systems, they showed that the rank position of 67% of universities in the THE ranking and of 60% in the Shanghai Jiao Tong Ranking are highly sensitive to the composition of the overall score. Variations in league table position by different indicator models in general is greater in the lower ranks, but even e.g. the Massachusetts Institute of Technology (MIT) can be classified between the 10th position and the 25th position with the THE data

---

[2] Cited after the download version: http://www.washingtonmonthly.com/features/2000/norc.html

(Saisana & D'Hombres, p. 53). Saisana and D'Hombres concluded that 'no conclusive inference regarding the relative performance for the majority of the universities can be drawn from either ranking' (p. 8).

4.2.5 The Problem of League Tables

Most rankings, both national and international, are based on constructing league tables, ordering universities on a continuous scale from numbers 1 to x. This model supposes that each difference in a rank position of an institution marks a difference in performance/quality—number 12 is better than number 14. In league tables 'minimal differences produced by random fluctuations may be misinterpreted as real differences' (Müller-Böling & Federkeil, 2007). Our empirical analysis of existing league tables suggests that in many cases small differences in the numerical value of indicators lead to quite substantial shifts in league table ranks. For example, in the 2008 edition of the THE World Rankings, the difference between the university ranked number 27 (Brown University) and that ranked 43rd (University of Queensland) is only 4.5 points on a 100-point scale. Only 10 points separate the institutions ranked number 50 and number 100. Hence league tables tend to exaggerate differences between institutions and push vertical stratification to the extreme. In statistical terms, the league table approach ignores the existence of standard errors in data. Meaningful rankings should be confined to establishing ranges (as the NRC rankings of PhD programs in the USA does), groups or clusters of institutions with similar profiles and/or programs.

League tables are also highly sensitive to changes in the methodology to compile tables, in particular with regard to methods of standardization of original scores. The introduction of 'z-score aggregation' as a new method of standardization in the THE ranking in 2008 led to a drop by the London School of Economics from 17th to 59th—yet still in publications and reactions the year-on-year changes are highlighted as if the same thing was measured.

4.2.6 The Problem of Field and Regional Biases in Publication and Citation Data

The problem of field and regional biases regards the—so far largely unsolved—challenge of existing rankings to address diversity related to cultural, language and contextual factors, especially when it comes to their handling of research performance.

First, the two major databases on publications and citations that are used for large-scale comparative bibliometric studies, Thomson Reuters' Web of Science

(WoS) (used in ARWU and in THE since 2010) and Elsevier's Scopus (underlying THE/QS until 2009), mainly include journal articles published in peer-reviewed journals. Publication cultures and modes vary considerably between different fields (e.g. Moed, 2005). These journals are the prime vehicles for knowledge dissemination in the natural sciences, medical sciences and life sciences. Focusing the data collection on those journal articles implies a bias in favor of research outputs in the sciences and medicine. CWTS studies have shown that even within the sciences, there are significant differences regarding publication cultures. In many of the applied sciences and in engineering, conference proceedings are often more important than journal articles. In the social sciences and humanities, book publications (both monographs and book chapters) play an important role in knowledge dissemination. As a result the existing WoS-based or Scopus-based indicators on the institutional level tend to disfavor universities that are strong in fields other than the sciences or do not have medical schools. So publication cultures have an impact on the outcomes of rankings. However, both databases are rapidly improving the major lacunas in their coverage of these underrepresented domains of knowledge production. Not only have numbers of journals increased, more and more conference proceedings are indexed as well. For example, as of 2009 the extended version of the Web of Science includes a Conference Proceedings Papers database. Comparative research by CWTS (Visser & Moed, 2008) on the overlap and differences of coverage with both databases indicates that Scopus exhibited a 50% 'surplus' of publications (above the WoS) in specific fields: Arts & Humanities; Engineering; Business, Management & Accounting; Energy. Nonetheless, the coverage of both databases is likely to remain unsatisfactory in those fields where neither journals nor conference proceedings papers are used by researchers and scholars as their main vehicle for knowledge dissemination: the arts and humanities in particular.

Second, the sets of journals in the databases used in the ARWU and THE are biased against non-English speaking countries. In particular the Thomson Reuters database (WoS) originated in the US and includes predominantly US and English-language journals. Hence publications from non-English speaking countries, including large countries with a long science tradition, are underrepresented (e.g. in French, German, Chinese, Japanese). As the sciences are mostly international in their modes of publication while several other fields (humanities, social sciences) are dealing more with national issues publishing in 'native' languages, the bias in favor of sciences is reinforced.

And third, both global league tables are implicitly used to assess the performance not only of universities but also of national higher education and research systems. Then the problem of different national approaches in the organization of higher education and research systems surfaces. For the citation databases implicitly refer to one particular model of higher education and research organization: they only include universities and largely exclude non-university research institutions (e.g. CNRS in France and Max Planck Institutes in Germany). Therefore, they may underestimate the research performance of major countries. A valid transparency tool would have to take into account the particular contextuality of national structures and for instance would have to include non-university research institutions. In addition, drawing an unequivocal line between research institutes and higher education institutions may be complicated if they share staff and facilities.

4.2.7 The Problem of Unspecified and Volatile Methodologies

The early league tables were published with little or no information on the methodology used to compile them. In recent years, increasing application of IREG's Berlin Principles (International Ranking Expert Group, 2006, see also next section) has ameliorated this situation. Most, though not all, websites of major global and national rankings now provide a section on their methodology. Nevertheless, a 2009 report complained: 'Research has found that the results of the Shanghai Jiao Tong Academic Ranking of World Universities (ARWU) are not replicable, thus calling into question the comparability and methodology used' (AUBR Expert Group, 2009). It has to be noted that the SJTU group was a founding member of the IREG; its methodology is explained on http://www.arwu.org/ARWUMethodology2010.jsp.

In addition, magazines publishing annual league tables have been accused of changing their methodology in order to achieve changes in their top positions, as there would be little news value in repeatedly having the same universities at the top and this could impact magazine sales (Dill & Soo, 2005).

4.3 Good Practice In and Around Ranking

Methodological critiques like the ones presented above and which echo observations in other research seem to indicate that all rankings and league tables are 'bad'. To counter that impression, we now turn to some examples of good practice, targeting the main points which were identified as problematic.

4.3.1 Berlin Principles on Ranking of Higher Education Institutions

In the second of a series of conferences of the International Ranking Expert Group (IREG), which is a group of individuals and organizations engaged in producing or researching rankings, convened in Berlin in 2006, a set of basic principles for good practice in rankings was agreed, labeled the *Berlin Principles on Ranking of Higher Education Institutions* (International Ranking Expert Group, 2006). The Berlin Principles refer to four aspects of rankings: the purposes and goals of rankings, design and weight of indicators, collection and processing of data and presentation of ranking results. In summary, the 16 principles call for:

- Clarity about purpose and target groups
- Recognition of the diversity of institutions
- Transparency regarding methodology
- The measurement of outcomes rather than inputs
- Providing consumers with a clear understanding of all the factors used to develop a ranking and offering a choice in how rankings are displayed
- The application of quality assurance principles to the ranking itself: facilitating understanding and intersubjective control by enabling feedback, providing feedback opportunities to end-users, and acting on feedback to correct errors and faults.

In general, the Berlin Principles are accepted as a set of relevant and appropriate indications of what should be seen as 'good' rankings. In our design of U-Multirank, we have applied such principles.

From 2011 onwards, the IREG audits and recognizes rankings to show that they are prepared 'in accordance with the highest quality standards – set up in the Berlin Principles' (IREG Observatory, 2011).

4.3.2 Rankings for Students: CHE and Studychoice123

In the area of transparency tools meant to support (prospective) students, some interesting alternatives to the league tables found in the USN&WR and its followers have been developed. The German-based rankings published by the CHE are internationally seen as good practice (Dill & Soo, 2005; Thibaud, 2009; Usher & Savino, 2006; Van Dyke, 2005); the Dutch Studychoice123 (SK123) is a very similar ranking issued in hard copy since the 1980s and available online since 2006. The main principles underlying this type of rankings include the following (see also Table 4.3):

- Definition of a stakeholder target group and explicit focus on aiding prospective students to find the study programs best matching their aims, needs and wants, selecting information in which they are interested (including investment and consumption motives);
- Ranking of units at the level of single disciplines or subject areas rather than presenting averages for higher education institutions as a whole;
- Interactive interfaces allowing end-users to decide which indicators weigh most heavily in their eyes, supported by web-based technologies allowing interactive rankings;
- Robust grouping of units into top, middle and bottom groups on each indicator rather than the spurious precision of league tables from number 1 to n;

- Use of different and where possible verified data sources (available statistics, factual information from higher education institutions, and opinion/satisfaction surveys among students, graduates and teaching staff, information about the university facilities, local amenities, etc.).

4.3.3 Leiden Ranking of University Research

The Centre for Science and Technology Studies (CWTS) of Leiden University in 2008 for the first time published a ranking entirely based on its own bibliometric indicators (www.cwts.nl/ranking). In its own words, the Leiden Ranking aims to compare research institutions with impact measures that take into account the differences between disciplines. The ranking focuses on all universities worldwide with more than 700 Web of Science indexed publications per year. This implies that the approximately 1,000 most productive (in terms of number of publications) universities in the world are covered.

There are in fact several rankings, because CWTS follows a multiple-indicator approach. On the basis of the same publication and citation data and the same technical and methodological starting points, different types of impact indicators can be constructed, for instance one focusing entirely on impact of the university as a whole, another in which also scale (size of the institution) is taken into account, or one normalized for the citation habits in a particular field of knowledge. Rankings based on these different indicators do not produce similar results, although they originate from exactly the same data. Moreover, rankings are strongly influenced by the size threshold used to define the set of universities for which the ranking is calculated. For instance, smaller universities that are not present in the top 100 (in size) may take high positions in impact ranking if the size threshold is lowered. Publishing multiple rankings is a way to give room to several perspectives on research performance in higher education and research institutions.

4.3.4 Qualifications Frameworks and Tuning Educational Structures

In the Bologna Process, attention has turned from degree restructuring to international cooperation in quality assurance and to qualifications frameworks as efforts to stimulate compatibility of studies across Europe increase (Westerheijden et al., 2010). Because of this, attention has increasingly focused on students' learning outcomes, and on the development and implementation of a qualifications framework for the whole Bologna area (the European Higher Education Area or EHEA), the so-called EHEA-QF. This EHEA-QF parallels the higher education levels of the qualifications framework developed in the European Union across all levels of (lifelong) learning, the EQF. However, the descriptors used in both European qualification frameworks developed to date are so abstract that they are not directly useful for the development of indicators for rankings.

In a less abstract and more field-based manner, the Socrates-supported project 'Tuning Educational Structures in Europe' (Tuning, for short: http://tuning.unideusto.org), has been working on developing descriptors of typical learning outcomes for graduates in 28 areas of knowledge. These descriptors are mostly content-based, e.g. in physics, a first-cycle graduate should 'have a good understanding of the most important physical theories (logical and mathematical structure, experimental support, described physical phenomena)' and in civil engineering an 'understanding of the interaction between technical and environmental issues and ability to design and construct environmentally friendly civil engineering works'. Where the European qualifications frameworks are too abstract to be useful for linking them to ranking indicators, Tuning may be too specific for that purpose. However, the Tuning descriptors do underpin our general focus on outcomes, as a part of the educational process that is eminently relevant for international comparison and compatibility.

4.3.5 *Comparative Assessment of Student Learning (AHELO)*

The OECD initiated a feasibility project to develop international comparative tests of what students at the end of their undergraduate studies have learned in their own field (the pilot fields are economics and engineering) as well as in general skills, the Assessment of Higher Education Learning Outcomes (AHELO).[3] AHELO extends the idea behind other international tests of competencies among pupils (TIMMS and PISA) and among adults (PIAAC), also organized under the auspices of the OECD. This is the first-ever effort to make an actual assessment of students' learning outcomes in higher education across countries. Potentially then, this would provide a highly relevant type of indicator for rankings that want to focus on student learning or added value (if combined with measures of quality of incoming students).

At the time of writing of this volume, the instruments for AHELO were being developed, so it is too early to reflect on its feasibility.

However AHELO, as it is being designed, will be administered to a relatively small sample of students in a small sample of higher education institutions' study programs (similar to PISA). As a consequence the data will be too fragmentary to

---

[3] http://www.oecd.org/document/22/0,3746,en_2649_35961291_40624662_1_1_1_1,00.html, last accessed May 19, 2011.

be used directly in a ranking of institutions or field-based units within institutions. For ranking purposes, samples of students from all institutions or fields involved in a ranking would have to be included in the tests.

4.3.6 Assessment of University-Based Research Expert Group

The DG Research and Innovation of the European Commission has been engaged in data collection about university-based research because of the key role of higher education institutions in the EU's innovation strategy. An Expert Group was appointed in 2008 'with a view to proposing a more valid comprehensive methodological approach', to 'promote and contribute to the development of multidimensional methodologies designed to facilitate the assessment of university-based research' (AUBR Expert Group, 2009, p. 5). The Expert Group's report concludes that there is no single set of indicators that responds to all information needs of all stakeholders, and goes on to propose guidelines for use in developing focused approaches to assessing university-based research:

- Fitness for purpose and objectives, which can be achieved through a matrix of possible indicators and which could be operationalized in a multidimensional, web-based tool;
- Quantitative and qualitative information should be combined;
- The appropriate scale should be 'knowledge clusters' e.g. faculties, departments, or interdisciplinary clusters.

For continued preparation of data collection, the Expert Group proposed to establish a European Observatory for Assessment of University-based Research. Finally, the Expert Group recommends that 'good practice' models, including its own proposed Multidimensional Research Assessment Matrix, should follow a number of principles (AUBR Expert Group, 2009, pp. 45–46):

- Consultation with researchers and universities;
- Data collection through digital repositories. Such non-obtrusive data collection might be extended beyond its current niches;
- Peer review panels to ensure a broader understanding of the research and its contribution to knowledge, including the importance of new disciplines and interdisciplinarity;
- Indicators: all 20 systems of research assessment surveyed by the AUBR Expert Group use bibliometric indicators, although many balance this with other information. Moreover, the AUBR Expert Group acknowledges that indicators measure past performance rather than potential, while decision-making by definition is about the future. And they draw attention to the limitation that '[e]mphasis on global impact can undermine the importance of regionally relevant outcomes' (AUBR Expert Group, 2009, p. 52);

- Purpose: the Expert Group assembled a matrix of instruments and purposes, enabling scenario-type recommendations of the type 'If one has purpose X, then instruments A, B, C are most appropriate';
- Self-evaluation: three research assessment schemes include self-evaluation as a key component in the process;
- Social and Economic Impact and Benefits: Several countries and universities are experimenting with measuring societal impact, demonstrated through case studies, end-user opinion, and appropriate indicators. This is most notable in the Australian Research Quality Framework (RQF), developed in 2005–2007, Aalto University in Finland, and the Netherlands;
- Unit of Assessment: research assessments should focus on the research discipline or unit, because it is necessary to accommodate differences in research quality within individual universities;
- Not mentioned by the Expert Group as a good practice, but important nevertheless is that positive attributes of research assessments include aiding strategic planning, international benchmarking, and bringing about greater cohesion and organization among discipline groupings (AUBR Expert Group, 2009). In other words, good assessments respond to information needs of important stakeholder groups.

Several of the good practices indicated by the Expert Group AUBR have been included in the design of U-Multirank (stakeholder consultation, purposefulness, being responsive to stakeholder information needs, focus on social and economic impact, and consideration of unit of assessment). As we will show in Chap. 6, U-Multirank is a multidimensional ranking tool that has taken many of the suggestions mentioned here on board.

4.4 Information, Indicators and Data Sources in Transparency Tools

In this section, we take a critical look at the types of data used in current classifications and rankings. We integrate the quality assurance aspect in this section, because this field shows relevant experiences with different data sources. The discussion focuses on data currently used but we will also include data originating in other contexts that could play a role for international rankings as well.

There is no neutral measurement of social issues; each measurement – the operationalization of constructs, the definition of indicators, and the selection of data sources – depends on the interest of research and the purpose of the measurement. International rankings in particular should be aware of possible biases and be precise about their objective. 'Not all nations or systems share the same values and beliefs about what constitutes 'quality' in tertiary institutions, and ranking systems should not be devised to force such comparisons' (International Ranking Expert Group, 2006, nr. 5). For instance, an evaluation of publication activities over a *past* period by bibliometric means would use a different approach to count publications of researchers who changed positions during the period of measurement than a ranking that wants to show the *potential* of researchers currently active at an institution, although the indicators may look the same at first glance. The appropriateness of data for the specific purpose of the ranking and the comparability of concepts, definitions and data between institutions are crucial issues, particularly in international rankings and must be checked very carefully.

4.4.1 Information Offered by Classifications

4.4.1.1 Carnegie Classification

The Carnegie Classification typifies higher education institutions along a large number of dimensions and indicators (www.carnegiefoundation.org/classifications). Describing all indicators goes beyond the scope of this discussion as some involve intricate analysis including factor analysis; they have to do with:

- Degree levels conferred by the higher education institution, absolute numbers and proportions of each level (from associate to doctorate);
- Fields of study (range, concentration, degrees per field, etc.);
- Location (town size and type, from metropolitan to rural);
- Numbers of students;
- Student profile (distribution of test scores of newly entering students; full-time or part-time status; degree-seeking or not; transfer origin [for higher degrees]; residential status [on-campus or otherwise]);
- Single or multiple campus;
- Research expenditure, research staff; combined into aggregate as well as per-capita measures.

The information needed to construct those indicators is derived entirely from publicly available databases in US higher education, in particular those collected in the Integrated Postsecondary Education Data System (IPEDS). The IPEDS is based on surveys conducted annually by the US Department of Education's National Center for Education Statistics (NCES; see http://nces.ed.gov/ipeds/). IPEDS gathers information from all higher education institutions in the US that benefit from federal student financial aid programs. There is a legal obligation for those higher education institutions to report data on enrolment, program completion, graduation rates, staff, finances, tuition fees and student financial aid. The federal agency checks the quality of the self-reported data. The Carnegie Foundation is thus neither responsible for the data collection nor for its verification; the data are freely available at the federal level in the US.

If higher education institutions do not provide the data, imputations are made by the Carnegie researchers. In some borderline cases regarding institutional profile, there is communication with the higher education institution to choose the best-fitting classification (e.g. mostly bachelor or mostly master degree institutions).

The only exception to using publicly-available databases in the Carnegie classification concerns the voluntary mention of higher education institutions as 'community engaged'; for this special category descriptive self-documentation was provided and reviewed by a US-wide consultation panel.

4.4.1.2 U-Map

The European U-Map tool (van Vught, 2009) is in a less advantageous position than the Carnegie Foundation, as there is no European database available at the level of higher education and research institutions. U-Map has put great effort into defining indicators and collecting the necessary information from several sources. However, national statistics often did not prove rich enough for the information needs, so ad hoc collection of information from higher education and research institutions has been the main data source in U-Map. U-Map's 23 indicators together make up six dimensions.

- Teaching and learning profile
  - Orientation of degree
  - Subject areas covered
  - Degree level focus
  - Expenditure on teaching
- Student profile
  - Mature or adult learners
  - Students enrolled (headcount)
  - Part-time students
  - Students enrolled in distance learning programs
- Research involvement
  - Expenditure on research
  - Peer-reviewed publications
  - Doctorate production
- Regional engagement
  - First-year bachelor students from the region
  - Importance of local/regional income sources
  - Graduates working in the region
- Involvement in knowledge exchange
  - Cultural activities
  - Income from knowledge exchange activities
  - Patent applications filed
  - Start-up firms

- International orientation
  - Foreign degree-seeking students
  - Importance of international sources of income
  - Outgoing students in European and other international exchange programs
  - Incoming students in European and other international exchange programs
  - Non-national teaching and research staff

U-Map has also tested 'pre-filling' higher education institutions' questionnaires, i.e. data available in national public sources are entered into the questionnaires sent to higher education institutions for data gathering. This should reduce the effort required from higher education institutions and give them the opportunity to verify the 'pre-filled' data as well. The U-Map test with 'pre-filling' from national data sources in several countries has appeared to be successful and resulted in a substantial decrease of the burden of gathering data at the level of higher education institutions.

4.4.2 Information Offered by Global Institutional Rankings

Global rankings and league tables share broad principles and approaches, although they are driven by different purposes and differ in relation to their methodologies, criteria, reliability and validity (Dill & Soo, 2005). The latter suggests that there is no commonly accepted definition of quality of higher education—as research on quality assurance found two decades ago (Brennan, Goedegebuure, Shah, Westerheijden, & Weusthof, 1992)—and hence a single, objective league table cannot exist (Brown, 2006; Usher & Savino, 2006; Van Dyke, 2005). This is shown even by a cursory comparison of the indicators that major global institutional rankings use (cf. Table 4.1), which we will go into in the following subsections.

All of the following rankings limit their range to several hundred pre-selected higher education institutions—universities, to be precise. We shall not go into the criteria used to establish a threshold, but generally they have to do with the research output in total of the institution; institutional size, and therefore its visibility, is generally seen as a prerequisite for being ranked.

In addition, the existing '[g]lobal rankings suggest that there is in fact only one model that can have global standing: the large comprehensive research university' (van der Wende & Westerheijden, 2009). The higher regard for research institutions cannot be blamed on the league tables or on the availability of citation data only, but also arises from the academy's own stance towards the importance of research. Although it can be argued that a league of world-class universities needs to exist as role models (on the concept of the world-class university cf. Salmi, 2009), the evidence that strong institutions inspire better performance is so far mainly found in the area of research rather than that of teaching (Sadlak & Liu, 2007). This means that in the existing rankings data are available only in this special type of higher education institution, which represents only a minority of the higher education and research institutions of the world.

Table 4.1 Indicators and weights in global university rankings

	HEEACT 2010	ARWU 2010	THE 2010	QS 2011	Leiden Rankings 2010
Research output	Articles past 11 years (10%) and last year (10%)	Articles published in *Nature* and *Science* (20%) [Not calculated for institutions specialized in humanities and social sciences]	Research income (5.25%) Ratio public research income/total research income (0.75%) Papers per staff member (4.5%)		Number of publications (P)
Research impact	Citations last 11 years (10%) and last 2 years (10%) Average annual number of citations last 11 years (10%) Hirsch-index last 2 years (20%) Highly-cited papers (15%) Articles last year in high-impact journals (15%)	Articles in Science Citation Index-expanded and Social Science Citation Index (20%)	Citations (normalized average citation per paper) (32.5%)	Citations per faculty member (20%)	Two versions of size-independent, field-normalized average impact ('crown indicator' CPP/FCSm, and alternative calculation MNCS2) Size-dependent 'brute force' impact indicator (multiplication of P with the university's field-normalized average impact): P * CPP/FCSm Citations-per-publication indicator (CPP)
Quality of education		Alumni of an institution winning Nobel Prizes and Fields Medals (10%)	PhDs awarded per staff (6%) Undergraduates admitted per staff (4.5%) Income per staff (2.25%) Ratio PhD awards/bachelor awards (2.25%)	Faculty/student ratio (20%)	
Quality of staff		Staff winning Nobel Prizes and Fields Medals (20%) Highly cited researchers in 21 broad subject categories (20%)			

Reputation			Peer review survey (19.5 + 15 = 34.5%) International staff score (5%) International students score (5%)	Academic reputation survey (40%) Employer reputation survey (10%)
			Ratio international mix, staff and students (5%) Industry income per staff (2.5%)	International faculty (5%) International students (5%)
General		Sum of all indicators, divided by staff number (10%)		
Website	http://ranking.heeact.edu.tw/en-us/2010/Page/Indicators	http://www.arwu.org/ARWUMethodology2010.jsp	http://www.timeshighereducation.co.uk/world-university-rankings/2010-2011/analysis-methodology.html	http://www.topuniversities.com/university-rankings/world-university-rankings	http://www.socialsciences.leiden.edu/cwts/products-services/leiden-ranking-2010-cwts.html
Notes					There are several rankings, each focusing on one indicator

4.4.2.1 Academic Ranking of World Universities (ARWU)

The Shanghai Academic Ranking of World Universities (ARWU) focuses on research. The publication concerns the top 500 of some 1,000 universities in the ARWU database. It is based on indicators about publications, citations and highly cited authors as registered in worldwide databases and on the lists (and CVs) of Nobel prize and Field medal winners, besides institutions' staff numbers. As all indicators are size-dependent an additional indicator was introduced to calculate productivity per staff member. Sixty percent of the composite score relies on bibliometric indicators, 30% on Nobel prize/Field medal winners and the remaining 10% on the size-independent indicator.

The indicators on research mainly refer to research *activity* measured by the number of publications rather than on research *impact* (citations). Publications in journals *Science* and *Nature* are counted twice (they are part of SCI publications, too). This implies a clear bias towards the natural sciences.

Nobel prizes are awarded for a limited number of academic fields only (physiology/medicine, chemistry, physics, economics; literature and peace do not refer to academic achievements). This means that 40% of the overall score refers to five fields of research only (including the Field medal for mathematics). Nobel prize winners since 1910 are taken into account, but with larger weights for more recent laureates. They are used for two indicators. First, as Nobel winners they are counted for the university to which they were affiliated at the time of winning the prize. Nobel prizes are usually awarded many years after the original research was undertaken and many prize winners could have changed university in the meantime. It can be questioned, therefore, if this indicator measures an institution's research excellence or rather its ability to attract researchers with high reputations. Second, Nobel prizes are counted for a university's graduates, which also has a tenuous and lengthy time lag relationship with the excellence of an institution at this moment: to what extent has becoming a Nobel prize winner been 'caused' by teaching in the university where they studied for their first or second degree?

Hence the institutional ARWU ranking has a strong bias in favor of the natural sciences due to the selection of indicators (e.g. the use of publications in *Science* and *Nature*). The use of the (mainly English language) bibliometric database in addition raises questions of language and cultural bias.

In addition to the institutional ranking, ARWU publishes rankings of broad academic fields for natural sciences/mathematics, engineering/technology and computer science, life and agricultural sciences, clinical medicine and pharmacy and social sciences. The indicators are slightly different from the institutional ranking: instead of articles in *Science* and *Nature* the broad field rankings are measuring the number of articles in top journals in the fields. As there are no Nobel prizes in engineering, external research funds are substituting this indicator (see Table 4.2).

In 2009 the first-time ARWU rankings for five fields were published: mathematics, physics, chemistry, computer science and economics/business. In these field-based rankings the indicators are the same as those used for the respective broad fields.

Table 4.2 Indicators and weights in ARWU field rankings

Indicator	Weight	Science	Engineering	Life sciences	Clinical medicine	Social sciences
Alumni	10%	X	–	X	X	X
Awards	15%	X	–	X	X	X
Publications (SCI, SSCI)	25%	X	X	X	X	X
Top journal publications	25%	X	X	X	X	X
Highly cited authors	25%	X	X	X	X	X
Research funds	25%	–	X	–	–	–

The methodology of the rankings is described in detail on the ARWU website (www.arwu.org). The rankings rely exclusively on existing, publicly available databases. Due to the limitations and biases inherent in the indicators the ranking gives valid information on research in the natural sciences and medicine; but validity is limited for engineering and very problematic for the social sciences and humanities (which are not included in the field-based rankings). To be fair, we must keep in mind that the Shanghai ranking was originally developed to compare the research performance in science and technology of Chinese universities with the rest of the world.

ARWU's presentation is on a website (www.arwu.org), but the ranking is fixed; there is no interactivity beyond choosing the global institutional ranking, the field ranking or the subject ranking. Registered users (registration is free) can also get a view of each university's profile, which gives the total ranking over the years since 2003 as well as the field and subject rankings in which the university figures since those started (2007 and 2009, respectively).

4.4.2.2 The Times Higher Education (THE) Ranking

The methodology of the *Times Higher Education*'s ranking changed somewhat after 2009, when THE split from the company that until then produced its rankings, QS, because of the continued criticism of the QS methodology (which will be described in the next subsection). Since 2010, the THE methodology has evolved towards a more sophisticated and larger set of indicators, in cooperation with Reuters Thomson, which shifted the weights of indicators towards bibliometric indicators and redesigned the academic worldwide survey. The survey remains the major data collection method and it also remains the heaviest weighted set of indicators, as they make up 34% of the ranking score—the difference with the old methodology in that sense is marginal. More importantly, the reputation questions in the survey are more directed, because THE now distinguishes research reputation from educational reputation (see Fig. 4.1)[4].

Research impact in terms of citations makes up an almost equal share of the index (32.5%). Smaller weights are accorded to several indicators of the learning

---
[4] http://www.timeshighereducation.co.uk/world-university-rankings/2010-2011/analysis-methodology.html

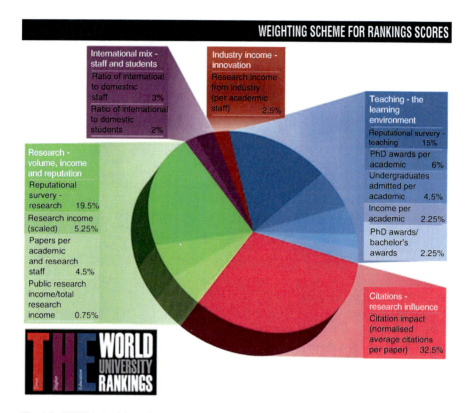

Fig. 4.1 THE Methodology 2010 (Supplied courtesy of the *Times Higher Education*)

environment (together 15%), research volume and income (together 10.5%), internationalization (5%) and industry-related research (2.5%).

The website on which the THE ranking is published (http://www.timeshighereducation.co.uk/world-university-rankings) by default gives the league table of the top 200 universities, but has added interactivity in recent years. It is possible for end-users to select league tables by one of the major dimensions of the ranking (teaching, research, citations, internationalization or industry research), next to a top 100 by reputation. Furthermore, there are six broad field-based rankings and continent-region rankings.

4.4.2.3 QS Top Universities Ranking

Quacquarelli Symonds Ltd used to produce the rankings published in the *Times Higher Education (Supplement)*, and after *THE* split off in 2009 continued to publish its own ranking for the USA in cooperation with *US News & World Report (USN&WR)*.

The QS methodology depends strongly on academics' opinions of the 'quality' or rather reputation of higher education institutions around the world, as its most important instrument (making up 40% of the ranking) was a worldwide survey. An additional reputational survey, among employers, makes up another 10% of the ranking. Regarding the academics' idea of reputation, the QSC survey was completely undirected. The survey simply stated that 'it is the informed views of the academic community that ensures the ranking recognizes excellence without rigidly dictating the form that excellence must take'. This statement takes the well-known paraphrase 'quality is in the eye of the beholder' completely from the wrong end because the 'beholder' is the end-user of the ranking, not the one who delivers data. But if it is not known what goes into the ranking, the only appropriate adage is 'garbage in, garbage out'.

The other half of the ranking outcome mainly depends on research impact and staff to student ratio (each 20%). The remainder is devoted to internationalization of staff and students (each 5%).

Besides a world institutional league table of 600 universities, visitors to the website (http://www.topuniversities.com/university-rankings) may find a league table of Asian universities, and world universities by subject area. There is no interactivity regarding weighting or selection of indicators on the website.

4.4.2.4 The Higher Education Evaluation and Accreditation Council, Taiwan (HEEACT)

The Higher Education Evaluation and Accreditation Council of Taiwan (HEEACT) publishes a ranking of the academic performance of higher education institutions in a five-year project which ran until 2010. The HEEACT pre-selected what it called 'the top 500' higher education institutions to calculate its ranking. The ranking was completely bibliometric; the dimensions involved were 'research productivity, research impact and research excellence' indicated by, respectively, published papers and citations, and highlighting highly-cited papers (for weights, see Table 4.1).

In contrast to most other rankings the time period taken into consideration was quite long (11 years) and thus the HEEACT ranking, more than others, referred to past performance rather than current potential, although it duplicated some indicators for the last year to emphasize current trends. Due to the structure of the underlying databases this ranking had a similar bias towards the natural sciences as the ARWU rankings. In its studies of the national universities, the HEEACT also looked at employers' satisfaction with graduates and at university-industry cooperation, using patents as an indicator, but those data were not included in its international ranking and more detailed information was not available in English.

The HEEACT website (http://ranking.heeact.edu.tw/en-us/2010/homepage) allows, among other things, for sorting the higher education institutions either according to their rank in the top 500, alphabetically by name, or by their scores on one of the 10 individual indicators.

4.4.2.5 Leiden Ranking

The Leiden rankings have been discussed above (Sect. 4.3.3). They indicate publications and—mostly—citations from a major international publications and citations database (the Thomson Reuters data underlying what was formerly known as the ISI Web of Science), which undergoes intensive checking and cleaning by the CWTS group to ensure that publications are ascribed to the correct authors in the correct higher education and research institutions.

4.4.3 Information Offered by Field-Based Rankings

In Table 4.3 we present an overview of the indicators used in major field-based rankings. Besides the rankings that cover many fields and which are included in the table, we have taken into consideration some specialized field rankings.

4.4.3.1 Field-Based Rankings Across Fields

Rankings of US higher education institutions are not international league tables, but one of the American rankings has set the whole rankings 'business' in motion, and another is mentioned for its focused approach. The former is of course the US News & World Report (www.usnews.com/sections/rankings). It lists the 'best colleges' and the 'best graduate schools', classifying higher education institutions on the basis of the Carnegie basic classification and using indicators collected through a questionnaire to higher education institutions. Joining the ranks of rankers in 2008, *Forbes* magazine takes a somewhat different, more economic approach (Vedder & Ewalt, 2009) to ranking 660 undergraduate colleges from what it defines as a student perspective. *Forbes* does not distinguish types of higher education institutions, apart from their funding base: public or private. Its production-oriented indicators (fast graduation, high earnings) result not in the 'usual suspects' such as Harvard or MIT at the top of the table, but military academy West Point instead.

Having been discussed in some detail before, we will not go into the CHE and SK123 rankings again (Sect. 4.3.2). Instead, let us summarize the major field-based rankings that include different fields here together.

Deriving from their explicit aim to inform prospective students in their own country about studies in all major fields, these rankings collect data that puts less emphasis on research than the institutional global rankings; in fact, only the CHE university rankings include any indicator of research at all.

Regarding quality of education, there are different emphases on objective versus subjective (student satisfaction) data, which are strongly present in SK123. There is one ranking, that produced by *USN&WR*, which uses a survey to assess reputation in the eyes of peers.

Table 4.3 Main indicators in major field-based rankings

	CHE Excellence Ranking	Studychoice 123	USN&WR 2009 'America's Best Colleges'	Forbes 2011 'America's Best Colleges'
Research output	Publications (P)			
Research impact	Citation 'crown indicator' (CPP/FCSm) Highly-cited books			
Quality of education	Students' overall satisfaction Student mobility Participation in an Erasmus Mundus program	Student opinion per course Student opinion on facilities by institution Job market by discipline	Retention (freshmen, graduation) (20.25%) Student selectivity (high-scoring entrants, acceptance rate) (15%) Financial resources for education (10%) Graduation rate performance (related to expected rate) (0.5%)	Student evaluations of professors from Ratemyprofessors.com (25%) Postgraduate success: Listing of alumni in the Who's Who in America (25%) Four-year graduation rates (16.7%)
Quality of staff	Teaching staff mobility in ERASMUS (incoming + outgoing) International staff		Faculty resources (class size, salary, staff degrees, full-time, staff-student ratio) (20%)	
Reputation			Peer assessment of academic excellence (25%)	

(continued)

Table 4.3 (continued)

	CHE Excellence Ranking	Studychoice 123	USN&WR 2009 'America's Best Colleges'	Forbes 2011 'America's Best Colleges'
General	International master's students International doctoral students	Accessibility and facilities by institution Admittance and selection per course	Alumni giving rate (5%)	Enrolment-adjusted numbers of students and faculty receiving nationally competitive awards (16.7%) Estimated average loan debt of students upon graduation (20%)
Websites	www.excellenceranking.org	www.studychoice123.nl	www.usnews.com/rankings	http://bestcollegerankings.org/popular-rankings/forbes-college-rankings/
Notes	More information is available in in-depth comparison of user-selected study programs	Mentioned here are headings, each encompassing 3–10 'rankable' indicators and/or 4–6 non-'rankable' items of information. There is also more information in the form of 'basic facts' for higher education institutions, locations, etc.	There are alternative weightings for master and baccalaureate colleges as opposed to liberal arts colleges and 'national universities' on retention and graduation	

Within the objective data, dependence on the context of national higher education systems becomes clear, as the US-based USN&WR includes an indicator of selectivity of access and of alumni giving, which would not make sense in the German or Dutch higher education systems.

In general, from the table it appears that the different field-based rankings show little overlap in the information they provide.

4.4.3.2 Business Studies Rankings

The field in which we find most specific, field-based rankings concerns business schools and MBA rankings. There are a number of rankings produced by newspapers and journals such as *Business Week*, *Financial Times*, *The Wall Street Journal*, *The Economist*, and *US News & World Report*. 'Each of those rankings has its own methodology and collects its own data. Some rankings are based on surveys of constituent groups, such as graduating students (e.g., BusinessWeek) or corporate recruiters (e.g. The Wall Street Journal). Others apply at least some weight to data reported directly by schools (e.g. US News & World Report, Financial Times)' (AACSB, 2005).

The most prominent ranking of MBA programs is published by the *Financial Times* (http://rankings.ft.com/businessschoolrankings). The ranking follows the traditional approach of calculating a composite overall indicator that is transformed into a league table. In contrast to the ARWU and THE/QS rankings, which confine themselves to a small number of indicators, FT's MBA ranking uses 20 indicators to calculate the composite overall score (and some indicators themselves are composite indicators out of a number of single measures). Related to the specific profiles of MBA programs 40% of the overall score comes from two indicators on graduates' salaries; 10% is due to the number of faculty publications in a list of 40 academic and practitioner journals weighted by size of institutions; the rest is distributed evenly across the various indicators (Table 4.4).

The single indicators are described on FT's website but the scores of the composite indicators are not published. Hence there is no information about the score differentials between the institutions.

The FT website among other things gives the option of sorting the institutions by each of the individual indicators shown on screen (which can be a standard subset or up to all of the indicators used); specific schools can be compared with one another, and the rankings can also be downloaded as a worksheet.

The report by the AACSB Task Force criticized special rankings of MBA programs because of the risk they run of creating a narrow view on universities and business schools (AACSB, 2005, p. 7).

This task force believes that media rankings have had other more serious negative impacts on business education. Because rankings of fulltime MBA programs are commonly presented under the label of 'best b-schools,' the public has developed a narrow definition about the breadth and value of business education. This diminishes the importance of faculty research, undergraduate programs and

Table 4.4 Indicators FT MBA ranking

Indicator	Weight
Weighted salary	20%
Salary percentage increase	20%
Value for money	3%
Career progress	3%
Aims achieved	3%
Placement success	2%
Employed at 3 months	2%
Alumni recommended	2%
Women faculty	2%
Women students	2%
Women board (1)	1%
International faculty	4%
International students	4%
International board	2%
International mobility	6%
International experience	2%
Languages	2%
Faculty with doctorates	5%
FT doctoral rank	5%
FT research rank	10%

doctoral education and compels schools to invest more heavily in highly-visible MBA programs.

But there is also criticism against the selection of indicators used in terms of relevance and the reliance on easy-to-measure indicators: 'Measures used in media rankings are often arbitrary, selected based on convenience, and definitely controversial. Characteristics that are of little importance are often included, while important characteristics are excluded because they are more difficult to measure' (AACSB, 2005, p. 7).

4.4.3.3 International Engineering Rankings

Up to now there are no original international rankings in engineering. What is available are the broad field rankings within the ARWU, THE and QS World Rankings. With regard to the selection of institutions in those rankings and their sets of indicators this means that their rankings for engineering are focusing on international research universities only. This has important implications:

- The available engineering rankings cover only the minority of all higher education institutions in the field that meet the criteria for inclusion in the world rankings.
- The focus is on research performance; performance in education and other dimensions of higher education (as e.g. lifelong learning, community outreach) are not taken into account.

Indicators of research performance are confronted with severe methodological problems in engineering. The indicators used are mainly bibliometric; the international bibliometric databases largely rely on journal articles whereas in (many fields of) engineering, other forms of publication, in particular conference proceedings, are more important than journal articles. Hence indicators based on bibliometric analysis only measure publication output and impact for some subfields of engineering.

4.4.4 Miscellaneous Other League Tables

The league tables and rankings mentioned above do not constitute the full set of international league tables, but they are the ones discussed most widely. Other global rankings include the Global University Ranking by Wuhan University, which is only available in Chinese, although on Wikipedia it is briefly mentioned as being based on 'Essential Science Indicators (ESI), which provides data of journal article publication counts and citation frequencies in over 11,000 journals around the world in 22 research fields' (http://en.wikipedia.org/wiki/College_and_university_rankings#Global_University_Ranking, accessed November 11, 2009).

There is also SCImago, a ranking of mainly higher education and research[!] institutions in the 17,000 journals in the Scopus bibliographic database (SCImago Research Group, 2009). It uses '… 5 indicators of institution research performance, stressing output (ordering criteria), collaboration and impact.'

Then there are some global rankings of a specialized nature (see following subsection) and national or regional rankings that deserve mention because of some special focus (see second subsection following).

4.4.4.1 The Scientist

Very clearly directed to a particular target group is *The Scientist's* ranking of higher education and research institutions by how attractive they are as workplaces for postdocs or scientists (http://www.the-scientist.com/bptw, accessed November 10, 2009), which has been published annually at least since the year 2000. Its data are collected through a survey, among readers of *The Scientist* and its website, on 119 higher education and research institutions (94 from the USA and 25 from the rest of the world). Its indicators included:

- Job Satisfaction
- Peers
- Infrastructure and Environment
- Research Resources
- Pay
- Management and Policies
- Teaching and Mentoring
- Tenure and Promotion

4.4.4.2 Webometrics

Much broader in its appeal but also narrow in its explicit aims and approach is the Webometrics league table (www.webometrics.info). Published since 2004, this league table indicates an institution's web presence through websites, repositories with documents (research reports and materials for students), etc. which on the website is claimed to be 'a good indicator of impact and prestige of universities'. It looks more democratic than most other global rankings, because based on its web techniques it can afford to include not a few hundred but over 17,000 higher education and research institutions. Somewhat similar is the 'G-Factor ranking', looking at higher education institutions' scores in Google. However, there is not a single, clear interpretation of what web presence measures with regard to the core functions of higher education and research institutions.

4.4.4.3 RatER

Finally here, we would like to mention Moscow-based agency RatER, not because of its influence, but because its ranking purports to be multidimensional. According to its website, RatER was 'initiated by Russian big private industry in March 2005 in order to investigate problems of higher professional education'. It ranks over 400 universities from around the world, which are selected by merging rankings in other international league tables (ARWU, THE, Webometrics and Taiwan National University) as well as a selection of Russian and CIS state universities and anyone willing to fill in RatER's online questionnaire on:

- Education (programs offered, staff and student numbers, student success in international competitions)
- Research (patents, Nobel and Field prizes of staff, staff members in Academies, international citations)
- Resources (total budget, total spending on training and laboratory facilities, data processing capacity of the university's computer center)
- Social recognition of university's graduates ('[t]otal number of the live graduates of the university who achieved public recognition: prominent men of science, culture and business, politicians, government officials, administrators of territories and cities (with population exceeding 100,000), managers and executives of major international organizations (UN, UNESCO, etc.).')
- International activities (partnerships with foreign universities, honorary doctorates abroad, student mobility).

The exclusive use of a questionnaire shows RatER's reliance on ad hoc data collection from higher education institutions. Scales and weights of indicators are then determined by RatER's experts, who subsequently individually rate institutions on each indicator—apparently this is a subjective procedure. Final scores are calculated as averages among the experts' ratings (www.globaluniversitiesranking.org/index.php?option = com_content&view = article&id = 68&Itemid = 128, accessed November 11, 2009).

References

AACSB. (2005). *The business school rankings dilemma*. A report from a task force of AACSB International's Committee on Issues in Management Education. Tampa: AACSB.

AUBR Expert Group. (2009). *Assessing Europe's university-based research – Draft*. s. l. Brussels: European Commission – DG Research.

Brennan, J., Goedegebuure, L. C. J., Shah, T., Westerheijden, D. F., & Weusthof, P. J. M. (1992). *Towards a methodology for comparative quality assessment in European higher education: A pilot study on economics in Germany, the Netherlands and the United Kingdom*. London/Enschede/Hannover: CNAA/CHEPS/HIS.

Brown, R. (2006). League tables – Do we have to live with them? *Perspectives, 10*(2), 33–38.

Cremonini, L., Westerheijden, D. F., & Enders, J. (2008). Disseminating the right information to the right audience: Cultural determinants in the use (and misuse) of rankings. *Higher Education, 55*, 373–385.

Dill, D. D., & Soo, M. (2005). Academic quality, league tables, and public policy: A cross-national analysis of university ranking systems. *Higher Education, 49*, 495–533.

Eccles, J. S., & Gootman, J. A. (2002). *Community programs to promote youth development*. Washington, DC: National Academy Press.

Enserink, M. (2007). Who ranks the university rankers? *Science, 317*(5841), 1026–1028.

Filliatreau, G. & Zitt, M. (s. a.). *Big is (made) Beautiful. Some comments about the Shanghai ranking of world-class universities*. s. l. Paris: OST.

Gottlieb, B. (2009). Cooking the School Books: How U.S. News cheats in picking its 'best American colleges'. *Slate*, September 1, 2009.

Hazelkorn, E. (2011). *Rankings and the reshaping of higher education: The battle for world-class excellence*. London: Palgrave Macmillan.

Högskolverket. (2009). *Ranking of universities and higher education institutions for student information purposes?* (No. 2009:27 R). Stockholm: Högskoleverket.

International Ranking Expert Group. (2006). *Berlin principles on ranking of higher education institutions*. Retrieved June 24, 2006, from http://www.che.de/downloads/Berlin_ Principles_ IREG_534. pdf

IREG Observatory (2011). *IREG Ranking Audit Manual*. IREG Observatory on Academic Rankings and Excellence, 2011. Available at: http://www.ireg-observatory.org/pdf/ranking_audith_audit.pdf

King, R., Locke, W., Puncher, M., Richardson, J., & Verbik, L. (2008). *Counting what is measured or measuring what counts? League tables and their impact on higher education institutions in England* (No. April 2008/14). s. l. Higher Education Funding Council for England, Bristo.

Klein, S. P., & Hamilton, L. (1998). *The validity of the U. S. News & World Report ranking of ABA Law Schools*. s. l. Association of American Law Schools.

Leeuw, F. L. (2002). Evaluating and the ranking of higher education studies. In J. Bevers & M. Hulshof (Eds.), *Willems & wetens, liber amicorum voor Jos Willems* (pp. 141–154). Nijmegen: IOWO/KUN.

Marginson, S. (2006, September 7–9). *Global university rankings: private and public goods*. Paper presented at the 19th Annual CHER conference, Kassel, Germany.

Marginson, S. (2008). *Global, multiple and engaged: Has the 'Idea of a University' changed in the era of the global knowledge economy?* Paper presented at the fifth international workshop on Higher Education Reforms 'The Internationalization of Higher Education and Higher Education Reforms', Shanghai, China.

Marginson, S. (2009). University rankings, government and social order: Managing the field of higher education according to the logic of the performative present-as-future. In M. Simons, M. Olssen, & M. Peters (Eds.), *Re-reading education policies: Studying the policy agenda of the 21st century*. Rotterdam: Sense Publishers.

Merisotis, J. P. (2003). On the ranking of higher education institutions. *Higher Education in Europe, 27*(4), 361–364.

Moed, H. F. (2005). *Citation analysis in research evaluation*. Dordrecht: Springer.

Müller-Böling, D., & Federkeil, G. (2007). The CHE-Ranking of German, Swiss and Austrian Universities. In J. Sadlak & L. N. Cai (Eds.), *The world-class university an ranking: Aiming beyond status* (pp. 189–203). Bucharest: CEPES.

National Opinion Research Center (1997). *A review of the methodology for the U.S. news & world report's rankings of undergraduate colleges and universities*. The Washington Monthly Review Online. Retrieved January 23, 2012, from http://www.washingtonmonthly.com/features/2000/norc.html

OECD (2008). *Handbook on constructing composite indicators*. Paris, OECD.

Sadlak, J., & Liu, N. C. (2007). *The world-class university and ranking: Aiming beyond status*. Bucharest, Romania/ Shanghai, China/ Cluj-Napoca, Romania: UNESCO-CEPES.

Saisana, M., & D'Hombres, B. (2008). *Higher education rankings: Robustness issues and critical assessment. How much confidence can we have in higher education rankings?* Luxembourg: Office for Official Publications of the European Communities.

Salmi, J. (2009). *The challenge of establishing world-class universities*. Washington, D. C.: World Bank.

SCImago Research Group. (2009). *SCImago Institutions Rankings (SIR): 2009 World Report*. Retrieved November 11, 2009, from http://www.scimagoir.com/pdf/sir_2009_world_report.pdf

Stigler, G. J. (1961). The economics of information. *Journal of Political Economy, LXIX*, 213–225.

Thibaud, A. (2009). *Vers quel classement européen des universités? Etude comparative du classement de Shanghai et des autres classements internationaux* (No. Note de Benchmarking 4). Brussels/Paris: Institut Thomas More.

Usher, A., & Savino, M. (2006). *A world of difference: A global survey of university league tables*. Toronto: Educational Policy Institute.

van der Wende, M. (2008). Rankings and classifications in higher education. A European perspective. In J. C. Smart (Ed.), *Higher education: Handbook of theory and research* (Vol. 23). Dordrecht: Springer.

van der Wende, M., & Westerheijden, D. F. (2009). Rankings and classifications: The need for a multidimensional approach. In F. A. van Vught (Ed.), *Mapping the higher education landscape: Towards a European classification of higher education* (pp. 71–86). Dordrecht: Springer.

Van Dyke, N. (2005). Twenty years of university report cards. *Higher Education in Europe, 30*(2), 103–125.

van Raan, A. F. J. (2005). Fatal attraction: Conceptual and methodological problems in the ranking of universities by bibliometric methods. *Scientometrics, 62*(1), 133–143.

van Vught, F. A. (2008). Mission diversity and reputation in higher education. *Higher Education Policy, 21*(2), 151–174.

van Vught, F. A. (Ed.). (2009). *Mapping the higher education landscape: Towards a European classification of higher education*. Dordrecht: Springer.

Vedder, R., & Ewalt, D. M. (2009). America's best colleges. *Forbes*, August 5, 2009.

Visser, M. S., & Moed, H. F. (2008). *Comparing web of science and scopus on a paper-by-paper basis*. Paper presented at the 10th international conference on Science & Technology Indicators, Vienna.

Westerheijden, D. F. (2009). Information of quality and quality of information to match students and programme. In J. Newton & R. Brown (Eds.), *The future of quality assurance*. Amsterdam: EAIR.

Westerheijden, D. F., Beerkens, E., Cremonini, L., Huisman, J., Kehm, B., Kovac, A., et al. (2010). *The first decade of working on the European Higher Education Area: The Bologna Process Independent Assessment – Executive summary, overview and conclusions*. s. l. Vienna: European Commission, Directorate-General for Education and Culture.

Yorke, M. (1998). The Times' league table of universities, 1997: A statistical appraisal. *Quality Assurance in Education, 6*(1), 58.

Chapter 5
Impact of Rankings

Frans A. van Vught and Don F. Westerheijden

5.1 Introduction

Rankings not only provide information on the performance of higher education and research institutions, either rightly or wrongly, but they also have major impacts on decision-making in higher education and research institutions and on the sector more broadly. According to many commentators, their effect on the sector is rather negative: encouraging wasteful use of resources, promoting a narrow concept of quality, and inspiring institutions to engage in 'gaming the rankings'. As will be shown near the end of this chapter, a well-designed ranking can have a positive effect on the sector, encouraging higher education and research institutions to improve their performance. While specific effects depend on the details of each ranking exercise, some common tendencies of current rankings nevertheless can be highlighted.

5.2 Impact on Student Demand

Many rankings intend to affect student demand and there is clear evidence that they indeed have an impact on student choices. It has been shown in the US that when an institution improves its position in the rankings, the next year it receives more applicants, sees a greater proportion of its accepted applicants enroll, and

---

F.A. van Vught (✉) • D.F. Westerheijden
Center for Higher Education Policy Studies, University of Twente,
Enschede, The Netherlands

F.A. van Vught and F. Ziegele (eds.), *Multidimensional Ranking: The Design and Development of U-Multirank*, Higher Education Dynamics 37,
DOI 10.1007/978-94-007-3005-2_5, © Springer Science+Business Media B.V. 2012

subsequently sees that the students in the incoming class have higher entrance scores (Monks & Ehrenberg, 1999). The experience of the CHE Ranking in Germany confirms this result. In some fields, e.g. psychology and medicine, the number of applications at the recommended universities increased significantly after publication of ranking results: in psychology the number of applications rose on average 19% in universities recommended as excellent in research and 15% in universities recommended as efficient and supportive in teaching (Federkeil, 2002).

Furthermore, it has been shown both in the US and Europe that rankings are not equally used by all types of students (Hazelkorn, 2011): less by domestic undergraduate entrants, more at the graduate and postgraduate levels. Especially at the undergraduate level, rankings appear to be used particularly by students of high achievement and by those coming from highly educated families (Cremonini, Westerheijden, & Enders, 2008; Heine & Willich, 2006; McDonough, Antonio, & Perez, 1998).

5.3 Impact on Institutional Management

Rankings strongly impact on the internal management in higher education institutions. The majority of higher education leaders—63%, according to Hazelkorn's survey (Hazelkorn, 2007)—report that they use potential improvement in rank to justify claims on resources, which is confirmed by a survey of strategic plans and annual reports (Espeland & Sauder, 2007). Moreover, lacking other benchmarks, some administrators use rankings as a heuristic to help allocate resources internally, particularly by rewarding current winners (an example of the 'Matthew effect'; see Sect. 5.7), e.g. by investing in laboratories that have had major research impact scores. In general, they tend to focus on targeting the indicators in league tables that are most easily influenced, e.g. the institution's branding, institutional data and choice of publication language (English) and channels (counted in the international databases such as Thomson Reuters or Scopus), in extreme cases leading to what Hazelkorn called 'Fetishization of particular forms of knowledge, contributors and outputs' and stimulating a return to Mode-1 research at the cost of Mode-2 research. At the same time, Mode-2 research is regarded as highly relevant for stimulating higher education and research institutions' role in the knowledge economy. From that perspective, turning towards Mode-1 research can be regarded as a perverse effect.

The changes in an institution's ranking position can have a major effect on the leadership of an institution. There are various examples of cases in which leaders' salary bonuses were directly linked to their institution's position in the ranking (Jaschik, 2007), or in which administrators had to step down because of a negative ranking outcome, even though the drop in the ranking may have been caused by erroneous data (see Siang, 2005; The Star, 2006).

5.4 Impact on Public Funding

Higher education and research rankings not only attract the attention of students, but they also are notably followed by national policy-makers and the public in general, more perhaps than foreseen in past decades (Hazelkorn, 2011). There are numerous examples from across the globe demonstrating that policy-makers are not satisfied with the position of their higher education institutions in the global rankings and therefore have begun to reform their higher education systems and adapt, differentiate or even increase funding to the sector. Within national systems, the rankings have prompted the desire for more and higher ranked higher education institutions ('world-class universities') both as symbols of national achievement and prestige and supposedly as engines of the knowledge economy (Marginson, 2006). Salmi (2009) discussed several patterns of reactions of countries to global higher education rankings. In his view (Salmi, p. 36):

> Adopting the goal of building world-class universities does not imply, however, that all universities in a given country can be or should aspire to be of international standing. A more attainable and appropriate goal would be, rather, to develop an integrated system of teaching, research, and technology-oriented institutions that feed into and support a few centers of excellence that focus on value-added fields and chosen areas of comparative advantage and that can eventually evolve into world-class institutions.

Ways to do this, according to Salmi, include upgrading existing institutions, merging institutions to concentrate strengths, or create new ones (or combinations of these strategies)—in order of increasing costs. Authorities appear to be willing to go to great lengths to get 'their' institutions into the top rankings. For instance, Vietnam used much of its World Bank loan for higher education to establish a new 'world class university'. Saudi Arabia used its own ample funds to create a 'world class university' in the area of technology. Similar initiatives exist in a number of countries (including China and South Korea); in some cases they refer to global rankings explicitly and define goals to have a certain number of higher education institutions among the top in the rankings in a given target year. In some countries (e.g. Denmark) mergers of universities were influenced by global rankings too, as their concepts and indicators favor large units. The minister in charge of higher education in France stated that France's poor showing in the rankings underlined the absolute necessity of reforming the country's higher education (Marshall, 2008). The French government has allocated additional funding to create centers of excellence and position France among the highest-ranking universities in the world. The German 'excellence initiatives' award grants to a number of universities to enhance their research performance; this too was influenced by global ranking results. Finally, it has been shown that after the USN&WR ranking was introduced in the US on a larger scale, state appropriations to public universities increased. State appropriations per student were more responsive to USN&WR rankings exposure if a state had more citizens who were politically active, cared more about higher education, and bought *USN&WR* from the newsstand (Jin & Whalley, 2007).

It can be questioned, however, if redirecting funds to a small set of higher education and research institutions to make them 'world class' benefits the whole higher education system: countries' policies seem to show quite different rates of inclusiveness (Cremonini, Benneworth, & Westerheijden, 2010; Hazelkorn, 2011). The consequences of lack of inclusiveness have not yet been researched empirically, but the hypothesis can be posed that an increase of vertical diversity among higher education and research institutions follows from the winners getting more, the losers less. If that hypothesis were corroborated, the next hypothesis could be that the gaps between institutions become bigger, and that this makes mobility across institutions more difficult for students.

5.5 Impact on the Higher Education Reputation Race

One of the major concerns surrounding rankings is their tendency to encourage a reputation race in the higher education sector (van Vught, 2008). The reputation race implies the existence of an ever-increasing search by higher education and research institutions and their funders for higher positions in the league tables. In Hazelkorn's survey of higher education institutions, 3% were ranked first in their country, but 19% wanted to get to that position (Hazelkorn, 2011). The reputation race has costly implications, and Ehrenberg (2002b) saw rankings as one reason for the escalation in the cost of higher education in the US over the last decades. Rankings exacerbate competition in the sector and as a result higher education institutions have to invest more and more into attracting the most talented students and staff and building the reputation of the school. Since the position in a ranking is not absolute but always relative to how others perform, there is no end to this race. The problem of the reputation race is that the investments do not always lead to better education and research, and that the resources spent might be more efficiently used elsewhere.

One aspect of the reputation race is the concentration of higher education and research institutions' efforts on research. Most rankings focus disproportionately on research, as shown above, either directly by using research output measures or indirectly by using measures that characterize research-intensive universities (e.g. low student/staff ratio, reputation among peers). Yet the link between the quality in research and quality in teaching is not particularly strong (see Dill & Soo, 2005). This misrepresentation leads not only to incomplete, misleading or bad decision-making (Marginson, 2006) but also—again—to a wasteful use of resources. It leads to a situation where even higher education institutions that see their mission primarily in teaching are forced to invest more in research only because research indicators 'signal' the quality of their education in the rankings.

The reputation race thus increases higher education costs significantly (van Vught, 2008). Massy (2003) described the situation in the USA as follows:

> Universities press their pricing up to the limits that markets, regulators, and public opinion will allow. They justify their actions in terms of the rising cost of excellence and other factors beyond their control, but that is only part of the story. The impetus for price hikes stems from the university's own choices.

If public policies in other countries continue to follow the US example and increase the competition in a system where reputation is the major driving force, similar cost explosions should be expected (van Vught, 2008).

5.6 Impact on Quality

Any ranking —or for that matter any indicator system, no matter how carefully designed— simplifies reality and offers an incomplete picture of institutional quality. The major problem with this is not so much a somewhat flawed picture of institutions, but that this incomplete framework tends to get rooted as a definition of quality. One of the greatest impacts of rankings might be their ability to redefine what 'quality' is in the higher education sector (e.g. Tijssen, 2003). 'Rankings define the purposes, outputs and values of higher education and interpret it to the world at large, in a fashion that is far more compelling than either the policy reports of governments or the reasoned analyses of scholars of higher education' (Marginson, 2006). This is particularly the case for league tables that use a single composite indicator for an institution. The characteristics that weigh less or that are not even captured in the rankings are in danger of becoming ignored by the institutions, its funders and by the public in general.

A study of American law schools showed that administrators took rankings heavily into consideration when they defined goals, assessed progress, evaluated peers, admitted students, recruited faculty, adopted new programs, and created budgets. In that way, rankings appeared to create self-fulfilling prophecies by encouraging schools to become more like what the rankings measured. 'Rankings impose a standardized, universal definition of law schools which creates incentives for law schools to conform to that definition' (Espeland & Sauder, 2007).

This standardization process is likely to reduce the horizontal diversity in higher education systems. As we mentioned before, the existing global rankings largely take the comprehensive research university as their model (Marginson, 2006). Alternative models, such as vocationally-oriented universities of applied sciences (*Fachhochschulen*) in Germany or liberal arts colleges in the US are underrated by such rankings. In the absence of policies to protect diversity by other means, attention to global research rankings may trigger the evolution of more uniform and mainly vertically differentiated systems.

5.7 Impact Through the 'Matthew Effect'

As a result of the vertical differentiation, rankings are likely to contribute to wealth inequality and expanding performance gaps among institutions (van Vught, 2008). On the one hand, rankings and especially league tables create inequality among institutions that would be hard to distinguish otherwise. They create artificial lines that imply the danger of becoming institutionalized and real (Espeland & Sauder, 2007). Similarly, rankings have exacerbated competition for the leading researchers and best younger talent, and are likely to drive up the price of high-performing researchers and research groups (Marginson, 2006) making these financially affordable only for the richest institutions.

In short, the competitive framework creates a 'Matthew effect' (Matthew 13:12), i.e. a situation where already strong institutions are able to attract more resources from students (e.g. increase tuition fees), government agencies (e.g. research funding), and third parties, and thereby strengthen their market position even further.

5.8 Impact on Institutional Responses to Ranking: Gaming the Results

In systems where the position of a higher education institution in a ranking is assumed to be important in the eyes of its main funders, institutional leaders are under great pressure to improve their institution's position in the league tables. In order to do so, these institutions sometimes may engage in activities that improve their positions in rankings, but which may have negligent or even harmful effect on the performance in its core activities. Experiences in the US regarding the UNS&WR league tables have shown that higher education institutions are very sensitive to the strategic importance of league tables, leading to actions to present themselves in a more favorable light than would be realistic, or even feel compelled to take recourse to 'gaming the rankings' (Dill & Soo, 2005) by manipulation. Ehrenberg (2002a) demonstrated that almost every indicator in the USN&WR ranking may lead to gaming by the institutions. Various examples could be mentioned. For instance, to raise their ranking score on selectivity (an indicator in the USN&WR rankings) some institutions invested in stimulating students to apply although they would never be accepted (Schreiterer, 2008). Also, since the standardized test score of applicants is considered in the ranking, some institutions make submitting the score voluntary to applicants, knowing that only students with a high score have the incentive to provide it, which increases the institution's average. Faculty salaries also count in the ranking, and there are examples of institutions increasing salaries without discussing whether this would improve teaching and learning or contribute to faculty retention, or if there could be a more effective use of these resources. Finally, since USN&WR counts full-time faculty for its student/staff ratio in the fall term, some departments appeared to encourage their faculty to take an academic leave in spring, not in fall (Espeland & Sauder, 2007).

Moreover, since ranking position is not absolute, but relative to how other institutions perform, institutions have an incentive to make their main competitors look worse. If a ranking has a survey element in it that asks for the reputation of other institutions, it is in the interests to manipulate these results. There are examples of institutions deliberately downgrading the academic reputation of their competitors (Hazelkorn, 2011; van der Werf, 2009).

5.9 Potential for a Positive Impact

Most of the effects discussed above are rather negative to students, institutions and the higher education sector more broadly. The problem is not so much the existence of rankings as such, or the fact that higher education institutions use rankings among other information sources to inform strategic decision-making (Hazelkorn, 2011), but the fact that many of the existing rankings and league tables are flawed and create dysfunctional incentives. What can be concluded from these results is that higher education and research institutions as well as policy-makers at the system level are very responsive to the rankings. If a ranking was able to create useful incentives, it could be a powerful tool for improving the performance in the sector.

The experience with e.g. the CHE Rankings shows that a well-designed ranking may provide institutions with the incentive to genuinely improve their core educational and research processes. Well-designed rankings may be used as a starting point for internal analysis of strengths and weaknesses. Rankings offer the possibility to compare one's own institution with others, either for partnership benchmarking or for positioning oneself against competitors. Some rankings offer institutions the possibility to get tailor-made analyses (e.g. CHE Ranking, SK123). Without rankings, higher education and research institutions have only data on their own institution at their disposal, which does not allow any positioning in the field. To fulfill this task rankings have to offer results on a level of aggregation that corresponds to the needs of internal strategic decision-making.

Similarly, rankings may provide useful stimuli to students to search for the best-fitting study programs, and to policy-makers to consider where in the higher education system investment should be directed for the system to fulfill its social functions optimally. The point of the preceding sections was not so much that all kinds of stakeholders react to rankings, but that the current rankings and league tables seem to invite overreactions on too few dimensions or indicators.

5.10 Consequences for the Design of a New Multidimensional Ranking Tool

In the previous chapters, we discussed positive and negative results with regard to existing transparency tools in the current, complex higher education systems. Some commentators have found it remarkable that such different rankings all have the same institutions in their top tiers. Does this indicate that an underlying concept of 'quality' is measured through all the proxies that those rankings define? Cynics may reply that all rankings ensure that the same institutions are at the top to gain credibility ('face validity' in its crude sense of reinforcing prestige). From our point of view, concerned as we are to design a meaningful ranking for higher education and research institutions, we would rather stay at the level of empirical and methodological critique. In particular, one-dimensional league tables prove to be neither informative nor a valid approach to measure differences between institutions; they do not correspond to the information needs of the different groups of external stakeholders and they do not correspond to the needs within universities for strategic decision-making. Instead we argue that multidimensional, robust rankings are needed to enable various groups of end-users to adapt them to their individual information needs, so that intended behavioral consequences may ensue without (many) unintended, perverse effects on the behavior of higher education and research institutions ('gaming the rankings'), students (being guided towards institutions which may have high reputations but offer low-quality programs) and decision-makers (adapting aims and decisions to available indicators).

In the previous chapters the methodologies of current international and national rankings, both institutional and field-based, have been discussed. In Part II of this volume we will present an alternative and new approach. With regard to the design of such an alternative model of a global, multidimensional ranking, the following general conclusions can be drawn with regard to the methodologies, the set of indicators and the calculation of the current rankings:

- Most international institutional rankings (such as ARWU and THE) focus on one 'type' of higher education institution: the large, international research university. First, they either focus exclusively on research (ARWU, Leiden, and HEEACT) or their selection criteria and/or indicators include a predominance of research (THE). There are only few international rankings that specialize on different aspects (labor market success—Ecôle des Mines; web presence—Webometrics) and hence include other types of institutions, too.
- As the most prominent and influential global rankings are mostly confined to measuring research performance, the global perception of a 'world-class university' is practically identical with research excellence (see Salmi, 2009).
- The availability of (bibliometric) databases, the indicators used and the procedures to select the institutions included in most current rankings imply biases in terms of fields as well as language and culture. In line with the Berlin Principles an alternative approach must give more attention to avoiding biases.
- With regard to biases in underlying databases as well as differences in concepts, indicators and measures, issues of validity and reliability are particularly problematic for international rankings.
- Institutional global rankings use either institutional information only or they calculate unweighted averages out of field-based data. (The only exception is the Leiden ranking where the so called 'crown indicator', the field-normalized citation rate, is field-specific by definition.) This raises the question of how to deal with differences between fields in aggregating information in institutional rankings.

Our critical review also resulted in points of departure for a better practice, both theoretically inspired and looking at existing good practices. They are as follows:

- Following the Berlin Principles, rankings should explicitly define and address target groups, as indicators and the way to present results have to be focused.
- Rankings and quality assurance mechanisms are complementary instruments. Rankings represent an external, quantitative view on institutions from a transparency perspective; traditional instruments of internal and external quality assurance are aiming at institutional accountability and enhancement. Rankings may help to ask the right questions for processes of internal quality enhancement.
- For some target groups, in particular students and researchers, information has to be field-based; for others, e.g. university leaders and national policy-makers, information about the higher education institution as a whole has priority (related to the strategic orientation of institutions); a multilevel set of indicators must reflect these different needs.
- Field-based comparisons must be made between higher education and research institutions of similar characteristics, leading to the need for a pre-selection per field-based ranking of a set of more or less homogeneous institutions.
- Rankings have to be multidimensional (see limitations of composite indicators; heterogeneity of preferences/priorities within target groups).
- There are neither theoretical nor empirical reasons for assigning fixed weights to individual indicators to calculate a composite overall score; within a given set of indicators the decision about the relative importance of indicators should be left to the users.
- International rankings have to be aware of potential biases of indicators; aspects of international comparability therefore are an important aspect of our study.
- Rankings should not use league tables from 1 to n but should differentiate between clear and robust differences in levels of performance. The decision about an adequate number of differentiated sets has to be taken with regard to the number of institutions included in a ranking and the distribution of data.
- Rankings have to use multiple databases to bring in different perspectives on institutional performance. As much as possible available data sources should be used, but currently their availability is limited. To create multidimensional rankings, gathering additional data from the institutions is necessary. Therefore, the quality of the data collection process is crucial.
- Rankings should be self-reflexive with regard to potential unintended consequences and undesirable/perverse effects.
- Involvement of stakeholders in the process of designing a ranking tool is crucial to keep feedback loops short, so as to avoid misunderstandings and so as to enable a high quality of the designed instruments.
- A major issue regards the measures to ensure quality of the ranking process and instruments. This includes statistical procedures as well as the inclusion of expertise of stakeholders, rankings and indicator experts, field experts (for the field-based rankings) and regional/national experts. A major condition for the acceptance of rankings is the transparency about their methodology. The basic

methodology, the ranking procedures, the data used (including information about survey samples) and the definitions of indicators have to be public for all users. Transparency includes informing about limitations of the rankings.

These general conclusions have been an important source of inspiration for how we designed U-Multirank, a new, global, multidimensional ranking instrument. In Part II we will present the design, construction and testing processes that have resulted in the development of U-Multirank.

References

Cremonini, L., Benneworth, P., & Westerheijden, D. F. (2010). *In the shadow of celebrity: The impact of world-class universities policies on national higher education systems*. Paper presented at the ASHE annual conference, Indianapolis, IL.
Cremonini, L., Westerheijden, D. F., & Enders, J. (2008). Disseminating the right information to the right audience: Cultural determinants in the use (and misuse) of rankings. *Higher Education, 55*, 373–385.
Dill, D. D., & Soo, M. (2005). Academic quality, league tables, and public policy: A cross-national analysis of university ranking systems. *Higher Education, 49*(4), 495–537.
Ehrenberg, R. G. (2002). Reaching for the brass ring: The U. S. News & World Report rankings and competition. *The Review of Higher Education, 26*(2), 145–162.
Ehrenberg, R. G. (2002). *Tuition rising: Why college costs so much*. Cambridge: Harvard University Press.
Espeland, W. N., & Sauder, M. (2007). Rankings and reactivity: How public measures recreate social worlds. *The American Journal of Sociology, 113*(1), 1–40.
Federkeil, G. (2002). *The CHE/Stern ranking*. Paper presented at the international roundtable on statistical indicators for the quality assessment of higher/tertiary education institutions, Warsaw, Poland.
Hazelkorn, E. (2007). The impact of league tables and ranking systems on higher education decision-making. *Higher Education Management and Policy, 19*(2), 87–110.
Hazelkorn, E. (2011). *Rankings and the reshaping of higher education: The battle for world-class excellence*. London: Palgrave Macmillan.
Heine, C., & Willich, J. (2006). *Informationsverhalten und Entscheidungsfindung bei der Studien- und Ausbildungswahl Studienberechtigte 2005 ein halbes Jahr vor dem Erwerb der Hochschulreife*. HIS: Forum Hochschule(3).
Jaschik, S. (2007, March 19). Should U. S. news make presidents rich? *Inside Higher Education*. Retrieved from http://www.insidehighered.com/news/2007/03/19/usnews
Jin, G. Z., & Whalley, A. (2007). *The power of information: How do U. S. News rankings affect the financial resources of public colleges?* Cambridge: NBER.
Marginson, S. (2006, September 7–9). *Global university rankings: Private and public goods*. Paper presented at the 19th annual CHER conference, Kassel, Germany.
Marshall, J. (2008, August 17). France: Jiao Tong rankings cause for concern. *University World News*.
Massy, W. F. (2003). *Honoring the trust: Quality and cost containment in higher education*. Boston: Anjer Publishing.
McDonough, P. M., Antonio, A. L., & Perez, L. X. (1998). College rankings: Democratized college knowledge for whom? *Research in Higher Education, 39*(5), 513–537.
Monks, G., & Ehrenberg, R. G. (1999). *The impact of U. S. News and World Report college rankings on admission outcomes and pricing decisions at selective private institutions*. Cornell Higher Education Research Institute (CHERI). Paper I. http://digitalcommons.ilr.cornell.edu/cheri/1.

Salmi, J. (2009). *The challenge of establishing world-class universities*. Washington, D. C.: World Bank.

Schreiterer, U. (2008). *Traumfabrik Harvard. Warum amerikanische Unis so anders sind*. Frankfurt am Main, Germany: Campus Verlag.

Siang, L. K. (2005). *Hashim Yaacob should resign as UM Vice Chancellor for his "I am not worried" statement over UM's 80-place drop in World's Top 200 Universities or sacked for his "tunnel vision" for the nation's premier university.* Retrieved 10–05, from http://www.limkitsiang.com/archive/2005/oct05/lks3686.htm

The Star. (2006, March 30). UM dons speak up for VC. *The Star.* Retrieved from http://thestar.com.my/news/story.asp?file=/20063/30/nation/13813040&sec=nation

Tijssen, R. F. W. (2003). Scoreboards of research excellence. *Research Evaluation, 12*(2), 91–104.

van der Werf, M. (2009). Researcher offers unusually candid description of university's effort to rise in rankings. *Chronicle of Higher Education*, June 3, 2009.

van Vught, F. A. (2008). Mission diversity and reputation in higher education. *Higher Education Policy, 21*(2), 151–174.

Part II
U-Multirank

Chapter 6
Background and Design

Gero Federkeil, Frans Kaiser, Frans A. van Vught, and Don F. Westerheijden

6.1 Introduction

On 2 June 2009 the European Commission announced the launching of a feasibility study to develop a multidimensional global university ranking.

Its aims were to 'look into the feasibility of making a multidimensional ranking of universities in Europe, and possibly the rest of the world too'. The Commission believes that accessible, transparent and comparable information would make it easier for students and teaching staff, but also parents and other stakeholders, to make informed choices between different higher education institutions and their programs. It would also help institutions to better position themselves and improve their quality and performance.

The Commission pointed out that existing rankings tend to focus on research in 'hard sciences' and ignore the performance of universities in areas like humanities and social sciences, teaching quality and community outreach. While drawing on the experience of existing university rankings and of EU-funded projects on transparency in higher education, the new ranking system should be:

- multidimensional: covering the various missions of institutions, such as education, research, innovation, internationalization, and community outreach;
- transparent: it should provide users with a clear understanding of all the factors used to measure performance and offer them the possibility to consult the ranking according to their needs;

G. Federkeil (✉)
Centre for Higher Education (CHE), Gütersloh, Germany

F. Kaiser • F.A. van Vught • D.F. Westerheijden
Center for Higher Education Policy Studies, University of Twente, Enschede, The Netherlands

- global: covering institutions inside and outside Europe (in particular those in the US, Asia and Australia).

The project would consist of two consecutive parts:

- In a first phase the consortium would design a multidimensional ranking system for higher education institutions in consultation with stakeholders.
- In a second phase the consortium would test the feasibility of the multidimensional ranking system on a sample of no less than 150 higher education and research institutions. The sample would focus on the disciplines of engineering and business studies and should have a sufficient geographical coverage (inside and outside of the EU) and a sufficient coverage of institutions with different missions.

In June 2011 our CHERPA-Network which was awarded the multidimensional ranking project submitted its final report to the European Commission. One of the report's major conclusions was that an enhanced understanding of the diversity in the profiles and performances of higher education and research institutions at a national, European and global level requires a new ranking tool. The new tool will promote the development of diverse institutional profiles. It will also address most of the major shortcomings of existing ranking instruments. The full report of the project is available on: http://ec.europa.eu/education/higher-education/doc/multirank_en.pdf. We called this new tool U-Multirank as this stresses three fundamental points of departure: it is multidimensional, recognizing that higher education institutions serve multiple purposes and perform a range of different activities; it is a ranking of university performances (although not in the sense of an aggregated league table like other global rankings); and it is user-driven (as a stakeholder with particular interests, you are enabled to rank institutions with comparable profiles according to the criteria important to you).

This chapter addresses the basic design aspects of the new, multidimensional global ranking tool. First, we present the general design principles that to a large extent have guided the design process. Secondly, we describe the conceptual framework from which we deduce the five dimensions of the new ranking tool. Finally, we outline a number of methodological choices that have a major impact on the operational design of U-Multirank.

6.2 Design Principles

U-Multirank aims to address the challenges identified as arising from the various currently existing ranking tools. Using modern theories and methodologies of design processes as our base (Bucciarelli, 1994; Oudshoorn & Pinch, 2003) and trying to be as explicit as possible about our approach, we formulated a number of design principles that guided the development of the new ranking tool. The following list contains the basic principles applied when designing and constructing U-Multirank.

- Our fundamental epistemological argument is that as all observations of reality are theory-driven (formed by conceptual systems) an 'objective ranking' cannot be developed (see Chap. 1). Every ranking will reflect the normative design and selection criteria of its constructors.
- Given this epistemological argument, our position is that rankings should be based on the interests and priorities of their users: rankings should be **user-driven**. This principle 'democratizes' the world of rankings by empowering potential users (or categories of users) to be the dominant actors in the design and application of rankings rather than rankings being restricted to the normative positions of a small group of constructors. Different users and stakeholders should be able to construct different sorts of rankings. (This is one of the *Berlin Principles*).
- Our second principle is **multidimensionality**. Higher education and research institutions are predominantly multipurpose, multiple-mission organizations undertaking different mixes of activities (teaching and learning, research, knowledge transfer, regional engagement, and internationalization are five major categories that we have identified; see the following section). Rankings should reflect this multiplicity of functions and not focus on one function (research) to the virtual exclusion of all else. An obvious corollary to this principle is that institutional performance on these different dimensions should never be aggregated into a composite overall ranking.
- The next design principle is **comparability**. In rankings, institutions and programs should only be compared when their purposes and activity profiles are sufficiently similar. Comparing institutions and programs that have very different purposes is worthless. It makes no sense to compare the research performance of a major metropolitan research university with that of a remotely located University of Applied Science; or the internationalization achievements of a national humanities college whose major purpose is to develop and preserve its unique national language with an internationally orientated European university with branch campuses in Asia.
- The fourth principle is that higher education rankings should reflect the **multi-level nature of higher education**. With very few exceptions, higher education institutions are combinations of faculties, departments and programs of varying strength. Producing only aggregated institutional rankings disguises this reality and does not produce the information most valued by major groups of stakeholders: students, potential students, their families, employers, academic staff and professional organizations. These stakeholders are mainly interested in information about a particular field. This does not mean that institutional-level rankings are not valuable to other stakeholders and for particular purposes. The new instrument should allow for the comparisons of comparable institutions at the level of the organization as a whole and also at the level of the disciplinary fields and multidisciplinary in which they are active.
- Finally we include the principle of **methodological soundness**. The new instrument should refrain from methodological mistakes such as the use of composite indicators, the production of league tables and the denial of contextuality.

In addition it should minimize the incentives for strategic behavior on the part of institutions to 'game the results'.

These principles underpin the design of U-Multirank, resulting in a user-driven, multidimensional and methodologically robust ranking instrument. In addition, U-Multirank aims to enable its users to identify institutions and programs that are sufficiently comparable to be ranked, and to undertake both institutional and field level analyses.

A fundamental question regarding the design of any transparency tool has to do with the choice of the 'dimensions': on which subject(s) will the provision of information focus? What will be the topics of the new ranking tool?

We take the position that any process of collecting information is driven by a – more or less explicit – conceptual framework. Transparency tools should clearly show what these conceptual frameworks are and how they have played a role in the selection of the broader categories of information on which these tools are focused.

For the design of U-Multirank we specify our own conceptual framework in the following section.

6.3 Conceptual Framework

A meaningful ranking requires a conceptual framework in order to decide on its content categories. We call these categories the 'dimensions' of the new ranking tool. We found a number of points of departure for a general framework for studying higher education and research institutions in the higher education literature. Four different conceptual perspectives have been combined in this approach.

First, a common point of departure is that processing knowledge is the general characteristic of higher education and research institutions (Becher & Kogan, 1992; Clark, 1983). 'Processing' can be the discovery of new knowledge as in research, or its transfer to stakeholders outside the higher education and research institutions (knowledge transfer) or to various groups of 'learners' (education). Of course, a focus on the overall objectives of higher education and research institutions in the three well-known primary processes or functions of 'teaching and learning, research, and knowledge transfer' is a simplification of the complex world of higher education and research institutions. These institutions are, in varying combinations of focus, committed to the efforts to discover, conserve, refine, transmit and apply knowledge (Clark). But the simplification helps to encompass the wide range of activities in which higher education and research institutions are involved. The three functions are a useful way to describe conceptually the general purposes of these institutions and therefore are the underlying three dimensions of our new ranking tool.

The second conceptual assumption is that the performance of higher education and research institutions may be directed at different 'audiences'. In the current higher education and research policy area, two main general audiences have been prioritized, the first through the international orientation of higher education and research institutions. This emphasizes how these institutions are seen as society's portals to the globalized world (both 'incoming' influences and 'outgoing' contributions to the international discourse). At the same time, the institutions' engagement with the region can be distinguished. Here the emphasis is on the involvement with and impact on the region in which a higher education institution operates. In reality these 'audiences' are of course often combined in the various activities of higher education and research institutions.

It is understood that the functions higher education and research institutions fulfill for international and regional audiences are manifestations of their primary processes, i.e. the three functions of education, research and knowledge transfer mentioned before. What we mean by this is that there may be educational elements, research elements and knowledge transfer elements to the international orientation. Similarly, regional engagement may be evident in an institution's education, research and knowledge transfer activities. International and regional orientations are two further dimensions of the multidimensional ranking.

The term 'processing' used above points to the third main conceptual assumption, namely the major stages in any process of creation or production: input, throughput (or the process in a narrow sense) and its results, which can be subdivided into immediate outputs and further reaching impacts. A major issue in higher education and research institutions, as in many social systems, has been that the transformation from inputs to performances is not self evident. One of the reasons why there is so much criticism of league tables is exactly the point that from similar sets of inputs, different higher education and research institutions may reach quite different types and levels of performance.

We make a general distinction between the 'enabling' stages of the overall creation stages on the one hand and the 'performance' stages on the other. The enabling stages consist of the inputs and processes of creation/production processes while the performance stages include their outputs and impacts. We have used the distinction of the various stages of a creation/production process to further elaborate the conceptual framework for the selection of indicators in the new ranking instrument.

A fourth assumption refers to the different stakeholders or users of rankings. Ranking information is produced to inform users about the value of higher education and research, which is necessary as it is not obvious that they are easily able to take effective decisions without such information. (Higher) education is not an ordinary 'good' for which the users themselves may assess the value a priori (using, e.g., price information). Higher education is to be seen as an experience good (Nelson, 1970): the users may assess the quality of the good only while or after 'experiencing' it (i.e. the higher education program), but such 'experience' is ex post knowledge. It is not possible for users to know beforehand whether the educational program meets their standards or criteria. Ex ante they only can refer to the perceptions of previous users. Some even say that higher education is a credence good (Dulleck & Kerschbamer, 2006): the value of the good cannot be assessed while experiencing it, but only (long) after. If users are interested in the value added of a degree program on the labor market, information on how well a class is taught is not relevant. They need information on how the competences acquired during higher education will improve their position on the career or social ladder. So stakeholders and users have to rely on information that is provided by a variety of transparency tools and quality assessment outcomes. However, different users require different types of information.

Some users are interested in the overall performance of higher education and research institutions (e.g. policy-makers) and for them the internal processes contributing to performance are of less interest. The institution may well remain a 'black box' for these users. Other stakeholders (students and institutional leaders are prime examples) are interested precisely in what happens inside the box. For instance, students may want to know the quality of teaching in the field in which they are interested. They may want to know how the program is delivered, as they may consider this as an important aspect of their learning experience and their time in higher education (consumption motives). Students might also be interested in the long term impact of taking the program as they may see higher education as an investment and are therefore interested in its future returns (investment motives).

Users engage with higher education for a variety of reasons and therefore will be interested in different dimensions and performance indicators of higher education institutions and the programs they offer. Rankings must be designed in a balanced way and include relevant information on the various stages of knowledge processing which are relevant to the different stakeholders and their motives for using rankings.

The conceptual grid shown below must be applied twice: once to the institution as a whole and once at the field level, and it has to accommodate interest in both performance and (to a lesser extent) process. For different dimensions (research, teaching & learning, knowledge transfer) and different stakeholders/users the relevance of information about different aspects of performance may vary.

The result of this elementary conceptual framework is a matrix showing the types of indicators that could be used in rankings and applied at both institutional and field levels (Table 6.1). Filtering higher education and research institutions into homogeneous groups requires contextual information rather than only the input and process information that is directly connected with enabling the knowledge processes. Contextual information for higher education and research institutions relates to their positioning in society and specific institutional appearances. It describes the conditions in which the primary processes of education, research and knowledge transfer operate. A substantial part of the relevant context is captured by applying another multidimensional transparency tool (U-Map) in pre-selecting higher education and research institutions (see below). Additional context information may be needed to allow for the valid interpretation of specific indicators by different stakeholders.

Using this conceptual framework we selected the following five dimensions as the major content categories of U-Multirank:

- Teaching & Learning
- Research
- Knowledge Transfer
- International Orientation
- Regional Engagement

6 Background and Design

Table 6.1 Conceptual grid U-Multirank

	Stages	Enabling		Performance	
	Functions & Audiences	Input	Process	Output	Impact
	Functions				
Context	Teaching & Learning				
	Research				
	Knowledge Transfer				
	Audiences				
	International Orientation				
	Regional Engagement				

In the next chapter we will discuss the various indicators to be used in these five dimensions.

An important factor in the criticism of rankings and league tables is the fact that often their selection of indicators is guided primarily by the (easy) availability of data rather than by relevance. This often leads to an emphasis on indicators of the enabling stages of the higher education production process, rather than on the area of performance, largely because governance of higher education and research institutions has concentrated traditionally on the bureaucratic (in Weber's neutral sense of the word) control of inputs: budgets, personnel, students, facilities, etc. Then too, inputs and processes can be influenced by managers of higher education and research institutions. They can deploy their facilities for teaching, but in the end it rests with the students to learn and, after graduation, work successfully with the competencies they have acquired. Similarly, higher education and research institution managers may make facilities and resources available for research, but they cannot guarantee that scientific breakthroughs are 'created'. Inputs and processes are the parts of a higher education and research institution's system that are best documented. But assessing the performance of these institutions implies a more comprehensive approach than a narrow focus on inputs and processes and the dissatisfaction among users of most current league tables and rankings is because they often are more interested in institutional performance while the information they get is largely about inputs. In our design of U-Multirank we focused on the selection of output and impact indicators. U-Multirank is a multidimensional *performance* assessment tool and thus includes indicators that relate to the performances of higher education and research institutions.

6.4 Methodological Aspects

There are a number of methodological aspects that have a clear impact on the way a new, multidimensional ranking tool like U-Multirank can be developed. In this section we explain the various methodological choices made when designing U-Multirank.

6.4.1 Methodological Standards

In addition to the content-related conceptual framework, the new ranking tool and its underlying indicators must be based also on methodological standards of empirical research, validity and reliability in the first instance. In addition, because U-Multirank is intended to be an international comparative transparency tool, it must deal with the issue of comparability across cultures and countries and finally, in order to become sufficiently operational, U-Multirank has to address the issue of feasibility.

6.4.1.1 Validity

(Construct) validity refers to the evidence about whether a particular operationalization of a construct adequately represents what is intended by the theoretical account of the construct being measured. When characterizing, e.g. the internationality of a higher education institution, the percentage of international students is a valid indicator only if scores are not heavily influenced by citizenship laws. Using the nationality of the qualifying diploma on entry has therefore a higher validity than using citizenship of the student.

6.4.1.2 Reliability

Reliability refers to the consistency of a set of measurements or measuring instrument. A measure is considered reliable if, repeatedly applied in the same population, it would always arrive at the same result. This is particularly an issue with survey data (e.g. among students, alumni, staff) used in rankings. In surveys and with regard to self-reported institutional data, the operationalizing of indicators and formulation of questions requires close attention – in particular in international rankings, where cross-cultural understanding of the questions will be an issue.

6.4.1.3 Comparability

A ranking is the comparison of institutions and programs using numerical indicators. Hence the indicators and underlying data/measure must be comparable between institutions; they have to measure the same quality in different institutions. In addition to the general issue of comparability of data across institutions, international rankings have to deal with issues of international comparability. National higher education systems are based on national legislation setting specific legal frameworks, including legal definitions (e.g. what/who is a professor). Additional problems arise from differing national academic cultures. Indicators, data elements and underlying questions have to be defined and formulated in a way that takes such contextual variations into account. For example, if we know that doctoral students are counted as academic staff in some countries and as students in others, we need to ask for the number of doctoral students counted as academic staff in order to harmonize data on academic staff (excluding doctoral students).

6.4.1.4 Feasibility

The objective of our project was to design a multidimensional global ranking tool that is feasible in practice. The ultimate test of the feasibility of our ranking tool has to be empirical: can U-Multirank be applied in reality and can it be applied with a favorable relation between benefits and costs in terms of financial and human resources? We report on the empirical assessment of the feasibility of U-Multirank in Chap. 9.

6.4.2 User-Driven Approach

To guide the readers' understanding of U-Multirank, we now briefly describe the way we have methodologically worked out the principle of being user-driven. We propose an interactive web based approach, where users will be able to declare their interests in a three step, user driven process:

1. select a set of institutions or fields in institutions ('units') that are homogeneous on descriptive issues judged by the users to be relevant given their declared interests;
2. choose whether to focus the ranking on higher education and research institutions as a whole (focused institutional rankings) or on fields within these institutions (field based rankings);

3. select a set of indicators to rank the chosen units. This will result in users creating their own specific and different rankings, according to their needs and wishes, from the entire database.

The first step can be based on the existing U-Map classification tool (see the following Sect. 6.4.3). We argue that it does not make sense to compare all institutions irrespective of their missions, profiles and characteristics, so a selection of comparable institutions based on U-Map should be the basis for any ranking.

In the second step, the users make their choices regarding the ranking level, i.e. whether a ranking will be created at the institutional level, creating a focused institutional ranking, or at the field level, creating a field-based ranking.

The final step is the selection of the indicators to be used in the ranking. There are two ways to organize this choice process. In the first option, users have complete freedom to select from the overall set of indicators, choosing any indicator, addressing any cell in the conceptual grid. We call this the 'personalized rankings'. Through this personalized approach the users may find information on those aspects in which they are particularly interested. Compared to existing league tables we see this as one of the advantages of our approach. However this kind of individualized, one off ranking (which may be different even if the same user applies different indicators) may not be attractive to all types of users, as there is no clear non-relative result for a particular institution or program. In the second option the indicators can be pre-selected. Such a selection can be undertaken from the perspective of a specific organization or institution, and will be called an 'authoritative ranking'. It is important that the selection of the indicators is made as transparent as possible.

6.4.3 U-Map and U-Multirank

The principle of comparability calls for a method that helps us in finding institutions the purposes and activity patterns of which are sufficiently similar in order to enable useful and effective rankings. Such a method, we suggest, can be found in the connection of U-Multirank with U-Map (see www.u-map.eu).

U-Map, being a classification tool, describes ('maps') higher education institutions on a number of dimensions, each representing an aspect of their activities. This mapping produces *activity profiles* of the institutions, displaying what the institutions do and how that compares to other institutions. U-Map prepares the ground for U-Multirank in the sense that it helps identify those higher education institutions that are comparable and for which, therefore, performance can be compared by means of the U-Multirank ranking tool.

Where U-Map is describing what the institutions do (and thus offers descriptive profiles), U-Multirank focuses on the *performance* aspects of higher education and research institutions. U-Multirank shows how well the higher education institutions are performing in the context of their institutional profile. Thus, the emphasis is on indicators of performance, whereas in U-Map it lies on the *enablers* of that performance – the inputs and activities. Despite the difference in emphasis, U-Map and U-Multirank share the same conceptual model. The conceptual model provides the rationale for the selection of the indicators in both U-Map and U-Multirank, both of which are complementary instruments for mapping diversity; horizontal diversity in classification and vertical diversity in ranking.

6.4.4 Grouping

U-Multirank does not calculate league tables. As has been argued in Chap. 4, league table rankings have severe flaws which make them, methodologically speaking, unreliable as transparency tools. As an alternative U-Multirank uses a grouping method. Instead of calculating 'exact' league table positions we will assign institutions to a limited number of groups.

Within groups there will be no further differentiation. Between the groups statistical methods guarantee that there is a clear difference between performance levels of different groups. The number of groups should be related to the number of institutions ranked. On the one hand the number of groups should express clear differences of performance; on the other hand the number should not be so low as to be restrictive, with the end result that many institutions end up clustered in one group. Last but not least, the number of groups and the methods for calculating the groups must be clear and comprehensible to users.

6.4.5 Design Context

In this chapter we have described the general aspects of the design process regarding U-Multirank. We have indicated our general design principles; we have described the conceptual framework from which the five dimensions of U-Multirank are deduced, and we have outlined a number of methodological approaches to be applied in U-Multirank. Together these elements form the design context from which we have constructed U-Multirank.

The design choices made here are in accordance with both the Berlin Principles and the recommendations by the Expert Group on the Assessment of University based Research. The Berlin Principles[1] emphasize (a. o.) the importance of being clear about the purpose of rankings and their target groups, of recognizing the diversity of institutional profiles, providing users the option to create tailor-made approaches, and of the need to focus on performance rather than on input factors. The AUBR Expert Group[2] (a. o.) underlines the importance of stakeholders' needs and

---

[1] http://www.ireg-observatory.org/index.php?option=com_content&task=view&id=41&Itemid=48
[2] Expert Group on Assessment of University-Based Research (2010), Assessing Europe's University-Based Research, European Commission, DG Research, EUR 24187 EN, Brussels.

involvement, as well as the principles of purposefulness, contextuality, and multidimensionality of rankings.

Based on our design context, in the following chapters we report on the construction of U-Multirank.

References

Becher, T., & Kogan, M. (1992). *Process and structure in higher education*. 2nd ed. London: Routledge.
Bucciarelli (1994): Louis L. Bucciarelli (1994): *Designing engineers*. Cambridge, MA: MIT Press.
Clark, B. R. (1983). *The Higher Education System: Academic Organization in Cross-National Perspective*. Berkeley: University of California Press.
Dulleck, U., & Kerschbamer, R. (2006). On doctors, mechanics, and computer specialists: The economics of credence goods. *Journal of Economic Literature, 44*(1), 5–42.
Nelson, P. (1970). "Information and consumer behavior." *The Journal of Political Economy, 78*(2), 311–329.
Oudshoorn, N., & Pinch, T. (Eds.). (2003), How Users Matter, the Co-construction of Users and Technology, Cambridge, MA: MIT Press

Chapter 7
Dimensions and Indicators

Gero Federkeil, Ben Jongbloed, Frans Kaiser, and Don F. Westerheijden

7.1 Introduction

Having set out the design context for U-Multirank in the previous chapter, we now turn to a major part of the process of constructing U-Multirank: the selection and definition of the indicators. These indicators need to enable us to measure the performances of higher education and research institutions both at the institutional and at the field level, in the five dimensions identified in our conceptual framework: teaching & learning, research, knowledge transfer, international orientation, and regional engagement. U-Multirank thus offers two levels of rankings (focused institutional rankings and field-based rankings) in five dimensions. This chapter provides an overview of the sets of indicators selected for the five dimensions, and briefly describes the selection process.

7.2 Stakeholders' Involvement

The indicator selection process was highly stakeholder-driven. Various categories of stakeholders (student organizations, employer organizations, associations and consortia of higher education institutions, government representatives, and international organizations) were involved in an iterative process of consultation to come to a stakeholder-based assessment of the relevance of various indicators.

The first step in the indicator selection process was a comprehensive inventory of potential indicators from the literature and from existing rankings and databases.

G. Federkeil (✉)
Centre for Higher Education (CHE), Gütersloh, Germany

B. Jongbloed • F. Kaiser • D.F. Westerheijden
Center for Higher Education Policy Studies, University of Twente,
Enschede, The Netherlands

This first list was exposed for feedback to stakeholders as well as to groups of specialist experts. Stakeholders were asked to give their views on the relative relevance of various indicators, presented to them as potential items in the five dimensions of U-Multirank.

The information gathered was fed into a second round of consultations with stakeholder organizations. To facilitate the consultation process we presented expert information on the availability of data, the perceived reliability of the indicators, and the frequency of their use in existing rankings.

The stakeholders' consultation process led to the selection of a set of indicators based on the criterion of *relevance* (according to stakeholders' perspectives). In addition, we applied four additional criteria to produce our list of indicators.

- *Validity* – The indicator measures what it claims to measure and is not confounded by other factors. This criterion is broken down into:
- *Concept* and *construct validity*: the indicator focuses on the *performance* of (programs in) higher education and research institutions and is defined in such a way that it measures 'relative' characteristics (e.g. controlling for size of the institution).
- *Face validity*: The indicator is used in other benchmarking and/or ranking exercises and thus may be regarded as a measure of performance, which already appears to be used.
- *Reliability*: The measurement of the indicator is the same regardless of who collects the data or when the measure is repeated. The data sources and the data to build the indicator are reliable.
- *Comparability*: The indicators allow comparisons from one situation/system/location to another; broadly similar definitions are used so that data are comparable.
- *Feasibility*: The required data to construct the indicator is either available in existing databases and/or higher education and research institutions, or can be collected with acceptable effort.

The selected indicators were tested in a pilot test on the basis of which the final selection of indicators was made.

7.3 Overview of Indicators

Following our conceptual framework, the five subsections that follow present the indicators for the five dimensions (teaching & learning, research, knowledge transfer, international orientation, regional engagement). For each indicator we include a number of comments that relate to the criteria (relevance, validity, reliability, comparability, feasibility) used for the selection of the indicator.

7.3.1 Teaching and Learning

Education is the core activity in most higher education and research institutions and comprises all processes to transmit knowledge, skills and values to learners (colloquially: students). Education can be conceived as a process subdivided in *enablers* (inputs,[1] process[2]) and *performance* (outputs and outcomes[3]). Teaching and learning ideally lead to the *impacts* or *benefits* that graduates will need for a successful career in the area studied and a successful, happy life as an involved citizen of a civil society. Career and quality of life are complex concepts, involving lifelong impacts. Moreover, the pace of change of higher education and research institutions means that long-term performance is of low predictive value for judgments on the future of those institutions. All we could aspire to in a ranking is to assess 'early warning indicators' of higher education's contribution, i.e. outcomes and outputs. Students' learning outcomes after graduation would be a good measure of outcomes. However, measures of *learning outcomes* that are internationally comparable are only now being developed in the AHELO project.[4] At this moment such measures do not exist, but if the AHELO project succeeds they would be a perfect complementary element in our indicator set.

Therefore, a combination of indicators was sought in order to reflect performance in the teaching and learning dimension. Teaching and learning can be looked at from different levels and different perspectives. As one of the main objectives of U-Multirank is to inform stakeholders such as students, their perspective is important too. From their point of view, the output to be judged is the educational process, so especially for the field-based rankings we include indicators that from a macro perspective are perceived as enablers.

Another approach to get close to learning outcomes lies in assessing the quality of study programs. Quality assurance procedures, even if they have become almost ubiquitous in this world's higher education, are too diverse to lead to comparable indicators (see Chap. 2): some quality assurance procedures focus on programs, others on entire higher education institutions; they have different foci, use different data, different performance indicators and different 'algorithms' to arrive at judgments. The qualifications frameworks currently being developed in the Bologna Process and in the EU may come to play a harmonizing role with regard to educational standards in Europe, but they are not yet effective (Westerheijden et al., 2010) and of course they do not apply in the rest of the world.

Indicators of the type of studies offered have been taken into consideration as objective bases for different qualities of programs, such as their interdisciplinary character. Besides, measures of students' progressing through their programs can be seen as indicators for the quality of their learning.

Proceeding from the adage that 'quality is in the eye of the beholder', indicators for quality can be sought in student and graduate assessments of their learning experience. The student/graduate experience of education is conceptually closer to what those same

---

[1] Inputs include resources for the education process: staff quality and quantity, facilities such as libraries, books, ICT, perhaps living and sports, funding available for those resources, and student quality and quantity.

[2] The process of education includes design and implementation of curricula, with formal teaching, self-study, peer learning, counseling services, etc.

[3] Outputs are direct products of a process, outcomes relate to achievements due to the outputs.

[4] http://www.oecd.org/document/22/0,3343,en_2649_35961291_40624662_1_1_1_1,00.html

students learn than judgments by external agents could be. Students' opinions may derive from investment or from consumption motives, but it is an axiom of economic theories as well as of civil society that persons know their own interest (and experience) best. Therefore we have chosen indicators reflecting both.

An issue might be whether student satisfaction surveys are prone to manipulation: do students voice their loyalty to the institution rather than their genuine (dis-) satisfaction? This is not seen as a major problem as studies show that loyalty depends on satisfaction (Athiyaman, 1997; Brown & Mazzarol, 2009; OECD, 2003).

Another issue about using surveys in international comparative studies concerns differences in culture that affect tendencies to respond in certain ways. Evidence from CHE rankings and from European surveys (e.g. EuroStudent[5]) shows, however, that student surveys can give valid and reliable information in a European context.

Table 7.1 lists the Teaching & Learning indicators that were selected for the pilot test of U-Multirank. The column on the right-hand side includes some of the comments and findings that emerged during the stakeholder/expert consultations.

One indicator dropped from the list during the stakeholder consultation was *graduate earnings*. Although the indicator may reflect the extent to which employers value the institution's graduates, it was felt by the majority of stakeholders that this indicator is very sensitive to economic circumstances and institutions have little influence on labor markets. In addition, data availability proved unsatisfactory for this indicator and comparability issues negatively affect its reliability.

For our field-based rankings, subject-level approaches to quality and educational standards do exist. In business studies, the 'triple crown' of specialized, voluntary accreditation by AACSB (USA), AMBA (UK) and EQUIS (Europe) creates a build-up of expectations on study programs in the field. In the field of engineering, the Washington Accord is an 'international agreement among bodies responsible for accrediting engineering degree programs. It recognizes the substantial equivalency of programs accredited by those bodies and recommends that graduates of programs accredited by any of the signatory bodies be recognized by the other bodies as having met the academic requirements for entry to the practice of engineering' (www.washingtonaccord.org).

In general, information on whether programs have acquired one or more of these international accreditations presents an overall, distant proxy to their educational quality. However, the freedom to opt for international accreditation in business studies may differ across countries, which makes an accreditation indicator less suitable for international comparative ranking. In engineering, adherence to the Washington Accord depends on national-level agencies, not on individual higher education institutions' strategies. These considerations have contributed to our decision not to include accreditation-related indicators in our list of Teaching & Learning performance indicators.

Instead, the quality of the learning experience is reflected in the student satisfaction indicators included in Table 7.1. These indicators can be based on a student

---

[5] http://www.eurostudent.eu:8080/index.html

7 Dimensions and Indicators

Table 7.1 Indicators for the dimension teaching & learning in the focused institutional and field-based rankings

		Definition	Comments
	Focused institutional ranking		
1	Expenditure on teaching	Expenditure on teaching activities (including expenditure on teaching related overhead) as a percentage of total expenditure	Data available. Indicator is input indicator. Stakeholders questioned relevance
2	Graduation rate	The percentage of a cohort that graduated x years after entering the program (x is the normal ('stipulated') time expected for completing all requirements for the degree times 1.5)	Graduation rate regarded by stakeholders as most relevant indicator. Shows effectiveness of schooling process. More selective institutions score better compared to (institutions in) open access settings. Sensitive to discipline mix in institution and sensitive to economic circumstances
3	Interdisciplinarity of programs	The number of degree programs involving at least two traditional disciplines as a percentage of the total number of degree programs	Based on objective statistics. Relevant indicator according to stakeholders: shows teaching leads to broadly-educated graduates. But sensitive to regulatory (accreditation) and disciplinary context. Data collection and availability problematic
4	Relative rate of graduate (un)employment	The rate of unemployment of graduates 18 months after graduation as a percentage of the national rate of unemployment of graduates 18 months after graduation (for bachelor graduates and master graduates)	Reflects extent to which institution is 'in sync' with environment. Sensitive to discipline mix in institution and sensitive to (regional) economic circumstances. Data availability poses problem
5	Time to degree	Average time to degree as a percentage of the official length of the program (bachelor and master)	Reflects effectiveness of teaching process. Availability of data may be a problem. Depends on the kind of programs
	Field-based ranking	*Definition*	*Comments*
6	Student-staff ratio	The number of students per fte academic staff	Fairly generally available. Is an input indicator. Depends on educational approaches. Sensitive to definitions of 'staff' and to discipline mix in institution
7	Graduation rate	The percentage of a cohort that graduated after x years after entering the program (x is the normal ('stipulated') time expected for completing all requirements for the degree times 1.5)	See above institutional ranking

(continued)

Table 7.1 (continued)

	Field-based ranking	Definition	Comments
8	Investment in laboratories [for Engineering FBR]	Investment in laboratories (average over last 5 years, in millions in national currencies) per student	High standard laboratories essential for offering high quality education. International comparisons difficult
9	Qualification of academic staff	The number of academic staff with PhD as a percentage of total number of academic staff (headcount)	Proxy for teaching staff quality. Generally available. Input indicator. Depends on national regulations and definitions of 'staff'
10	Relative rate of graduate (un)employment	The rate of unemployment of graduates 18 months after graduation as a percentage of the national rate of unemployment of graduates 18 months after graduation (for bachelor graduates and master graduates)	See above institutional ranking
11	Interdisciplinarity of programs	The number of degree programs involving at least two traditional disciplines as a percentage of the total number of degree programs	See above institutional ranking
12	Inclusion of issues relevant for employability in curricula	Rating existence of inclusion into curriculum (minimum levels/standards) of: project based learning; joint courses/projects with business students (engineering); business knowledge (engineering); project management; presentation skills; existence of external advisory board (including employers)	Problems with regard to availability of data
13	Inclusion of work experience into the program	Rating based on duration (weeks/credits) and modality (compulsory or recommended)	Data easily available
14	Computer facilities: internet access	Index including: hardware; internet access, including WLAN; (field specific) software; access to computer support	Data easily available
15	Student gender balance	Number of female students as a percentage of total enrolment	Indicates social equity (a balanced situation is considered preferable). Generally available But indicator of social context, not of educational quality

7 Dimensions and Indicators 103

	Student satisfaction indicators	Indicators reflecting students' appreciation of several items related to the teaching & learning process	Student satisfaction is of high conceptual validity. It can be made available in a comparative manner through a survey. An issue might be whether student satisfaction surveys are prone to manipulation: do students voice their loyalty to the institution rather than their genuine (dis-)satisfaction? Global comparability problematic: cross-cultural differences may affect the students' answers to the questions
16	Student satisfaction: overall judgment of program	Overall satisfaction of students with their program and the situation at their higher education institution	Refers to single question to give an 'overall' assessment; no composite indicator
17	Student satisfaction: research orientation of educational program	Index of four items: research orientation of the courses, teaching of relevant research methods, opportunities for early participation in research and stimulation to give conference papers	
18	Student satisfaction: evaluation of teaching	Satisfaction with regard to student's role in the evaluation of teaching, including prevalence of course evaluation by students, relevance of issues included in course evaluation, information about evaluation outcomes, impact of evaluations	
19	Student satisfaction: facilities	The satisfaction of students with respect to facilities, including: Classrooms/lecture halls: index including: availability/access for students; number of places; technical facilities/devices; Laboratories: index including: availability/access for students; number of places; technical facilities/devices; Libraries: index including: availability of literature needed; access to electronic journals; support services/e-services	

(continued)

Table 7.1 (continued)

	Field-based ranking	Definition	Comments
20	Student satisfaction: organization of program	The satisfaction of students with the organization of a program, including possibility to graduate in time, access to classes/courses, class size, relation of examination requirements to teaching	
21	Student satisfaction: promotion of employability (inclusion of work experience)	Index of several items: students assess the support during their internships, the organization, preparation and evaluation of internships, the links with the theoretical phases	
22	Student satisfaction: quality of courses	Index including: range of courses offered, coherence of modules/courses, didactic competencies of staff, stimulation by teaching, quality of learning materials, quality of laboratory courses (engineering)	
23	Student satisfaction: social climate	Index including: – Interaction with other students – Interaction with teachers – Attitude towards students in city – Security	
24	Student satisfaction: support by teachers	Included items: availability of teachers/professors (e.g. during office hours, via email); informal advice and coaching; feedback on homework, assignments, examinations; coaching during laboratory/IT tutorials (engineering only); support during individual study time (e.g. through learning platforms); suitability of hand-outs	

25	Student satisfaction: opportunities for a stay abroad	Index made up of several items: the attractiveness of the university's exchange programs and the partner universities; availability of exchange places; support and guidance in preparing for stay abroad; financial support (scholarships, exemption from study fees); transfer of credits from exchange university; integration of the stay abroad into studies (no time loss caused by stay abroad) and support in finding internships abroad
26	Student satisfaction: student services	Quality of a range of student services including: general student information, accommodation services, financial services, career service, international office and student organizations/associations
27	Student satisfaction: University webpage	Quality of information for students on the website. Index of several items including general information on institution and admissions, information about the program, information about classes/lectures; English-language information (for international students in non-English speaking countries)

survey carried out among a sample of students from specific fields (in our pilot study: Business Studies and Engineering). As shown in the bottom half of the Table 7.1, this survey focuses on provision of courses, organization of programs and examinations, interaction with teachers, facilities, etc. Stakeholders' feedback on the student satisfaction indicators revealed that they have a positive view overall of the relevance of the indicators on student satisfaction.

In the field-based rankings, some specific indicators are used in addition to the student satisfaction indicators. Most are similar to the indicators in the focused institutional rankings. Some additional indicators are included to pay attention to the facilities and services provided by the institution to enhance the learning experience (e.g. laboratories, curriculum).

7.3.2 Research

Selecting indicators for capturing the research performance of a higher education and research institution or a disciplinary unit (e.g. department, faculty) within that institution has to start with a clear definition of *research*. We take the definition set out in OECD's *Frascati Manual*[6]:

> Research and experimental development (R&D) comprise creative work undertaken on a systematic basis in order to increase the stock of knowledge, including knowledge of man, culture and society, and the use of this stock of knowledge to devise new applications.

The term R&D covers three activities: basic research, applied research and experimental development. Given the increasing complexity of the research function of higher education institutions and its extension beyond PhD awarding institutions, U-Multirank adopts a broad definition of research, incorporating elements of both basic and practice-oriented (applied) research. There is a growing diversity of research missions across the classical research universities and the more vocational oriented institutions (university colleges, institutes of technology, universities of applied sciences, Fachhochschulen, etc.). This is reflected in the wide range of research outputs and outlets mapped across the full spectrum, from discovery to knowledge transfer to innovation.

Research performance indicators may be distinguished into:

- *Output indicators,* measuring the quantity of research products. Typical examples are the number of papers published or the number of PhDs delivered.
- *Outcome indicators,* relating to a level of performance or achievement. For instance the contribution research makes to the advancement of scientific scholarly knowledge. Typical examples are citation rates, awards and prizes.
- *Impact indicators,* referring to the contribution of research outcomes to society, culture, the environment and/or the economy.

---

[6] http://browse.oecdbookshop.org/oecd/pdfs/browseit/9202081E.PDF

Table 7.2 Primary form of written communications by discipline group

	Natural sciences	Life sciences	Engineering sciences	Social sciences & humanities	Arts
Journal article	X	X	X	X	X
Conference proceedings	–	–	X	–	–
Book chapters	–	–	–	X	–
Monographs/books	–	–	–	X	–
Artefacts	–	–	–	–	X
Prototypes	–	–	X	–	–

Source: Expert Group on Assessment of University-Based Research (2009)

Given that in most disciplines publications are often seen as the single most important research output of higher education institutions, research performance measurement frequently takes place through bibliometric data. Data on publications, texts and citations is readily available for building bibliometric indicators (see Table 7.2). This is much less the case for data on research awards and data underlying impact indicators. In addition to performance measures, sometimes input-related proxies such as the volume of research staff and research income are in use to describe the research taking place in a particular institution or unit. Compared to such input indicators, bibliometric indicators may be more valid measures for the output or productivity of research teams and institutions. Increasingly sophisticated indicators such as citation indexes and co-citation indicators have been developed over time. However, an important issue in the production of bibliometric indicators lies in the definition of items that are considered as relevant.

The Expert Group on Assessment of University Based Research[7] defines research output as referring to individual journal articles, conference publications, book chapters, artistic performances, films, etc. While journals are the primary publication channel for almost all disciplines, their importance differs across disciplines. In some fields, books (monographs) play a major role, while book chapters or conference proceedings have a higher status in other fields (see Table 7.2). Therefore, focusing only on journal articles may not do justice to the research performance in particular disciplines. Moreover, the complexity of knowledge has led to a diverse range of output formats and research outlets. One may mention audio visual recordings, computer software and databases, technical drawings, designs or working models, major works in production or exhibition and/or award-winning design, patents or plant breeding rights, major art works, policy documents or briefs, research or technical reports, legal cases, maps, translations or editing of major works within academic standards.

Apart from using existing bibliometric databases, there is also the option to ask institutions themselves to list their research products, without restrictions on the type, medium or quality. While this may improve data coverage, such self-reported accounts may not be standardized or reliable, because respondents may interpret the

---

[7] See: http://www.kowi.de/Portaldata/2/Resources/fp/assessing-europe-university-based-research.pdf

definitions differently. For example, they may overestimate unpublished but accepted articles. This means that in the case of field-based rankings, the choice of one of these options will depend on the field.

The indicators for research performance in the focused institutional rankings and the field-based rankings are listed below (Table 7.3), along with some comments reflecting their assessment (by stakeholders and experts) against the criteria discussed in the first section of this chapter. The indicators in the table were used in the pilot test (see Chap. 9). The majority of the indicators were normalized by taking into account measures of an institution's (or a department's) size – that is: referring to total staff (in fte or headcount), total revenues or other volume measures.

Bibliometric indicators (citations, publications) are part of every research-based ranking. To acknowledge the output in the arts, an indicator reflecting arts-related output is included in U-Multirank as well. However, data availability is posing some challenges here. Research publications other than peer-reviewed journal publications are included, but this requires self-reporting by institutions based on clear definitions of the types of publications.

An indicator that was considered for use but dropped was 'Presence of research-related promotion schemes for academic staff'. A performance-based appraisal/incentive system (e.g. tenure track system) may increase the attractiveness of an institution to strong researchers, but it proved difficult to define such an indicator in a uniform way across multiple contexts (institutions, borders, disciplines).

Yet another indicator excluded during the process was 'Share of within-country joint research publications'. The number of publications that involve at least one author from another organization in the same country reflects successful national research cooperation. While such data is available, it is limited only to national authors. During the indicator selection process the relevance of the indicator was questioned, more so given the fact that research often is an international endeavor.

Some of the indicators in Table 7.3 are of an input type, such as expenditure on research, competitive grants and post-doc positions. However, stakeholders regarded them as relevant, even though data availability and definitions may sometimes pose a challenge. Therefore it was decided to keep them in the list of indicators for U-Multirank's institutional ranking.

Indicators for reflecting research performance in the field-based rankings are fewer in number. The ones that are included are largely overlapping with indicators for the institutional ranking. The fact that they are relating to a particular field opens up the door for additional indicators, i.e. doctoral productivity.

7.3.3 Knowledge Transfer

Knowledge transfer has become increasingly relevant for higher education and research institutions as many nations and regions strive to make more science output readily available for economic, social and cultural development. There are

7 Dimensions and Indicators

Table 7.3 Indicators for the dimension research in the focused institutional and field-based rankings

	Focused institutional ranking	Definition	Comments
1	Expenditure on research	The amount of money spent on research activities in the reference year as a percentage of total expenditure	Reflects involvement in (and priority attached to) research. Thus input indicator. Data mostly available. Recommended by Expert Group on University-based Research. Difficult to separate teaching and research expenditure in a uniform way
2	Research income from competitive sources	Income from European research programs + income from other international competitive research programs + income from research councils + income from privately funded research contracts as a share of total income	Success in winning grants indicates quality of research. Expert Group regards the indicator as relevant. Levels of external funding may vary greatly across disciplines and countries. Lack of clear delineation affects comparability. In some countries, competitive public funding may be difficult to separate from other public funding
3	Research publication output	Frequency count of research publications with at least one author address referring to selected institution (within Web of Science)	Broadly accepted. Data largely available. Widely used in research rankings (Shanghai, Leiden ranking, HEEACT). Different disciplinary customs cause distortion. Since publications are in peer-reviewed journals, they also signify a certain degree of research quality. However, focus on peer reviewed journal articles is too narrow for some disciplines
4	Post-doc positions (share)	Number of post-doc positions /fte academic staff	Success in attracting post-docs indicates quality of research. Reliability affected by the contextual characteristics of a country's science system. Definitions may vary across countries. Data availability may be weak
5	Interdisciplinary research activities	Share of research publications authored by multiple units from the same institution (based on self-reported data)	Research activities are increasingly becoming interdisciplinary. Indicator may be difficult to define (and collect) satisfactory

(continued)

Table 7.3 (continued)

	Focused institutional ranking	Definition	Comments
6	Field-normalized citation rate	Field-normalized citation impact score, where the fields are equivalent to the Thomson Reuters Journal Categories. 'Actual' citation counts are compared to 'expected' counts based on the average impact score of all journals assigned to a field. A score larger than one represents a citation impact above world average within that field of science, whereas scores below one represent below average impact	Indicates international scientific impact. Widely used and accepted indicator, especially in the exact sciences. Certain parts of social sciences, humanities and engineering are less well covered by citation indexes. Disregards impact of publications in journals aimed at professional audience
7	Share of highly cited research publications	Share of top 10% most highly cited publications; comparing 'actual' citation counts to 'expected' counts per field; citation impact distributions are calculated by applying a fixed citation-window, for two 'research-based' document types: articles, reviews. These data refer to database years	Publishing in top-ranked, high impact journals reflects quality of research. Indicator relevant primarily for exact/natural sciences. Data largely available. Books and proceedings are not considered. Never used before in any international classification or ranking
8	Number of art related outputs	Count of all relevant research-based tangible outputs in creative arts /fte academic staff	Recognizes outputs other than publications (e.g. exhibition catalogues, musical compositions, designs). This allows musical academies and art schools to be covered in ranking. Data suffers from lack of agreed definitions and lack of availability. Quantities difficult to aggregate
9	Number of international awards and prizes won for research work	Prizes, medals, awards and scholarships won by employees for research work and in (inter-) national cultural competitions, including awards granted by academies of science	Indicator of peer esteem. Recognition of quality. Data suffers from lack of agreed definitions and lack of availability. Quantities difficult to aggregate. Comparison across disciplines difficult

7 Dimensions and Indicators   111

	Field-based ranking	Definition	Comments
10	External research income	Level of funding attracted by researchers from contracts with external sources, including competitive grants and research income from government, industry, business and community organizations, as a percentage of total income	Success in winning grants indicates quality of research. Lack of clear delineation affects comparability. Annual and accurate numbers hard to retrieve, research contracts may run over several years
11	Research publication output	Frequency count of (Web of Science) research publications with at least one author address referring to selected institutional unit (relative to fte academic staff)	Frequently used indicator. However, research findings are not just published in journals
12	Doctorate productivity	Number of completed PhDs per number of professors (head count)*100 (3-year average)	Indicates aspects of the quantity and quality of a unit's research. Indicator affected by the contextuality of a country's science system
13	Field-normalized citation rate	See definition under institutional ranking	See comments made above for corresponding entry under institutional ranking
14	Highly cited research publications	See definition under institutional ranking	Top-end citation indices are less useful in some fields where high-profile research findings are also published in other outlets (books, reports, conference proceedings)

large differences between efforts and performance of individual institutions in this respect, partly because of the official mandate of an institution and partly because of the strategic profile chosen by individual institutions. *Knowledge transfer* is a broader and more encompassing concept than *technology transfer*. It may be defined as:

> The process by which the knowledge, expertise and intellectually linked assets of Higher Education Institutions are constructively applied beyond Higher Education for the wider benefit of the economy and society, through two-way engagement with business, the public sector, cultural and community partners. (Holi et al., 2008)

Measuring the impact of the knowledge transfer (or knowledge exchange) process in higher education and research institutions and ultimately on users, i.e. business and the economy, has now become a preoccupation of many governing and funding bodies, as well as policy-makers. So far, most attention has been devoted to measuring Technology Transfer (TT) activities. Traditionally TT is primarily concerned with the management of intellectual property (IP) produced by universities and other higher education and research institutions. TT means identifying, protecting, exploiting and defending intellectual property (OECD, 2003). Higher education and research institutions often have *technology transfer offices* (TTOs) (Debackere & Veugelers, 2005), which are units that liaise with industry and assist higher education and research institutions' personnel in the *commercialization* of research results. TTOs provide services in terms of assessing inventions, patenting, licensing IP, developing and funding spin-offs and other start-ups and approaching firms for contract-based arrangements.

The broader nature of Knowledge Transfer compared to TT also means it includes other forms – *channels* – of transfer than those requiring strong IP protection. A typical classification of mechanisms and channels for knowledge transfer between higher education and research institutions and other actors would include four main interaction channels for communication between higher education and research institutions and their environment:

- Texts, including scientific, professional and popular,
- People, including students and researchers,
- Artefacts, including equipment, protocols, rules and regulations,
- Money.

Texts are an obvious knowledge transfer channel. Publishing in scientific or popular media is, however, already covered under the research dimension in U-Multirank. In the case of texts, it is customary to distinguish between two forms: *publications*, where copyright protects how ideas are expressed but not the ideas themselves, and *patents*, which grant exclusive rights to use the inventions explained in them. While publications are part of the research dimension in U-Multirank, patents will be included under the Knowledge Transfer dimension.

People are another channel of knowledge transfer. People carry with them competences, skills and *tacit* knowledge. Indeed, many knowledge exchanges will be person-embodied. This type of knowledge transfer, however, is captured through the

Teaching & Learning and Regional Orientation dimensions included in U-Multirank. Knowledge transfer through people also takes place through networks, continuous professional development (CPD)[8] and research contracts.

Money flows are an important interaction channel, next to texts and people. Unlike texts and people, money is not a carrier of knowledge, but a way of valuing the knowledge transferred in its different forms. The money involved in contract research, CPD, consultancy and commercialization is one of the traditional indicators of knowledge exchange, often used in surveys of TTOs, such as the one carried out by the US-based Association of University Technology Managers (AUTM) for its Annual Licensing survey.

Artefacts make up the fourth major channel of interaction. Artefacts are concrete, physical forms in which knowledge can be carried and transferred. They are more or less 'ready to use', such as machinery, software, new materials or modified organisms. This is often called 'technology'. Artefacts may also extend to art-related outputs produced by scholars working in the arts and humanities disciplines. These works of art, including artistic performances, films and exhibition catalogues have been included in the scholarly outputs covered in the Research dimension of U-Multirank.

Most approaches to knowledge transfer measurement primarily address revenues obtained from the commercialization of Intellectual Property (IP). Clearly the measurement of income from IP is an incomplete reflection of knowledge transfer performance. For this reason, new approaches have been developed, such as the Higher Education-Business and Community Interaction (HE-BCI) Survey in the UK.[9] This UK survey began in 2001 and recognizes a broad spectrum of activities with both financial and non-financial objectives. However, it remains a fact that many indicators in the area of Knowledge Transfer are still in their infancy— in particular the ones that try to go beyond the IP issues.[10] Moreover, there is a need to define knowledge transfer more clearly in order to delineate it from dimensions such as Teaching, Research and Regional Engagement. Like research, knowledge transfer is a process, where inputs, throughputs, outputs and outcomes may be distinguished. Most knowledge transfer measurements focus on the input, some on the output and even fewer on the outcome (or impact) side of this process.

---

[8] CPD may be defined as: The means by which members of professional associations maintain, improve and broaden their knowledge and skills and develop the personal qualities required in their professional lives, usually through a range of short and long training programs (offered by education institutions), some of which have an option of accreditation.

[9] http://ec.europa.eu/invest-in-research/pdf/download_en/knowledge_transfer_web.pdf. The HE-BCI survey is managed by the Higher Education Funding Council for England (HEFCE) and used as a source of information to inform the funding allocations to reward the UK universities' third stream activities. See: http://www.hefce.ac.uk/econsoc/buscom/hebci

[10] The European Commission-sponsored project E3M (Montesinos et al., 2008) aims to create a ranking methodology for measuring university third mission activities along three subdimensions: Continuing Education (CE), Technology Transfer & Innovation (TT&I) and Social Engagement (SE).

U-Multirank particularly wants to capture aspects of knowledge transfer *performance*. However, given the state of the art in measuring knowledge transfer (Holi et al., 2008) and the near absence of (internationally comparable) data (see Chap. 4),[11] it proved extremely difficult to do so. Most candidates for additional indicators are of an input-type.

The knowledge transfer indicators are presented in Table 7.4, together with – in the right-hand column – some of the pros and cons of the indicators expressed by experts and stakeholders during the indicator selection process. The first selection of indicators was inspired by the international literature on knowledge transfer metrics and existing surveys in this area. An important reference is the report published in 2009 by the Expert Group on Knowledge Transfer Metrics (EGKTM) set up by DG Research of the European Commission.[12]

Cultural awards and prizes won in (inter)national cultural competitions would be an additional indicator that goes beyond the traditional technology-oriented indicators. However, the indicator is difficult to define uniformly and data is difficult to collect. Therefore this indicator was not kept in the list for the pilot.

While there is a large overlap in terms of indicators between the institutional ranking and the field-based ranking, the indicators related to licensing were felt to be less relevant for the institution as a whole. Licensing income is part of the third party funding indicator for the institutional level though. The number of collaborative research projects (university-industry) is another example of a knowledge transfer indicator that was not selected for the Focused Institutional Ranking.

7.3.4 International Orientation

Internationalization is a widely discussed and complex phenomenon in higher education. The rise of globalization and Europeanization have put growing pressure on higher education and research institutions to respond to these trends and develop an international orientation in their activities. Internationalization activities can be categorized in three types (Teichler, 2004):

- Activities to develop and promote international mobility of students and staff,
- Activities to develop and enhance international cooperation,
- Activities to develop and increase international competition.

---

[11] See also the brief section on the EUMIDA project, included in this report. One of EUMIDA's findings is that data on technology transfer activity and patenting is difficult to collect in a standardized way (using uniform definitions, etc.).

[12] See: http://ec.europa.eu/invest-in-research/pdf/download_en/knowledge_transfer_web.pdf

7 Dimensions and Indicators

Table 7.4 Indicators for the dimension knowledge transfer (KT) in the focused institutional and field-based rankings

	Focused institutional ranking	Definition	Comments
1	Incentives for knowledge exchange	Presence of knowledge exchange activities as part of the performance appraisal system	Such a scheme encourages staff to engage in KT. Information available in institutions. Difficult to define uniformly across institutions, borders, disciplines. New indicator
2	Third party funding	The amount of income for cooperative projects that are part of public programs (e.g. EC Framework programs) plus direct industry income as a proportion of total income	Signals KT success. Some data do exist (although definitions may vary). Is regarded as relevant indicator by EGKTM
3	University-industry joint publications	Relative number of research publications that list an author affiliate address referring to a business enterprise or a private sector R&D unit; relative to fte academic staff	Indicates appreciation of research by industry. Reflects successful partnerships. Less relevant for HEIs oriented to humanities, social sciences. ISI databases available. Used in CWTS University-Industry Research Cooperation Scoreboard
4	Patents	The number of patent applications for which the university acts as an applicant related to number of academic staff	Widely used in KT surveys. Included in U-Map. Depends on disciplinary mix of HEI. Data are available from secondary (identical) data sources
5	Size of technology transfer office	Number of employees (FTE) at Technology Transfer Office related to the number of FTE academic staff	Reflects priority for KT. Input indicator, could also show inefficiency. Data are mostly directly available. KT function may be dispersed across the HEI. Not regarded as core indicator by EGKTM
6	CPD courses offered	Number of CPD courses offered per academic staff (fte)	Captures outreach to professions. Relatively new indicator. CPD difficult to describe uniformly
7	Co-patents	Percentage of university patents for which at least one co-applicant is a firm, as a proportion of all patents	Reflects extent to which HEI shares its IP with external partners. Not widely used in TT surveys. Depends on disciplinary mix of HEI. Data available from secondary sources (PatStat)

(continued)

Table 7.4 (continued)

		Definition	Comments
8	Number of spin-offs	The number of spin-offs created over the last 3 years per academic staff (fte)	EGKTM regards Spin-offs as core indicator. Data available from secondary sources. Clear definition and demarcation criteria needed. Does not reveal market value of spin-offs
	Field-based ranking		
9	Academic staff with work experience outside higher education	Percentage of academic staff with work experience outside higher education within the last 10 years	Signals that HEI's staff is well-placed to bring work experience into their academic work. Data difficult to collect
10	Annual income from licensing	The annual income from licensing agreements as a percentage of total income	Licensing reflects exploiting of IP. Indicator is used widely. HEIs not doing research in natural sciences/engineering/medical sciences hardly covered
11	Co-patents	Percentage of university patents for which at least one co-applicant is a firm, as a proportion of all patents	See above institutional ranking
12	Joint research contracts with private sector	Budget and number of joint research projects with private enterprises per fte academic staff	Indicator of (applied) R&D activities. Indicator only refers to the size of projects, not their impact in terms of KT
13	Number of licence agreements	The number of licence agreements as a percentage of the number of patents	Licensing reflects exploiting of IP. Indicator is used widely. HEIs not doing research in natural sciences/engineering/medical sciences hardly covered. Number of licences more robust than licensing income
14	Patents awarded	The number of patents awarded to the university related to number of academic staff	Widely used KT indicator. Data available from secondary (identical) data sources. Patents with an academic inventor but another institutional applicant(s) not taken into account. Not relevant for all fields
15	University-industry joint publications	Number of research publications that list an author affiliate address referring to a business enterprise or a private sector R&D unit, relative to fte academic staff	See above institutional ranking. Differences in relevance by fields

7 Dimensions and Indicators

The rationales that drive these activities are diverse. Among others, they comprise (IAU, 2005):

- The increasing emphasis on the need to prepare students international labor markets and to increase their international cultural awareness,
- The increasing internationalization of curricula,
- The wish to increase the international position and reputation of higher education and research institutions (Enquist, 2005).

In the literature (Brandenburg and Federkeil, 2007; Enquist, 2005; IAU, 2005; Nuffic, 2010) many indicators have been identified, most of which refer to inputs and processes. The outcomes and impacts of internationalization activities are not very well covered by existing internationalization indicators.

For many of the indicators data are available in the institutional databases. Hardly any of such data can be found in national or international databases.

The various manifestations and results of internationalization are captured through the list of indicators shown in Table 7.5. The table includes some comments made during the consultation process that led to the selection of the indicators.

It should be pointed out here that one of the indicators is a *student satisfaction indicator*: 'Student satisfaction: Internationalization of programs'. This describes the opportunities for students to go abroad. Student opinion on the availability of opportunities for a semester or internship abroad is an aspect of the internationalization of programs. This indicator is relevant for the field level.

An indicator that was considered, but dropped during the stakeholders' consultation process is 'Size of international office'. While this indicates the commitment of the higher education and research institution to internationalization, and data is available, stakeholders consider this indicator not very important. Moreover, the validity is questionable as the size of the international office as a facilitating service is only a very crude indicator of internationalization.

The indicator 'international graduate employment rate' was dropped from the list for focused institutional rankings because a large majority of stakeholders judged this to be insufficiently relevant. At the field level this indicator was however seen as an attractive indicator for the international orientation of the program.

'International partnerships', that is the number of international academic networks a higher education and research institution participates in, is a potential indicator of the international embeddedness of the institution (department). However, it was dropped from the list during the stakeholder consultation as there is no clear internationally accepted way of counting partnerships. The same argument was used to exclude the indicator 'Joint international research projects'.

7.3.5 Regional Engagement

The *region* has become an important entity in the processes of economic and social development and innovation. Gaps between regions in terms of these processes are growing and regions that have skilled people and the infrastructure for innovation

Table 7.5 Indicators for the dimension international orientation in the focused institutional and field-based rankings

		Definition	Comments
	Focused institutional ranking		
1	Educational programs in foreign language	The number of programs offered in a foreign language as a percentage of the total number of programs offered	Signals the commitment to international orientation in teaching and learning. Data availability good. Relevant indicator. Used quite frequently. Sensitive to relative 'size' of national language
2	International academic staff	Foreign academic staff members (headcount) as percentage of total number of academic staff members (headcount). Foreign academic staff is academic staff with a foreign nationality, employed by the institution or working on an exchange basis	Considered to be relevant by stakeholders. Nationality not the most precise way of measuring international orientation
3	International doctorate graduation rate	The number of doctorate degrees awarded to students with a foreign nationality, as a percentage of the total number of doctorate degrees awarded	Indicator not used frequently. Some stakeholders see it as less relevant. Availability of data problematic
4	International joint research publications	Relative number of research publications that list one or more author affiliate addresses in another country relative to research staff	Only indicator addressing research internationalization. Data available in international databases, but bias towards certain disciplines and languages
5	Number of joint degree programs	The number of students in joint degree programs with foreign university (including integrated period at foreign university) as a percentage of total enrolment	Integration of international learning experiences is central element of internationalization. Data available. Indicator not often used
	Field-based ranking	Definition	Comments
6	Incoming and outgoing students	Incoming exchange students as a percentage of total number of students and the number of students going abroad as a percentage of total number of students enrolled	Important indicator of the international 'atmosphere' of a faculty/department. Addresses student mobility and curriculum quality. Data available
7	International graduate employment rate	The number of graduates employed abroad or in an international organization as a percentage of the total number of graduates employed	Indicates the student preparedness on the international labor market. Data not readily available. No clear international standards for measuring
8	International academic staff	Percentage of international academic staff in total number of (regular) academic staff	See above institutional ranking

7 Dimensions and Indicators 119

9	International research grants	Research grants attained from foreign and international funding bodies as a percentage of total income	Proxy of the international reputation and quality of research activities. Data are available. Stakeholders question relevance
10	Student satisfaction: internationalization of programs	Index including the attractiveness of the university's exchange programs, the attractiveness of the partner universities, the sufficiency of the number of exchange places; support and guidance in preparing the stay abroad; financial support; the transfer of credits from exchange university; the integration of the stay abroad into studies (no time loss caused by stay abroad)	Addresses quality of the curriculum. Not used frequently
11	Joint international publications	Relative number of research publications that list one or more author affiliate addresses in another country relative to academic staff	See above institutional ranking, but no problems of disciplinary distortion because comparison is made within the field
12	Percentage of international students	The number of degree-seeking students with a foreign diploma on entrance as percentage of total enrolment in degree programs	Reflects attractiveness to international students. Data available but sensitive to location (distance to border) of HEI. Stakeholders consider the indicator important
13	Student satisfaction: international orientation of programs	Rating including several issues: existence of joint degree programs, inclusion of mandatory stays abroad, international students (degree and exchange), international background of staff and teaching in foreign languages	Good indicator of international orientation of teaching; composite indicators depend on the availability of each data element

have a competitive advantage (Ischinger and Puukka, 2009). Higher education and research institutions can play an important role in the process of creating the conditions for a region to prosper. Creating and expanding this role in the region has become highly relevant for many public policymakers at the national and regional level, as well as for institutional administrators. How well a higher education and research institution is engaged in the region is increasingly considered to be an important part of the mission of higher education institutions.

Regional engagement is part of the broader concept of the 'third mission' of an institution. In the European project on third mission ranking (Montesinos et al. 2008) this 'third mission' consists of three dimensions: a social dimension, an enterprise dimension and an innovation dimension. The latter two dimensions are covered in the U-Multirank dimension 'Knowledge Transfer'. Indicators for the social dimension of the third mission comprise indicators on international mobility (that are covered in the U-Multirank dimension International Orientation) and a very limited number of indicators on regional engagement.

Activities and indicators on regional and community engagement can be categorized in three groups: outreach, partnerships and curricular engagement.[13] Outreach focuses on the application and provision of institutional resources for regional and community use, benefitting both the university and the regional community. Partnerships focus on collaborative interactions with the region/community and related scholarship for the mutual beneficial exchange, exploration, discovery and application of knowledge, information and resources. Curricular engagement refers to teaching, learning and scholarship that engage faculty, students and region/community in mutual beneficial and respectful collaboration.

Both enabling indicators and performance indicators are suggested in the literature on regional and community engagement. However, most attention is paid to the enablers and to indicators addressing the way an institution organizes its engagement activities. These indicators are based on checklists assessing the extent to which regional engagement is part of the institutional mission and integrated in the routines and procedures of the institution. Do the reward and promotion schemes of the institution acknowledge regional engagement activities? Are there visible structures that function to assist with region-based teaching and learning? Is there adequate funding available for establishing and deepening region-based activities? Are there courses that have a regional component (such as service-learning courses)? Are there mutually beneficial, sustained partnerships with regional community partners? These are typical items on such checklists (Furco & Miller, 2009; Hollander et al., 2001). The problem with these checklists is that the information is not readily available. Institutional or external assessors need to collect the information, which makes the robustness and reliability of the results in an international comparative setting highly questionable.

---

[13] See: http://classifications.carnegiefoundation.org/details/communityengagement.php

7   Dimensions and Indicators   121

Other indicators for regional engagement capture the relative size of the interaction. How much does the institution draw on regional resources (students, staff, funding) and how much does the region draw on the resources provided by the higher education and research institution (graduates and facilities)?

Clarification is required as to what constitutes a region. U-Multirank starts with the existing list of regions in the Nomenclature of Territorial Units for Statistics (NUTS) classification developed and used by the European Union,[14] in particular the NUTS 2 level. For non-European countries the lower level (Territorial level 3) of the OECD classification of its member states is used. This is composed of microregions.[15] As with most standard lists, these work fine in the majority of cases, but there are always cases where a different definition is more appropriate. In the pilot study we allowed higher education and research institutions to specify their own delimitation of region if they felt there were valid reasons for doing so. Table 7.6 includes the indicators on regional engagement, along with the comments made during the stakeholder and expert consultations.

In the dimension Regional Engagement there are a number of indicators were considered but not included in the pilot test:

- 'Co-patents with regional firms' reflect cooperative research activities between higher education institutions and regional firms. While data may be found in international patent databases, the indicator is not often used and stakeholders did not particularly favor the indicator. Therefore it was dropped from our list.
- The same holds for measures of the regional economic impact of a higher education institution, such as the number of jobs generated by the university. Assessing what the higher education and research institution 'delivers' to the region (in economic terms) is seen as most relevant but data constraints prevent us from the use of such an indicator.
- Public lectures that are open to an external, mostly local audience, are a way to intensify contacts to the local community. However, stakeholders felt this indicator not to be relevant.
- A high percentage of new entrants from the region may be seen as the result of the high visibility of regionally active higher education and research institutions. It may also be a result of the engagement with regional secondary schools. This indicator however was not included in our list, mainly because it was not considered to be that relevant.

The above discussion makes it clear that regional engagement is a dimension that poses many problems with regard to availability of performance-oriented indicators and their underlying data. In the next chapter we will discuss the data gathering instruments that are available more extensively.

---

[14] http://epp.eurostat.ec.europa.eu/portal/page/portal/region_cities/regional_statistics/nuts_classification
[15] http://www.oecd.org/document/62/0,3343,en_2649_34413_36878718_1_1_1_1,00.html

Table 7.6 Indicators for the dimension regional engagement in the focused institutional and field-based rankings

	Focused institutional ranking	Definition	Comments
1	Graduates working in the region	The number of graduates working in the region, as a percentage of all graduates employed	Frequently used in benchmarking exercises. Stakeholders like indicator. No national data on graduate destinations
2	Income from regional/local sources	Institutional income from local regional authorities, local/regional charities and local/regional contracts as a percentage of total institutional income	Reflects connection and engagement with regional/local society. Sensitive to way public funding for HEI is organized (national versus regional/federal systems). Availability of data problematic
3	Regional joint research publications	Number of research publications that list one or more author-affiliate addresses in the same NUTS2 or NUTS3 region, relative to fte academic staff	Reflects 'local' research cooperation. Data available (Web of Science), but professional (laymen's) publications not covered
4	Research contracts with regional business	The number of research projects with regional firms, as a proportion of the total number of collaborative research projects	Seen as valid and relevant indicator, hardly any records kept on (regional) contracts. New type of indicator
5	Student internships in local/regional enterprises	The number of student internships in regional enterprises as a percentage of total enrolment (with defined minimum of weeks and/or credits)	Internships open up communication channels between HEI and regional/local enterprises. Stakeholders see this as important indicator. Definition of internship problematic and data not readily available. Disciplinary bias

	Field-based ranking	Definition	Comments
6	Degree theses in cooperation with regional enterprises	Number of degree theses in cooperation with regional enterprises as a percentage of total number of degree theses awarded, by level of program	Reflects regional cooperation and curricular engagement. Indicator hardly ever used
7	Graduates working in the region	The number of graduates working in the region, as a percentage of all graduates employed	See above institutional ranking
8	Regional participation in continuing education	Number of regional participants (coming from NUTS3 region where HEI is located) as percentage of total number of population in NUTS3 region aged 25+	Indicates how much the HEI draws on the region and vice versa. Covers important aspect of curricular engagement. Data not readily available. Indicator hardly ever used
9	Student internships in local/regional enterprises	Number of internships of students in regional enterprises (as percentage of total students)	See above institutional ranking, but disciplinary bias not problematic at field level
10	Summer school/courses for secondary education students	Number of participants in schools/courses for secondary school students as a percentage of total enrolment	Addresses outreach activities. Limited availability of data. Lack of internationally accepted definition of summer school courses

References

Athiyaman, A. (1997). Linking student satisfaction and service quality perceptions: the case of university education. *European Journal of Marketing, 31*(7), 528–540.

Brandenburg, U., & Federkeil, G. (2007). *How to measure internationality and internationalisation of higher education institutions! Indicators and key figures.* CHE Working Paper 92, Gütersloh.

Brown, R. M., & Mazzarol, T. W. (2009). The importance of institutional image to student satisfaction and loyalty within higher education. *Higher Education, 58*(1), 81–95.

Debackere, K., & Veugelers, R. (2005). The role of academic technology transfer organizations in improving industry-science links. *Research Policy, 34*, 321–342.

Enquist, G. (2005). The internationalisation of higher education in Sweden, the National Agency for Higher Education. *Högskoleverkets rapportserie* 2005:27 R. Stockholm.

Expert Group on Knowledge Transfer Metrics. (2009). *Metrics for knowledge transfer from public research organizations in Europe.* Brussels: European Commission DG for Research. See: http://ec.europa.eu/invest-in-research/pdf/download_en/knowledge_transfer_web.pdf.

Furco, A., & Miller, W. (2009). *Issues in benchmarking and assessing institutional engagement.* New Directions for Higher Education, No. 147, Fall 2009, p. 47–54.

Holi, M. T., Wickramasinghe, R., & van Leeuwen, M. (2008). *Metrics for the evaluation of knowledge transfer activities at universities.* Cambridge: Library House.

Hollander, E. L., Saltmarsh, J., & Zlotkowski, E. (2001), "Indicators of Engagement." In L. A. Simon, M. Kenny, K. Brabeck, & R. M. Lerner (Eds.), *Learning to serve: promoting civil society through service-learning.* Norwell, Mass.: Kluwer.

IAU, International Association of Universities (2005). *Global survey report, internationalization of higher education: new directions, new challenges*, Paris: IAU.

Ischinger, B., & Puukka, J. (2009), Universities for Cities and Regions: Lessons from the OECD Reviews, Change: *The Magazine of Higher Learning, 41*(3), 8–13.

Montesinos, P., Carot, J. M., Martinez, J. M., & Mora, F. (2008). Third mission ranking for world class universities: beyond teaching and research, *Higher Education in Europe, 33*(2), 259–271.

Nuffic (2010) Mapping internationalization, http://www.nuffic.nl/internationalorganizations/services/quality-assurance-and-internationalization/mapping-internationalization-mint

OECD. (2003). *Turning science into business: patenting and licensing at public research organizations.* Paris: OECD.

Teichler, U. (2004). The changing debate on internationalisation of higher education. *Higher Education, 48*(1), 5–26.

Westerheijden, D. F., Beerkens, E., Cremonini, L., Huisman, J., Kehm, B., Kovac, A., et al. (2010). *The first decade of working on the European Higher Education Area: The Bologna Process Independent Assessment - Executive summary, overview and conclusions.* s. l. Vienna: European Commission, Directorate-General for Education and Culture.

Chapter 8
Data Collection

Julie Callaert, Elisabeth Epping, Gero Federkeil, Ben Jongbloed, Frans Kaiser, and Robert Tijssen

8.1 Introduction

In this chapter we will describe the data collection instruments used in the development of U-Multirank. The first section is an overview of existing databases – mainly on bibliometrics and patents. The second describes the questionnaires and survey tools used for collecting data from the institutions (the self-reported data) – at the institutional and department levels – and from students. The next chapter outlines the design of the pilot test through which the feasibility of a multidimensional global ranking was assessed and presents the major outcomes.

8.2 Databases

8.2.1 Existing Databases

One of the activities in the U-Multirank project was to review existing rankings and explore their underlying databases. If existing databases can be relied on for quantifying the U-Multirank indicators this would be helpful in reducing the overall

---

J. Callaert (✉)
Center for Research & Development Monitoring (ECOOM),
Catholic University of Leuven, Leuven, Belgium

E. Epping • B. Jongbloed • F. Kaiser
Center for Higher Education Policy Studies, University of Twente,
Enschede, The Netherlands

G. Federkeil
Centre for Higher Education (CHE), Gütersloh, Germany

R. Tijssen
Science and Innovation Studies, Leiden University, Leiden, The Netherlands

burden for institutions in responding to U-Multirank data requests. However, from the overview of classifications and rankings presented in Chap. 3 it is clear that international databases holding information at institution level or at lower aggregation levels are currently available only for particular aspects of the dimensions Research and Knowledge Transfer. For other aspects and dimensions, U-Multirank needs to rely on self-reported data. Regarding research output and impact, there are worldwide databases on journal publications and citations. For knowledge transfer, the database of patents compiled by the European Patent Office is available. In the next two subsections, available bibliometric and patent databases will be discussed.

To further assess the availability of data covering individual higher education and research institutions, the results of the EUMIDA project – which seeks to develop the foundations of a coherent data infrastructure at the level of individual European higher education institutions – were also taken into account (see Sect. 8.2.4). In addition, a group of international experts were asked to give their assessment of data availability in some of the non-EU countries to be included in the pilot study.

8.2.2 Bibliometric Databases

There are a number of international databases which can serve as a source of information on the research output of a higher education and research institution (or one of its departments). An institution's quantity of research-based publications (per capita) reflects its research output and can also be seen as a measure of scientific merit or quality. In particular, if its publications are highly cited within the international scientific communities this may characterize an institution as high-impact and high-quality. The production of publications by a higher education and research institute not only reflects research activities in the sense of original scientific research, but usually also the presence of underlying capacity and capabilities for engaging in sustainable levels of scientific research.[1] The research profile of a higher education and research institution can be specified further by taking into account its engagement in various types of research collaboration. For this, one can look at joint research publications involving international, regional and private sector partners. The subset of jointly authored publications is a testimony of successful research cooperation.

Data on numbers and citations of research publications are covered relatively well in existing databases. Quantitative measurements and statistics based on information drawn from bibliographic records of publications are usually called 'bibliometric data'. These data concern the quantity of scientific publications by an author or organization and the number of citations (references) these publications

---

[1] This is why research publication volume is a part of the U-Map indicators that reflect the activity profile of an institution.

have received from other research publications. There is a wide range of research publications available for characterizing the research profile and research performance of an institution by means of bibliometric data: lab reports, journal articles, edited books, monographs, etc. The bibliometric methodologies applied in international comparative settings such as U-Multirank usually draw their information from publications that are released in scientific and technical journals. This part of the research literature is covered ('indexed') by a number of international databases. In most cases the journals indexed are internationally peer-reviewed, which means that they adhere to international quality standards. U-Multirank therefore makes use of international bibliometric databases to compile some of its research performance indicators and a number of research-related indicators belonging to the dimensions of Internationalization, Knowledge Transfer and Regional Engagement.

Two of the most well-known databases that are available for carrying out bibliometric analyses are the Web of Science and Scopus.[2] Both are commercial databases that provide global coverage of the research literature and both are easily accessible. The Web of Science database is maintained by ISI, the Institute for Scientific Information, which was taken over by Thomson Reuters a few years ago. The Web of Science currently covers about 1 million new research papers per year, published in over 10,000 international and regional journals and book series in the natural sciences, social sciences, and arts and humanities. According to the Web of Science website, 3,000 of these journals account for about 75% of published articles and over 90% of cited articles.[3] The Web of Science claims to cover the highest impact journals worldwide, including Open Access journals and over 110,000 conference proceedings.

The Scopus database was launched in 2004 by the publishing house Elsevier. It claims to be the largest abstract and citation database containing both peer-reviewed research literature and web sources. It contains bibliometric information covering some 17,500 peer-reviewed journals (including 1,800 Open Access journals) from more than 5,000 international publishers. Moreover it holds information from 400 trade publications and 300 book series, as well as data about conference papers from proceedings and journals.

To compile the publications-related indicators in the U-Multirank pilot study, bibliometric data was derived from the October 2010 edition of the Web of Science bibliographical database. An upgraded 'bibliometric version' of the database is housed and operated by the CWTS (one of the CHERPA Network partners) under a full license from Thomson Reuters. This dedicated version includes the 'standardized institutional names' of higher education and research institutes that have been checked ('cleaned') and harmonized in order to ensure

---

[2] Yet another database is Google Scholar. This is a service based on the automatic recording by Google's search engine of citations to any author's publications (of whatever type) included in other publications appearing on the worldwide web.

[3] See: http://thomsonreuters.com/products_services/science/science_products/a-z/web_of_science/

that as many as possible of the Web of Science-indexed publications are assigned to the correct institution. This data processing of address information is done at the aggregate level of the entire 'main' organization (not for sub-units such as departments or faculties). All the selected institutions in the U-Multirank pilot study produced at least one Web of Science-indexed research publication during the years 1980–2010.

The Web of Science, being both an international and multidisciplinary database, has its pros and cons. The bulk of the research publications are issued in peer-reviewed international scientific and technical journals, which mainly refer to discovery-oriented 'basic' research of the kind that is conducted at universities and research institutes. There are relatively few conference proceedings in the Web of Science, and no books or monographs whatsoever; hence, publications referring to 'applied research' or 'strategic research' are underrepresented. It has a relatively poor coverage of non-English language publications. The coverage of publication output is quite good in the medical sciences, life sciences and natural sciences, but relatively poor in many of the applied sciences and social sciences and particularly within the humanities. The alternative source of bibliographical information, Elsevier's Scopus database, is likely to provide an extended coverage of the global research literature in those underrepresented fields of science.

For the following six indicators selected for inclusion in the U-Multirank pilot test data can be obtained from the CWTS/Thomson Reuters Web of Science database:

1. total publication output
2. university-industry joint publications
3. international joint publications
4. field-normalized citation rate
5. share of the world's most highly cited publications
6. regional joint publications

This indicator set includes four new performance indicators (#2, #3, #5, #6) that were specially constructed for U-Multirank and have not been used before in any international classification or ranking.

8.2.3 Patent Databases

As part of the indicators in the Knowledge Transfer dimension, we selected the number of *patent applications* for which a particular higher education and research institution acts as an applicant and (as part of that) the number of *co-patents* applied for by the institution together with a private organization.

Data for the co-patenting and patents indicators can be derived from patent databases. For U-Multirank, patent data were retrieved from the European Patent Office

(EPO). Its Worldwide Patent Statistical Database (version October 2009),[4] also known as PATSTAT, is designed and published on behalf of the OECD Taskforce on Patent Statistics. Other members of this taskforce include the World Intellectual Property Organization (WIPO), the Japanese Patent Office (JPO), the United States Patent and Trademark Office (USPTO), the US National Science Foundation (NSF), and the European Commission represented by Eurostat and by DG Research.

The PATSTAT patent database is especially designed to assist in advanced statistical analysis of patent data. It contains patent data from over 80 countries; adding up to 70 million records (63 million patent applications and 7 million granted patents). The patent data are sourced from offices worldwide, including of course the most important and largest ones such as the EPO, the USPTO, the JPO and the WIPO. Updates of PATSTAT are produced every 6 months, around April and October.

PATSTAT is a relational database: 20 related tables contain information on relevant dates (e.g. of patent filing, patent publication, granting of patent), on patent applicants and inventors, technological classifications of patents, citations from patents to other documents, family links,[5] etc. Updates of PATSTAT are produced twice a year.

8.2.4 Data Availability According to EUMIDA

Like the U-Multirank project, the EUMIDA project (see http://www.eumida.org) collects data on individual higher education and research institutions. The EUMIDA project is meant to test whether a data collection effort can be undertaken by EUROSTAT in the foreseeable future. EUMIDA covers 29 countries (the 27 EU member states plus Switzerland and Norway) and has demonstrated that a regular collection of institutional data by national statistical authorities is feasible across (almost) all EU-member states, albeit for a limited number of mostly input indicators.

The EUMIDA and U-Multirank project teams agreed to share information on issues such as definitions of data elements and data sources, given that the two projects share a great deal of data (indicators). The overlap lies mainly in the area of data related to the inputs (or activities) of higher education and research institutions. A great deal of this input-related information is used in the construction of the indicators in U-Map. The EUMIDA data elements therefore are much more similar to

---

[4] This version is held by the K.U. Leuven (Catholic University Leuven) and was licensed to its ECOOM unit (Expertise Centrum O&O Monitoring).

[5] A patent family is a set of patents taken in various countries to protect a single invention (when a first application in a country – the priority – is then extended to other offices). In other words, a patent family is the same invention disclosed by (a) common inventor(s) and patented in more than one country (see: US Patent and Trademark Office: www.uspto.gov).

Table 8.1 Data elements shared between EUMIDA and U-Multirank: their coverage in national databases

Dimension	EUMIDA and U-Multirank data element	European countries where data element is available in national databases
Teaching & learning	Relative rate of graduate unemployment	CZ, FI, NO, SK, ES
Research	Expenditure on research	AT*, BE, CY, CZ*, DK, EE, FI, GR*, HU, IT, LV*, LT*, LU, MT*, NO, PL*, RO*, SI*, ES, SE, CH, UK
	Research publication output	AT, BE-FL, CY, CZ, DK, FI, FR, DE, GR, HU, IE, IT, LV, LT, LU, NO, NL, PL, PT*, RO*, SK, SI, ES, SE*, CH, UK
Knowledge transfer	Number of spin-offs	BE-FL, FR*, GR, IT (p), PT (p), ES
	Third party funding	CY, CZ, DE, IT, NL, NO, PL, PT, ES, CH
	Patents	AT, BE-FL, CZ, EE*, FI, FR*, GR, HU, IE*, IT, LU, MT*, NO, NL (p), PL*, SI, ES, UK
International orientation	(No overlap between U-Multirank and EUMIDA)	
Regional engagement	(No overlap between U-Multirank and EUMIDA)	

Source: Based on EUMIDA Deliverable D2 – *Review of Relevant Studies* (dated 20 February 2010 and submitted to the Commission on 1 March 2010).
* indicates: There are confidentiality issues (e.g. national statistical offices may not be prepared to make data public without consulting individual HEIs).
(p) indicates: Data are only partially available (e.g. only for public HEIs or only for [some] research universities).
The list of EUMIDA countries with abbreviations: Austria (*AT*), Belgium (*BE*), [Belgium-Flanders community (*BE-FL*)], Bulgaria (*BG*), Cyprus (*CY*), Czech Republic (*CZ*), Denmark (*DK*), Estonia (*EE*), Finland (*FI*) France (*FR*), Germany (*DE*), Greece (*GR*), Hungary (*HU*), Ireland (*IE*), Italy (*IT*), Latvia (*LV*), Lithuania (*LV*), Luxembourg (*LU*), Malta (*MT*), Netherlands (*NL*), Norway (*NO*), Poland (*PL*), Portugal (*PT*), Romania (*RO*), Slovakia (*SK*), Slovenia (*SI*), Spain (*ES*), Sweden (*SE*), Switzerland (*CH*), United Kingdom (*UK*).

the U-Map indicators, since U-Map aims to build *activity profiles* for individual institutions whereas U-Multirank constructs *performance profiles*.

The findings of EUMIDA point to the fact that for the more research intensive higher education institutions, data for the dimensions of Education and Research are relatively well covered, although data on graduate careers and employability are sketchy. Some data on scientific publications is available for most countries. However, overall, performance-related data is less widely available compared to input-related data items. The role of national statistical institutes is quite limited here and the underlying methodology is not yet consistent enough to allow for international comparability of data.

Table 8.1 above shows the U-Multirank data elements that are covered in EUMIDA and whether information on these data elements may be found in national databases (statistical offices, ministries, rectors' associations, etc.). The table shows that

EUMIDA primarily focuses on the Teaching & Learning and Research dimensions, with some additional aspects relating to the Knowledge Transfer dimension. Since EUMIDA was never intended to cover all dimensions of an institution's activity (or its performance), it is only natural that dimensions such as International Orientation and Regional Engagement are less prominent in the project.

The table illustrates that information on only a few U-Multirank data elements is available from national databases and, moreover, what data exists is available only in a small minority of European countries. This implies, once again, that the majority of data elements will have to be collected directly from the institutions themselves.

8.3 Data Collection Instruments

Due to the lack of adequate data sets, the U-Multirank project had to rely largely on self-reported data (both at the institutional and field-based levels), collected directly from the higher education and research institutions. The main instruments to collect data from the institutions were four online questionnaires: three for the institutions and one for students.

The four surveys are:

- U-Map questionnaire
- institutional questionnaire
- field-based questionnaire
- student survey.

The U-Map questionnaire had already been tested and fully documented in its design phase. The remaining three surveys were designed, pre-tested, modified where necessary and a full set of supporting instruments (data-collection protocols, glossaries, FAQ, help desk) were developed for their use in the pilot study.

8.3.1 U-Map Questionnaire

As explained earlier, the U-Map questionnaire is an instrument for identifying similar subsets of higher education institutions within the U-Multirank sample. Data is collected in seven main categories:

- general information: name and contact person; public/private character and age of institution;
- students: numbers; modes of study and age; international students; students from region;
- graduates: by level of program; subjects; orientation of degrees; graduates working in region;
- staff data: fte and headcount; international staff;

- income: total income; income by type of activity; by source of income;
- expenditure: total expenditure; by cost centre; use of full cost accounting;
- research and knowledge exchange: publications; patents; concerts and exhibitions; start-ups.

8.3.2 Institutional Questionnaire

The institutional questionnaire collects data on the performance of the institution. The questionnaire is divided into the following categories:

- general information: name and contact; public/private character and age of institution; university hospital
- students: enrolment
- program information: bachelor/master's programs offered; CPD courses
- graduates: graduation rates; graduate employment
- staff: fte and headcount; international staff; technology transfer office staff
- income: total; income from teaching; income from research; income from other activities
- expenditure: total expenditure; by cost centre; coverage
- research and knowledge transfer: publications; patents; concerts and exhibitions; start-ups.

8.3.3 Field-Based Questionnaire

The field-based questionnaire includes information on individual faculties/departments and their programs in the pilot fields of business studies, mechanical engineering and electrical engineering.

The following categories are distinguished:

- overview: name and address of unit responsible for organizing the field; contact person
- staff & PhD: academic staff; number of professors; international visiting/guest professors; professors offering lectures abroad; professors with work experience abroad; number of PhDs; number of post-docs
- funding: external research funds; license agreements/income; joint R&D projects with local enterprises
- students: total number (female, international degree and exchange students); internships secured; degree theses in cooperation with local enterprises
- regional engagement: continuing education programs/professional development programs; summer schools/courses for secondary students
- description: accreditation of department; learning & teaching profile; research profile.

A second part of the questionnaire asks for details of the *individual study programs* to be included in the ranking. In particular the following information was collected:

- basic information about the program (e.g. degree, length); interdisciplinary characteristics; full-time/part-time;
- number of students enrolled in the program; number of study places and level of tuition fees; periods of work experience integrated in program; international orientation; joint study program;
- credits earned for achievements abroad; number of exchange students from abroad; courses held in foreign language; special features;
- number of graduates; information about labor market entry.

8.3.4 Student Survey

The main instrument for measuring student satisfaction is an online survey. The student questionnaire uses a combination of open questions and predefined answers. Its main focus is on the assessment of the teaching and learning experience and on the facilities of the institution (see Table 7.1 in the previous chapter for more detailed information).

Chapter 9
The Pilot Test and Its Outcomes

Julie Callaert, Elisabeth Epping, Gero Federkeil, Jon File,
Ben Jongbloed, Frans Kaiser, Isabel Roessler, Robert Tijssen,
Frans A. van Vught, and Frank Ziegele

9.1 Introduction

In this chapter we describe the design and outcomes of the pilot test specifically undertaken to analyze the feasibility of implementing U-Multirank and particularly of the application of the four data collection instruments just described on a global scale. First we outline the construction of the global sample of institutions that participated in the pilot test. Next we discuss the feasibility of the data collection procedures and use of the various indicators presented in Chap. 7. Finally we discuss the level of institutional interest in participating in the pilot and the potential upscaling of U-Multirank to a globally applicable multidimensional ranking tool.

J. Callaert
Center for Research & Development Monitoring (ECOOM),
Catholic University of Leuven, Leuven, Belgium

E. Epping • J. File • B. Jongbloed • F. Kaiser • F.A. van Vught (✉)
Center for Higher Education Policy Studies, University of Twente,
Enschede, The Netherlands

G. Federkeil • I. Roessler • F. Ziegele
Centre for Higher Education (CHE), Gütersloh, Germany

R. Tijssen
Science and Innovation Studies, Leiden University Leiden, The Netherlands

9.2 The Global Sample

A major task of the feasibility study was the selection of institutions to be included in the pilot study. The selection of the 150 pilot institutions (as broadly specified by the European Commission) needed to be informed by two major criteria: including a group of institutions that reflects as much institutional diversity as possible; and making sure that the sample was regionally and nationally balanced. In addition we needed to ensure sufficient overlap between the pilot institutional ranking and the pilot field-based rankings to be conducted in business studies and two engineering fields (also specified by the European Commission).

U-Map is an effective tool to identify institutional activity profiles and thereby to map institutional diversity. Yet at this stage of its development U-Map includes only a limited number of provisional (European) institutional profiles which makes it insufficiently applicable for the selection of a global sample of pilot institutions. We needed to find another way to create a sample with a sufficient level of diversity in institutional profiles. Our solution was to have national experts recommend a diverse range of institutions in their respective countries that could be invited to participate in the pilot study. We do not claim to have designed a sample that is fully representative of the diversity in higher education across the globe (particularly as there is no adequate description of this diversity) but we have succeeded in including a wide variety of institutional types in our sample.

Looking at the final group of participating institutions, we are confident that the group has sufficient institutional diversity. The U-map profiles of the institutions reflect variation regarding all five dimensions. Participating institutions include an Institute for Water and Environment; an agricultural university; a School of Petroleum and Minerals; a military academy; several music academies and art schools; research intensive universities, universities of applied sciences and a number of technical universities.

A total of 316 institutions were invited to participate in the pilot test. The 159 institutions that agreed to take part were spread over 57 countries. The distribution between European and non-European countries was as follows: 94 institutions were from countries of the European Union; 15 were from non-EU European countries and 50 institutions were from outside Europe. Eventually 115 institutions (72%) submitted the data for the institutional ranking. Of these institutions 57 participated in the business studies field-based ranking, 50 in electrical engineering and 58 in mechanical engineering.

In total 6,770 students provided data via the online student questionnaire. After data cleaning we were able to include 5,901 student responses in the analysis: 45% in business studies; 23% in mechanical engineering; and 32% in electrical engineering.

In two countries the participation of institutions turned out to be limited: the US and China. US institutions are already part of mature national classification and ranking systems and the institutions we approached did not see a great deal of added value in participating in a European-based pilot project. In China we encountered major communication difficulties and a reluctance to participate in an untested global ranking with unpredictable outcomes for the institutions – despite our assurances that these would not be made public. On the other hand there was an interest from regions/countries that were not initially intended to be included, i.e. Africa, Latin America and the Middle East.

During the pilot study there was some criticism that top research institutions were underrepresented in our sample. For this reason we performed an additional check on the representativeness of our sample in terms of the inclusion of internationally-oriented top research institutions. We analyzed how the institutions of our sample perform in existing international rankings focusing on research excellence. The analyses showed that a significant number of institutions in our sample are listed: 19 institutions are in the top 200 of the Times Higher Education ranking, 47 in the top 500 of the ARWU ranking and 47 in the top 500 of the QS ranking. The exact number of higher education institutions in the world is not known. If we use a rough estimate of 15,000 institutions worldwide then the top 500 comprises only 3% of all higher education institutions. In our sample 29% of the participating institutions were in the top 500, which indicates an overrepresentation rather than an underrepresentation of research intensive institutions in our sample.

9.3 Outcomes in Terms of Data Collection Processes

The data collection for the pilot test took place via two different processes: the collection of self-reported data from the institutions through the four surveys described in Chap. 8 and the collection of data on these same institutions from the international databases on publications/citations and patents as also outlined earlier. In our final report to the European Commission we describe the mechanics of the data collection process in detail (including the procedures introduced for data checking and validation and a detailed discussion of the technical challenges in generating reliable and valid bibliometric and patent data). (See http://ec.europa.eu/education/higher-education/doc/multirank_en.pdf).

9.3.1 Data Collection from the Four Surveys

After the completion of the data collection process we asked institutions to share their experience of the process. One particular concern in terms of feasibility was the burden for institutions of data delivery. Responses indicate that this burden differed substantially between the pilot institutions with the average time per questionnaire being around 5–6 days with European institutions spending significantly less time than institutions from outside Europe.

Other questions in the follow-up survey referred to the efficiency of data collection and the clarity of the questionnaires. In general the efficiency of data collection was reported to be good by the pilot institutions; some institutions were critical about the clarity of questions particularly concerning staff data (e.g. the concept of full-time equivalents) and to aspects of research and knowledge transfer (e.g. international networks, international prizes, cultural awards and prizes). Most institutions reported no major problems with regard to student, graduate and staff data. If they had problems these were mostly with research and third mission data (knowledge transfer, regional engagement). We return to these issues in the Sect. 9.4 where we look at the indicators in more detail.

One of the major challenges regarding the feasibility of our global student survey is whether the subjective evaluation of their own institution by students can be compared globally or whether there are differences in the levels of expectations or respondent behavior. Survey research among different groups of respondents with different national and cultural background must take into account that the respondents may have different standards by which they evaluate situations or events.

In our student questionnaire we used 'anchoring vignettes' to control for such effects. Anchoring vignettes is a technique designed to ameliorate problems that occur when different groups of respondents understand and use ordinal response categories to evaluate services and social situations in general (cf. King & Wand, 2007; King et al., 2004). Anchoring vignettes make it possible to construct a common scale of measurement across respondent groups by constructing a hypothetical situation which is assessed by these respondents. Anchoring vignettes have been tested and used e.g. in health service research; up to now they have not been used in comparative higher education research. Hence we had to develop our own approach to this research technique. (For a detailed description see the final project report to the European Commission.)

Our general conclusion from the anchoring vignettes analysis was that no correlation could be found between the students' evaluation of the situation in their own institutions and the expectation levels as reflected in our anchoring vignettes. This implies that the student assessments were not systematically influenced by differences in levels of expectation (related to different national backgrounds or cultures), and thus that the feasibility of the data collection through a global-level student survey is sufficiently feasible.

9.3.2 Data Collection from International Databases

The data collection regarding the bibliometric and patent indicators took place by studying the relevant international databases and extracting from these databases the information to be applied to the institutions and fields in the sample. For the bibliometric analysis we analyzed the October 2010 edition of the Web of Science database (WoS) to compile the bibliometric data of the institutions involved in the sample. A crucial aspect of this analysis was the identification of the sets of publications produced by one and the same institution, which is then labeled by a single, 'standardized' name tag.

The institutions were delimitated according to the set of WoS-indexed publications that contain an author affiliate address explicitly referring to that institution. The address information may comprise full names, name variants, acronyms or misspellings. The identified institutions may also comprise multiple affiliations (branches) – including hospitals, clinics or other medical centers – located elsewhere within the same city, region or country. For the pilot study this information was gathered without an external verification of the addresses or publications with representatives of each institution. As a result, 100% completeness for the selected set of publications cannot be guaranteed.

With respect to the bibliometric analysis of our sample it should be noted that although all the higher education institutions that participated in the U-Multirank pilot study produced at least one WoS-indexed research publication during the years 1980–2010, in some cases the quantities are very low (i. e. less than five publications on average in recent years). Many institutions in the pilot study are clearly not research-intensive institutes, at least not in terms of research with documented outputs in the form of research articles in scientific serial literature. Hence, in these cases the available bibliometric data were insufficient to create valid and reliable information for the bibliometric performance indicators, especially when the data is drawn from the WoS database for just a single (recent) publication year. In follow-up stages of U-Multirank the threshold values for WoS-indexed publication output should be changed in order to discard those institutions, or fields of science, where the bibliometric indicators or measurements are no longer amenable to detailed analysis of publication output or citation impact performance.

Our analysis of patents was based on data from the October 2009 version of the international PATSTAT-database. In this database the institutions participating in the sample were identified and studied in order to extract the institutional-level patent-data. The development of patent indicators on the micro-level of specific universities is complicated by the heterogeneity of patentee names that appear in patent documents within and across patent systems. Inconsistencies such as spelling mistakes, typographical errors and name variants (often also reflecting idiosyncrasies in the organization of intellectual property activities within organizations) considerably complicate analyses at the institutional level.

Several measures were taken to minimize the consequential chance of missing hits. First and foremost, all queries were performed on a table with *a priori* harmonized PATSTAT applicant names. The comprehensive and automated name cleaning method from which this table results was developed by ECOOM (Centre for R&D Monitoring, Leuven University; partner in CHERPA), in partnership with Sogeti,[1] in the framework of the EUROSTAT work on Harmonized Patent Statistics. Second, and specifically for our U-Multirank pilot, keyword searches were designed and tailored for each institute individually, to include as many as possible known name variants. Finally, each resulting list of retrieved name variants was checked manually and, if needed, false hits were eliminated. As a result, although these harmonization steps

---

[1] http://www.sogeti.com

imply high levels of accuracy and coverage (see Magerman et al., 2009; Peeters et al., 2009), we cannot guarantee 100% completeness for the extracted sets of patents.

We have argued that the field-based rankings of indicators in each dimension contribute significantly to the value and the usability of U-Multirank. At present, however, the breakdown of patent indicators by the fields defined in the U-Multirank pilot study (business studies, mechanical engineering and electrical engineering) is not feasible due to a lack of concordance with the field classification that is present in the patent database. The latter is organized according to the technological breakdown of the International Patent Classification. The classification of patents is based on technologies or products which use specific technologies. The overview of higher education fields is based on educational programs, research fields and other academically-oriented criteria. As a result the consequential large differences in notions that underlie 'higher education field' versus 'technology field' make a concordance between both meaningless. Therefore we were unable to produce patent analyses at the field-based level of U-Multirank.

9.4 Feasibility of Indicators

In the pilot study we analyzed the feasibility of the various indicators that were selected after the multi-stage process of stakeholder consultation. This analysis thus refers to the list of indicators presented in Chap. 7.

As described in Chap. 7, the selection of indicators was based on the application of a number of criteria: relevance; validity; reliability; comparability and feasibility. Using these criteria the indicators were 'pre-selected' as the basis for the pilot test. In the following tables we present both this 'pre-selection' and the results from the empirical feasibility test. For reasons of comprehension and to avoid confusion we have redefined and reordered the criteria applied in the original selection as follows:

- relevance
- concept/construct validity
- face validity
- robustness consisting of reliability and comparability
- availability (of data), instead of feasibility (because feasibility was the major subject of the pilot test).

These five criteria are presented in the left-hand columns of the tables in this section allowing a 'preliminary' (pre-pilot) rating. Rating 'A' expresses a consensus on the fitness for purpose of the indicator; rating 'B' indicates that some stakeholders and/or experts expressed some doubts regarding one or two selection criteria. The 'relevance' criterion was the major reason to keep these indicators on the list for the pilot study.

In the right-hand columns of the tables, the result of the empirical assessment of the feasibility of the indicators is summarized in a (post-pilot) final feasibility score.

9 The Pilot Test and Its Outcomes

Score 'A' indicates that the feasibility is judged to be high; score 'B' indicates that there are some problems regarding the feasibility but in most cases data on the indicators can be collected and interpreted. Score 'C' indicates that there are serious problems in collecting data on the indicator.

The (post-pilot) feasibility score is based on three criteria:

- **data availability**: the relative actual existence of the data needed to build the indicator. If information on an indicator or the underlying data elements is/are missing for a relatively large number of cases, the data availability is assumed to be low.
- **conceptual clarity**: the relative consistency across individual questionnaires regarding the understanding of the indicator. If, in the information collected during the pilot study, there was a relatively large and/or diversified set of comments on the indicator in the various questionnaires, the conceptual clarity is assumed to be low.
- **data consistency**: the relative consistency regarding the actual answers in individual questionnaires to the data needs of the indicator. If in the information collected during the pilot study, there was a relatively high level of inconsistencies in the information provided in the individual questionnaires, the data consistency is assumed to be low.

Indicators which were rated 'A' or 'B' during (pre-pilot) preliminary rating but which received a 'C' in terms of the (post-pilot) feasibility score were reconsidered in consultation with stakeholders with regard to their inclusion in the final list of indicators. For indicators with a problematic feasibility score there were two options:

1. The indicators were judged highly relevant despite the problematic score and therefore efforts to enhance the data situation will be proposed; these indicators have been retained ('in').
2. The indicators were not regarded as (very) relevant and in light of the feasibility problems they were deleted from the list of indicators ('out').

9.4.1 Teaching & Learning

The first dimension of U-Multirank is Teaching & Learning. Tables 9.1, 9.2 and 9.3 provide an overview of the indicators in this dimension according to the criteria and assessments described above.

Observations from the pilot test:

- Much to our surprise there were few comments on the indicators on graduation rate and time to degree.
- Most comments concerned graduate employment. The fact that in many countries/ institutions different measurement periods (other than 18 months after graduation) are used seriously hampers the interpretation of the results on this indicator.

Table 9.1 Focused institutional ranking indicators: teaching & learning

Teaching & learning	Rating of indicators (pre-pilot)					Feasibility score (post-pilot)				
Focused institutional ranking	Relevance	Concept/ construct validity	Face validity	Robustness	Availability	Preliminary rating	Feasibility score	Data availability	Conceptual clarity	Data consistency	Recommendation on feasibility 'C'
Graduation rate	◀	■	◀	■	■	A	B	■	◀	◀	
Time to degree	■	▶	▶	■	■	B	A	◀	◀	◀	
Relative rate of graduate (un)employment	◀	◀	■	◀	▶	B	C	■	■	▶	In
Interdisciplinarity of programs	■	■	■	▶	▶	B	B	■	■	◀	
Expenditure on teaching	■	▶	▶	◀	▶	B	B	■	■	■	

Table 9.2 Field-based ranking indicators: teaching & learning (departmental questionnaires)

Teaching & learning	Rating of indicators (pre-pilot)					Preliminary rating	Feasibility score (post-pilot)				Recommendation on feasibility 'C'
Field-based ranking Departmental questionnaire	Relevance	Concept/ construct validity	Face validity	Robustness	Availability		Feasibility score	Data availability	Conceptual clarity	Data consistency	
Student/staff ratio	◀	■	◀	■	◀	A	A	◀	◀	◀	
Graduation rate	◀ ■	■ ▶	◀ ▶	■ ◀	■ ■	A	B	■ ◀	■ ◀	◀ ◀	
Qualification of academic staff						B	A				
Percentage graduating within norm period	■	◀	▶	■	■	B	B	■	■	■	
Relative rate of graduate unemployment	◀	▶	▶	▶	▶	B	C	◀	◀	▶	In
Interdisciplinarity of programs	◀	▶	▶	■	■	B	B	■	■	■	
Inclusion of work experience	■	▶	▶	■	■	B	A–B	◀	◀	■	
Gender balance	▶	■	▶	◀	◀	B	A	◀	◀	◀	

Table 9.3 Field-based ranking indicators: teaching & learning (student satisfaction scores)

Teaching & learning	Rating of indicators (pre-pilot)						Feasibility score (post-pilot)				
Field-based ranking Student survey	Relevance	Concept/ construct validity	Face validity	Robustness	Availability	Preliminary rating	Feasibility score	Data availability	Conceptual clarity	Data consistency	Recommendation on feasibility "C"
Organization of program	◄	◄	■	■	◄	A	A	◄	◄	◄	
Inclusion of work experience	◄	◄	■	■	◄	A	A	◄	◄		
Evaluation of teaching	◄	◄	■	■	◄	A	A	◄	◄	◄	
Social climate	◄◄	◄◄	■	■■	◄◄	A	A	◄◄	◄◄	◄◄	
Quality of courses	◄	◄	■	■	◄	A	A	◄	◄	◄	
Support by teacher	◄	◄	■	■	◄	A	A	◄	◄	◄	
Computer facilities	◄	◄	■	■	◄◄	A	A	◄	◄	◄	
Overall judgment											
Libraries	◄◄	◄◄	■	■	◄◄	B	A	◄◄	◄◄	◄◄	
Laboratories	◄◄	◄◄	■	■	◄◄	B	A	◄◄	◄◄	◄◄	

- A relatively high number of respondents commented that 'interdisciplinarity of programs' requires more clarification.
- The breakdown of expenditure by activity (teaching, research) appeared to be problematic in a number of institutions. For those institutions that did provide data on the breakdown, a number of institutions indicated that the estimates were rather crude.

For the field-based rankings two subsets of indicators have been distinguished: the indicators that have been built using the information from departmental questionnaires and the indicators related to student satisfaction data.

Observations from the pilot test:

- A number of institutions did not have information on graduate employment/ unemployment at the field level. In addition, both institutional and national data, to which some institutions could refer, use different time periods in measuring employment status (e.g. 6, 12 or 18 months after graduation). As normally the rate of employment is increasing continuously over time, particularly during the first year after graduation, comparability of data is seriously hampered by different time periods. In accordance with the institutional ranking the indicator was nevertheless regarded as highly relevant by stakeholders.
- The indicator 'inclusion of work experience' is a composite indicator using a number of data elements (e.g. internships, teachers' professional experience outside HE) on employability issues; if one of the data elements is missing, the score for the indicator cannot be calculated.

There are no major problems with regard to the feasibility of individual indicators from the student survey. General aspects of the feasibility of a global student survey are discussed in Sect. 9.4.

9.4.2 Research

Indicators on research include bibliometric indicators (institutional and field-based) as well as indicators derived from institutional and field-based surveys. In general the feasibility of the research indicators, which are the main focus of existing international rankings, is judged to be good; nevertheless some indicators turned out be problematic.

Observations from the pilot test:

- The comments regarding expenditure on research refer to the problem of breaking down the basic government funding provided as a lump sum (Table 9.4).
- The comments on the 'post-doc' positions mainly regarded the clarity of definition and the lack of proper data.

Table 9.4 Focused institutional ranking indicators: research

Focused institutional ranking	Rating of indicators (pre-pilot)					Preliminary rating	Feasibility score (post-pilot)				Recommendation on feasibility "C"
	Relevance	Concept/construct validity	Face validity	Robustness	Availability		Feasibility score	Data availability	Conceptual clarity	Data consistency	
Percentage of expenditure on research	◀	▶	■	▶	■	A	B	■	■	◀	
Field-normalized citation rate[a]	◀	◀	■	◀	◀	A	A	◀	◀	◀	
Post-docs per fte academic staff	◀	◀	■	◀	■	A	B	■	■	◀	
Percentage research income from competitive sources	■	◀	▶	■	■	B	B	■	◀	◀	
Art-related outputs per fte academic staff	▶	■	▶	▶	▶	B	C	▶	▶	◀	In

9 The Pilot Test and Its Outcomes

											Out
Total publication output	▶	■	▶	▶	■	◀	B	B	■	■	◀
International awards and prizes won	◀	■	▶	▶	■	▶	B	C	▶	■	◀
Highly cited research publications[a]	◀	■	■	◀	◀	◀	B	A	◀	◀	◀
Interdisciplinary research activities	◀	■	▶	◀	◀	■	B	A	◀	◀	◀

[a]Data source: bibliometric analysis

- The large amount of missing data and frequent comments regarding the art-related output was no surprise. The lack of clarity in the definition corroborated the high number of missing values in this indicator. Stakeholders, in particular representatives of art schools, stressed the relevance of this indicator despite the poor data situation. The neglect of research performance in the arts and art-related fields is a major flaw of existing rankings. Even if this deficit cannot be overcome immediately, efforts should be made to enhance the data situation on cultural research outputs of higher education institutions. This cannot be done by producers of rankings alone; initiatives should also come from providers of (bibliometric) databases as well as stakeholder associations in the sector.
- On the field level, the proposed indicators do not encounter any major feasibility problems. In general, the data delivered by faculties/departments revealed some problems in clarity of definition of staff data. In particular the understanding and handling of the concept of 'full-time equivalents' (fte), which is used as a reference point to standardize indicators for size effects, proved difficult. Here a clearer yet concise explanation (including an example) should be used in future data collection (Table 9.5).
- It was also noted that the relevance and the exactness of the definition of 'post-doc' positions differs across fields. The data on post-doc positions proved to be more problematic in business studies than in engineering. With regard to future applications in other fields this must be kept in mind: while post-doc positions are very common in the sciences they are less widespread in the social sciences and not clearly defined in the humanities.

9.4.3 Knowledge Transfer

The dimension of knowledge transfer is, together with the regional engagement dimension, almost completely neglected in existing rankings, both nationally and internationally.

Observations from the pilot test:

- The indicators related to knowledge transfer did not cause much comment. Comments on TTO staff were mainly on the different way technology transfer activities are organized at the institutional level, making it difficult to compare the data (Table 9.6).
- In contrast to the findings at institutional level, the feasibility of the knowledge transfer indicators turned out to be highly problematic for field-based rankings. The only indicator with an 'A'-rating – indicating a high degree of feasibility – comes from bibliometric analysis (Table 9.7).

Table 9.5 Field-based ranking indicators: research

Research Field-based ranking	Rating of indicators (pre-pilot)					Preliminary rating	Feasibility score (post-pilot)				Recommendation on feasibility "C"
	Relevance	Concept/ construct validity	Face validity	Robustness	Availability		Feasibility score	Data availability	Conceptual clarity	Data consistency	
External research income	◄	◄	■	■	◄	A	A	◄	■	◄	
Total publication output[a]	◄	◄	■	■	■	A	A	◄	◄	◄	
Student satisfaction: research orientation of program	■	■	►	■	◄	A	A	◄	◄	◄	
Doctorate productivity	►	◄	►	◄	◄	B	A	◄	◄	◄	
Field-normalized citation rate[a]	◄	◄	■	◄	◄	B	A	◄	◄	◄	

(continued)

Table 9.5 (continued)

Research	Rating of indicators (pre-pilot)					Feasibility score (post-pilot)				
	Relevance	Concept/ construct validity	Face validity	Robustness	Availability	Preliminary rating	Feasibility score	Data availability	Conceptual clarity	Data consistency	Recommendation on feasibility "C"
Field-based ranking	▲	■	■	▲	▲	B	A	▲	▲	▲	
Highly cited research publications[a]											
Post-docs per PhD completed			*New indicator*				B	■	■	▲	

[a]Data source: bibliometric analysis

9 The Pilot Test and Its Outcomes

Table 9.6 Focused institutional ranking indicators: knowledge transfer

Knowledge transfer	Rating of indicators (pre-pilot)					Preliminary rating	Feasibility score (post-pilot)				Recommendation on feasibility "C"
Focused institutional ranking	Relevance	Concept/ construct validity	Face validity	Robustness	Availability		Feasibility score	Data availability	Conceptual clarity	Data consistency	
Percentage of income from third party funding	◄	■	►	►	■	A	C	►	◄	■	In
Incentives for knowledge transfer	◄	■	►	►	■	A	A	◄	◄	◄	
Patents awarded[a]	■	◄	◄	◄	◄	A	B	■	◄	◄	
University-industry joint research publications[b]	◄	◄	■	◄	◄	A	A	◄	◄	◄	
CPD courses offered per fte academic staff	◄	■	►	►	►	B	B	■	◄	◄	

(continued)

Table 9.6 (continued)

Knowledge transfer Focused institutional ranking	Rating of indicators (pre-pilot)					Preliminary rating	Feasibility score (post-pilot)				Recommendation on feasibility "C"
	Relevance	Concept/ construct validity	Face validity	Robustness	Availability		Feasibility score	Data availability	Conceptual clarity	Data consistency
Start-ups per fte academic staff	■	▶	■	■	■	B	B	■	◀	◀
Technology transfer office staff per fte academic staff	■	■	■	■	◀	B	B	■	■	◀
Co-patenting[a]	■	◀	■	◀	◀	B	A	◀	◀	◀

[a]Patent analysis
[b]Data source: bibliometric analysis

Table 9.7 Field-based ranking indicators: knowledge transfer

Knowledge transfer	Rating of indicators (pre-pilot)					Preliminary rating	Feasibility score (post-pilot)				Recommendation on feasibility "C"
Field-based ranking	Relevance	Concept/construct validity	Face validity	Robustness	Availability		Feasibility score	Data availability	Conceptual clarity	Data consistency	
University-industry joint research publications[a]	◄	◄	►	◄	◄	A	A	◄	◄	◄	
Academic staff with work experience outside HE	◄	◄	►	■	■	A	B	■	■	■	
Joint research contracts with private enterprise	◄	◄	►	■	◄	A	B	■	◄	◄	
Patents awarded[b]	►	◄	◄	◄	►	C	C	►	◄	►	Out
Co-patenting[b]	►	◄	►	◄	◄	B	C	►	◄	►	Out

(continued)

Table 9.7 (continued)

Knowledge transfer	Rating of indicators (pre-pilot)					Preliminary rating	Feasibility score (post-pilot)				Recommendation on feasibility "C"
Field-based ranking	Relevance	Concept/ construct validity	Face validity	Robustness	Availability		Feasibility score	Data availability	Conceptual clarity	Data consistency	
Annual income from licensing	▶	◀	▶	■	▶	B	C	▶	■	■	Out
Number of licensing agreements	◀	◀	▶	■	▶	B	C	▶	■	■	Out

[a]Data source: bibliometric analysis
[b]Patent analysis

- Availability of data on 'joint research contracts with private sector' is a major problem, but primarily in business studies and less in engineering.
- The indicators based on data from patent databases are feasible only for institutional ranking due to discrepancies in the definition and delineation of fields in the databases.
- Only a small number of institutions could deliver data on licensing.
- There was an agreement among stakeholders, therefore, that those indicators should be used for focused institutional rankings only.

9.4.4 International Orientation

Most of the indicators on the dimension 'international orientation' proved to be relatively unproblematic in terms of feasibility.

Observations from the pilot test:

- There were some problems reported with availability of information on the nationality of qualifying diplomas and students in international joint degree programs. In the latter, problems related primarily to the inaccuracy of the definition and the problems in interpretation stemming from this (Table 9.8).
- Not all institutions have clear data on outgoing students. In some cases only those students participating in institutional or broader formal programs (e.g. ERASMUS) are registered and institutions do not record numbers of students with self-organized stays at foreign universities (Table 9.9).
- Availability of data was relatively low regarding the student satisfaction indicator as only a few students had already participated in a stay abroad and could assess the support provided by their university.
- The indicator 'international orientation of programs' is a composite indicator referring to several data elements; feasibility is limited by missing cases for some of the data elements.
- Some institutions could not identify external research funds from international funding organizations.
- In order to test alternative means of measuring percentages of international staff, we used different definitions in the institutional and field-based rankings. The institutional questionnaire referred to the nationality of staff; the level of staff with foreign nationality was easy to identify for most institutions. In the field questionnaires, the definition 'international' referred to staff hired from abroad. This excludes foreign staff hired from another institution in the same country rather than from abroad. Some universities encountered difficulties in identifying their international staff based on this definition.

Table 9.8 Focused institutional ranking indicators: international orientation

International orientation	Rating of indicators (pre-pilot)					Preliminary rating	Feasibility score (post-pilot)				Recommendation on feasibility "C"
Focused institutional ranking	Relevance	Concept/ construct validity	Face validity	Robustness	Availability		Feasibility score	Data availability	Conceptual clarity	Data consistency	
Percentage of programs in foreign language	◄	■	■	■	◄	A	A	◄	◄	◄	
International joint research publications[a]	◄	◄	■	◄	◄	A	A	◄	◄	◄	
Percentage of international staff	◄	■	■	■	■	B	A	◄	◄	◄	
Percentage of students in international joint degree programs	◄	◄	■	■	◄	A	B	■	■	◄	
International doctorate graduation rate	►	■	►	■	■	B	A	◄	◄	◄	

Percentage foreign degree-seeking students	*New indicator*	B	■	▲	▲
Percentage students coming in on exchanges	*New indicator*	A	▲	▲	▲
Percentage students sent out on exchanges	*New indicator*	A	▲	▲	▲

[a]Data source: Bibliometric analysis

Table 9.9 Field-based ranking indicators: international orientation

International orientation	Rating of indicators (pre-pilot)					Feasibility score (post-pilot)				Recommendation on feasibility "C"
Field-based ranking	Relevance	Concept/ construct validity	Face validity	Robustness	Availability	Preliminary rating	Feasibility score	Data availability	Conceptual clarity	Data consistency
Percentage of international students	■	◄	■	■	◄	A	A	◄	◄	◄
Incoming and outgoing students	◄	◄	■	■	◄	A	A-B	■	■	◄
Opportunities to study abroad (student satisfaction)	■	■	►	■	◄	A	B	■	◄	◄
International orientation of programs	◄	◄	►	■	■	A	B	■	◄	◄
International academic staff	◄	■	■	■	■	B	A-B	■	◄	■
International joint research publications[a]	◄	■	►	◄	◄	B	A	◄	◄	■

9 The Pilot Test and Its Outcomes

International research grants	▶	■	■	■	◀	B	B	■	◀	◀	
International doctorate graduation rate	◀	■	▶	■	■	B	A	◀	◀	◀	

[a]Data source: Bibliometric analysis

9.4.5 Regional Engagement

Up to now the regional engagement role of universities has not been included in rankings. There are a number of studies on the regional economic impact of higher education and research institutions, either for individual institutions and their regions or on higher education in general. Those studies do not offer comparable institutional indicators or indicators disaggregated by fields.

Observations from the pilot test:

- A general comment regarding the indicators of regional engagement on both institutional and field levels related to the delineation of the region. The NUTS regions are not applicable outside Europe, which caused some problems in non-European higher education institutions. But even within Europe NUTS regions are seen as problematic by some institutions, in particular those from smaller countries having only one or two NUTS 2 regions. Although the conceptual clarity on the issue is good, the low level of data consistency showed that there is a wide variety of region definitions used by institutions, which may harm the interpretation of the related indicators (Table 9.10).
- Both in institutional and in field-based data collection information on regional labor market entry of graduates could not be delivered by most institutions. Here the problems concerning the availability of comparable information on graduate employment in general and the problems with the definition/delineation of 'region' were combined. There is a clear perception of the relevance of employability issues, and the relevance of higher education and research to the regional economy and the regional society at large, and stakeholders were strongly in favor of keeping the indicator (both for institutional and for field-based rankings).
- The most feasible indicator is the bibliometric indicator 'Regional co-publications'. Here region can be defined either by NUTS regions or in a more flexible way by the distance between locations of the collaborating institutions.

Less than half of the pilot institutions could deliver data on regional participation in continuing education programs (and only one fifth in mechanical engineering programs). Based on feedback from institutions and stakeholders, this indicator cannot be seen as feasible; there is probably no way to improve the data situation in the short term (Table 9.11).

While far from good, the data situation on student internships in local enterprises and degree theses in cooperation with local enterprises turned out to be less problematic in business studies than in the engineering field. Both internships and degree theses enable the expertise and knowledge of local higher education institutions to be utilized in a regional context, in particular in small- and medium-sized enterprises. At the same time they are a link to potential future employees and in many non-metropolitan regions they play an important role in the recruitment of higher education graduates.

9 The Pilot Test and Its Outcomes 161

Table 9.10 Focused institutional ranking indicators: regional engagement

Regional engagement	Rating of indicators (pre-pilot)						Feasibility score (post-pilot)				
Focused institutional ranking	Relevance	Concept/ construct validity	Face validity	Robustness	Availability	Preliminary rating	Feasibility score	Data availability	Conceptual clarity	Data consistency	Recommendation on feasibility "C"
Percentage of income from regional sources	◄	■	■	■	◄	A	C	►	■	◄	In
Percentage of graduates working in the region	◄	◄	►	►	►	B	C	►	■	►	In
Research contracts with regional partners	◄	■	►	►	■	B	B	■	◄	◄	
Regional joint research publications[a]	►	■	►	◄	◄	B	A	◄	◄	◄	

(continued)

Table 9.10 (continued)

Regional engagement Focused institutional ranking	Rating of indicators (pre-pilot)					Feasibility score (post-pilot)			
	Relevance	Concept/ construct validity	Face validity	Robustness	Availability	Preliminary rating	Feasibility score	Data availability	Conceptual clarity	Data consistency	Recommendation on feasibility "C"
Percentage of students in internships in local enterprises	■	◀	▶	▶	▶	B	C	▶	■	◀	In

[a] Data source: Bibliometric analysis

9 The Pilot Test and Its Outcomes

Table 9.11 Field-based ranking indicators: regional engagement

Regional engagement	Rating of indicators (pre-pilot)					Feasibility score (post-pilot)				
Field-based ranking Departmental questionnaire	Relevance	Concept/ construct validity	Face validity	Robustness	Availability	Preliminary rating	Feasibility score	Data availability	Conceptual clarity	Data consistency	Recommendation on feasibility "C"
Graduates working in the region	◀	◀	▶	▶	▶	B	C	▶	■	▶	In
Regional participation in continuing education	◀	■	▶	▶	▶	B	C	▶	■	■	Out
Student internships in local enterprises	◀	■	▶	▶	■	B	B-C	■	■	◀	In
Degree theses in cooperation with regional enterprises	■	■	▶	▶	■	B	B-C	■	■	◀	In
Summer schools	▶	▶	▶	▶	■	C	C	▶	■	◀	Out
Regional joint research publications[a]				*New indicator*			A	◀	◀	◀	

[a]Data source: bibliometric analysis

9.5 Feasibility of Upscaling

The pilot test included a limited number of institutions and only two fields. An important feasibility issue is upscaling: is it possible to extend U-Multirank to a comprehensive global coverage and how easy would it be to add additional fields?

In terms of the feasibility of U-Multirank as a potential new global ranking tool, the results of the pilot study are positive, but with one important caveat.

The level of institutional interest in participating in the new transparency tool was encouraging. In broad terms, half of the institutions invited to participate in the pilot study agreed to do so. Given that a significant number of these institutions (32%) were from outside Europe, and taking into account that it is clear that U-Multirank is a Europe-based initiative, this represents a strong expression of worldwide interest.

However, it is important to recognize that a pilot study is not a real ranking. The institutions participating in the pilot project have access to the institutional performance profiles of all the institutions in the pilot, as well as the dimension and indicator outcomes. While this provides a unique opportunity to compare and benchmark with over 100 other institutions worldwide, the outcomes of the pilot rankings will not be made public. The overall objective of the pilot study was to design a multidimensional ranking tool and to test the feasibility of this instrument, not to publish a ranking. We may assume that the interest in a real multidimensional ranking will be substantially greater.

Our single caveat concerns an immediate global-level introduction of U-Multirank. The pilot study suggests that a global multidimensional ranking is unlikely to prove feasible in the sense of achieving extensive coverage levels across the globe in the short term. It proved particularly difficult to recruit institutions from the USA and China for the pilot project. On the other hand, institutions in Australia and in a number of developing countries, largely invisible in existing global rankings, were enthusiastic about the project.

The prospects for widespread European coverage are encouraging. A substantial number of institutions both from EU and non-EU European countries participated in the project. From their participation in the various stakeholder meetings, we can conclude that there is also broad stakeholder interest in the further development and implementation of U-Multirank.

We anticipate that there will be continuing interest from outside Europe from institutions wishing to benchmark themselves against European institutions. And we believe that there are opportunities for the targeted recruitment of groups of institutions from outside Europe of particular interest to European higher education.

The other aspect of the potential up-scaling of U-Multirank is the extension to other fields. Any extension of U-Multirank to new fields must deal with two questions:

- the relevance and meaningfulness of existing indicators for those fields, and,
- the identification and development of new field-specific indicators.

While the U-Multirank feasibility study focused on the pilot fields of business studies and engineering, some issues of up-scaling to other fields have been discussed in the course of the stakeholder consultation. Experience from other field-based rankings also shows that there is a core set of indicators that is relevant and meaningful for (virtually) all fields.

However, these issues do not concern all dimensions in the same way. While students can be asked about their learning experience in the same way across different fields (although questions should refer to field-specific aspects as e.g. quality of laboratory courses in technical and experimental fields) and while internationalization can be measured in similar ways across fields, the culture of communicating research results differs greatly between disciplinary fields. A well-known example is the difference between publication cultures in the sciences/medicine and those in the humanities/social sciences (cf. van Raan, 2006). One of the major problems in scaling up U-Multirank in terms of fields seems to be the definition of indicators of research output across different disciplinary fields.

Any extension to additional fields has to address the issue of additional specific indicators relevant to those fields. In medicine, for instance, specific indicators referring to bedside teaching and clinical education are relevant indicators in the teaching and learning dimension. Following the user- and stakeholder-driven approach of U-Multirank, we suggest that field-specific indicators for international rankings should be developed together with stakeholders from these fields. We encourage stakeholders and organizations to actively participate in the development of relevant field-specific indicators, in particular in those areas and fields which so far have largely been neglected in international rankings due to the lack of adequate data and indicators.

In the two pilot fields of business studies and engineering we were able to use 86% of the final set of indicators in both fields. We expect that when additional fields are addressed in U-Multirank, some specific field indicators will have to be developed. Based on the experience of the CHE Ranking this will vary by field with some fields requiring no additional indicators and other specialized fields (such as medicine) needing up to 30% of the indicators to be tailor-made.

In general terms, we conclude that upscaling in terms of addressing a larger number of fields in U-Multirank is certainly feasible.

Finally, in terms of operational feasibility, our experience with the pilot study suggests that while a major 'upscaling' will bring significant logistical, organizational and financial challenges, there are no inherent features of U-Multirank that rule out the possibility of such future growth.

9.6 Overall Conclusion from the Pilot Test

In summary, the pilot test demonstrates that in terms of the feasibility of the dimensions and indicators, potential institutional interest in participating, and operational feasibility we have succeeded in developing a U-Multirank 'Version 1.0' that is ready to be implemented in European higher education and research and for institutions outside Europe that are interested in participating. As has been outlined above, further development work is needed on some dimensions and indicators – hence Version 1.0. This project has demonstrated the complexity of developing transparency instruments in higher education and it is unrealistic to expect a perfect new tool to be designed at the first attempt. Furthermore, in the long run U-Multirank needs to remain a dynamic instrument that responds to new developments in higher education, the changing interests of users and new possibilities offered by improved data collection systems.

References

King, G., Murray, C. J. L., Salomon, J. A., & Tandon, A. (2004). Enhancing the validity and Cross-Cultural comparability of measurement in survey research. *American Political Science Review, 98*, 191–207.

King, G., & Wand, J. (2007). Comparing incomparable survey responses: evaluating and selecting anchoring vignettes. *Political Analysis, 15*, 46–66.

Magerman T., Grouwels J., Song X., & Van Looy B. (2009). *Data production methods for harmonized patent indicators: Patentee Name Harmonization*. EUROSTAT Working Paper and Studies, Luxembourg.

Peeters B., Song X., Callaert J., Grouwels J., & Van Looy B. (2009). *Harmonizing harmonized patentee names: an exploratory assessment of top patentees*. EUROSTAT Working Paper and Studies, Luxembourg.

van Raan, A. (2006). Challenges in the Ranking of Universities. In J. Sadlak & L.N. Cai (eds.), *The World class university and ranking: aiming beyond status*. Bucharest, UNESCO-CEPES (2007).

Chapter 10
An Interactive Multidimensional Ranking Web Tool

Gero Federkeil, Jon File, Frans Kaiser, Frans A. van Vught, and Frank Ziegele

10.1 Introduction

The quality of a ranking to a large extent depends on the quality and user-friendliness of the presentation of its results. In the past, rankings were mainly published in static print form, but for a number of years many rankings have opted for online publication (replacing or in addition to print publication). In most rankings the tables can now be sorted by individual indicators as a minimum degree of interactivity. A few rankings (e.g. the Taiwanese College Navigator published by HEEACT[1] and CHE Ranking) have implemented tools to produce a personalized ranking, based on user preferences and priorities with regard to the set of indicators. This approach is consistent with the user-driven notion of ranking which is a basic feature of U-Multirank.

The presentation of U-Multirank results outlined in this chapter strictly follows this user-driven approach. But by relating institutional profiles (created in U-Map) with multidimensional rankings, U-Multirank introduces a second level of interactive ranking beyond the user-driven selection of indicators: the selection of a sample of institutions to be compared in focused rankings. Existing international rankings are largely limited to one 'type' of institution only: internationally-oriented research universities. U-Multirank has a much broader scope and intends to include a wider variety of institutional profiles. We argue that it does not make much sense to compare institutions across diverse institutional profiles. Hence U-Multirank offers a tool to identify and select institutions that are truly comparable in terms of their institutional profiles.

---

[1] College Navigator: http://cnt.heeact.edu.tw/site1/index2.asp?method=eintro; CHE Ranking: http://ranking.zeit.de/che2011/en/ (both retrieved on 9 May 2011).

G. Federkeil • F. Ziegele (✉)
Centre for Higher Education (CHE), Gütersloh, Germany

J. File • F. Kaiser • F.A. van Vught
Center for Higher Education Policy Studies, University of Twente,
Enschede, The Netherlands

10.2 Mapping Diversity: Combining U-Map and U-Multirank

From the beginning of the U-Multirank project one of the basic aims was that U-Multirank should be – in contrast to existing global rankings which brought about a dysfunctional short-sightedness on 'world-class research universities' – a tool to create transparency regarding the diversity of higher education institutions. The bias of existing rankings towards one specific institutional profile appears to result in the devaluing of other institutional profiles and decreasing diversity in higher education systems (see Chap. 4).

Our pilot sample includes institutions with quite diverse missions, structures and institutional profiles. We applied the U-Map profiling tool to specify these profiles. U-Map offers a multidimensional description of profiles in six dimensions. It is user-driven in the sense that there are no fixed categories or types of institutions. Instead, users can create their own profiles by selecting indicators relevant to them out of the six dimensions.

The combination of U-Map and U-Multirank offers a new approach to user-driven rankings. Users can not only select performance indicators according to their own preferences and priorities; they can also define the institutional profile they are interested in and hence the sample of institutions to be compared in U-Multirank (Fig. 10.1).

We envisage the public face of U-Multirank being a user-driven interactive web tool. This tool has yet to be developed but we have designed a simple prototype to

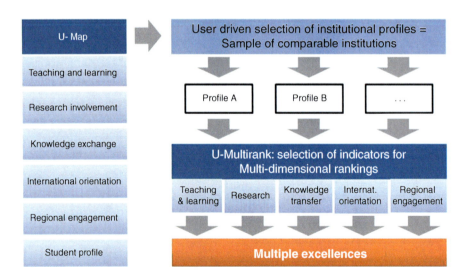

Fig. 10.1 Combining U-Map and U-Multirank

illustrate in broad terms what we think it will look like. The tool will include the two steps outlined above. Users will be offered the option to decide if they want to produce a focused institutional ranking or a field-based ranking, and in the latter case they can select the field(s). The next step will be the selection of the institutional profile the user is interested in. This selection defines the sample of institutions that will be included in the ranking. The user will have the option of selecting criteria from all U-Map dimensions or focusing on a specified set of dimensions. In a third step the user selects the ways the results will be presented. U-Multirank will include different ways of presenting the results.

10.3 The Presentation Modes

Presenting ranking results requires a general model for accessing the results, including provision for guiding users through the data and a visual framework to display the result data. In U-Multirank the presentation of data allows for both:

- a comparative overview on indicators across institutions, and
- a detailed view of institutional profiles.

The ideas presented below are mainly inspired by the existing U-Map visualizations and the way results are presented in the CHE Ranking.

U-Multirank produces indicators and results at different levels of aggregation leading to a hierarchical data model:

- Data at the level of institutions (results of focused institutional rankings)
- Data at the level of departments (results of field-based rankings)
- Data at the level of programs (results of field-based rankings)

The presentation format for ranking results should be consistent across the three levels while still accommodating the particular data structures on those levels. We suggest the following modes of presentation: interactive overview (Sect. 10.3.1), personalized ranking tables (Sect. 10.3.2), institutional results at a glance (Sect. 10.3.3) and a detailed listing of results for single institutions, departments and programs (Sect. 10.3.4).

10.3.1 Interactive Tables

The most common format used in ranking results is a table listing all institutions included in the ranking and all (or a selection of) indicators. In league table rankings tables are usually sorted by rank position. In U-Multirank we present the results alphabetically or by rank groups (see Chap. 6).

Table 10.1 Default table with three indicators per dimension

	Teaching & learning			Research			Knowledge transfer			International orientation			Regional engagement		
	Student/staff ratio	Graduation rate	Qualification of academic staff	Research publication output	External research income	Field-normalized citation rate	% Income third party funding	CPD courses offered	Start-up firms	International academic staff	% International students	Joint international publications	Graduates working in region	Internships in local enterprise	Regional co-publication
Institution 1	🟡	–	–	🟢	🟢	🟢	🟢	🟡	🟢	🟡	🟡	🟢	🟢	🟡	🟢
Institution 2	🔴	🟡	🟡	🟢	🟢	🟢	–	🟡	🟢	🟡	🟢	🟡	🟢	🔴	🟢
Institution 3	🟡	🟢	🟢	🟡	🟢	🟡	🟡	🟢	🟡	🟡	🟢	🟡	🟡	–	🟡
Institution 4	🔴	🟡	🟡	🟢	🔴	🟡	🔴	🟡	🟡	🟡	🟡	🟢	🟢	🟢	🟡
Institution 5	🟡	🟢	🟢	🔴	🟢	🟡	🟡	🟢	🔴	🟢	🟢	🟡	🟡	🟢	–
Institution 6	🔴	🟢	🟡	🟢	–	🟢	🟢	🟡	🟢	🟢	🟡	🟢	🟡	🟡	🟢
Institution 7	🟡	🟡	🟢	🟡	–	🟢	🟡	–	🟡	–	🟡	🟡	🟡	🟢	🟡
Institution 8	🟢	🟡	🟡	🟡	–	🟡	🟡	🔴	🟡	🟢	🟡	–	🟡	🟢	🟢
Institution 9	🟡	🟢	🟢	🟡	🟢	🟢	🟡	🟡	🟢	🟢	🟡	🟢	🟢	🟡	🟢

In the first layer of the table (field-based ranking), an overview is presented comprising three selected indicators per dimension, a total of 15 indicators. The table displays the ranking groups representing the relative scores on the indicators. The current table is a 'default' table. The selection of the indicators in this table will eventually be user-driven. Based on the actual choices made by users in formulating their personalized ranking tables (see Sect. 10.3.2) the indicators chosen most frequently will be presented in the default table (Table 10.1).

Of course, tables can be sorted by a single indicator. Following the grouping approach, institutions are sorted alphabetically within groups – the ranking does not produce a league table, only groups. In the following example the institutions are sorted by the indicator 'research publication output' (Table 10.2).

In Chap. 1 we discussed the necessity of multidimensional and user-driven rankings for epistemological reasons. Empirical evidence from the feasibility study strongly supports this view. The overview table above shows several institutions from the pilot sample and demonstrates that no institution performs in the top group (or bottom group) on all dimensions and indicators. While some institutions demonstrate average performance in many indicators, others show a clear performance profile with marked strengths and weaknesses.

Users may examine one or more dimensions in depth, drilling down to the second layer of the table by clicking on a single dimension, e.g. 'Research', which will then display the complete list of all indicators in that dimension (Table 10.3).

Table 10.2 Default table with three indicators per dimension; sorted by indicator 'research publication output'

	Teaching & learning			Research			Knowledge transfer			International orientation			Regional engagement		
	Student/staff ratio	Graduation rate	Qualification of academic staff	Research publication output	External research income	Field-normalized citation rate	% Income third party funding	CPD courses offered	Start-up firms	International academic staff	% International students	Joint international publications	Graduates working in region	Internships in local enterprise	Regional co-publication
Institution 2	●	●	●	●	●	●	–	●	●	●	●	●	●	●	●
Institution 4	●	●	●	●	●	●	●	●	●	●	●	●	●	●	●
Institution 1	●	–	–	●	●	●	●	●	●	●	●	●	●	●	●
Institution 3	●	●	●	●	●	●	●	●	●	●	●	●	●	–	●
Institution 7	●	●	●	●	–	●	●	–	●	–	●	●	●	●	●
Institution 8	●	●	●	●	–	●	●	●	●	●	●	–	●	●	●
Institution 9	●	●	●	●	●	●	●	●	●	●	●	●	●	●	●
Institution 5	●	●	●	●	●	●	●	●	●	●	●	●	●	●	–
Institution 6	●	●	●	●	–	●	●	●	●	●	●	●	●	●	●

Table 10.3 Default table for one dimension

	Research				
	External research income	Research publication output	Doctorate productivity	Field-normalized citation rate	Highly cited research publications
Institution 1	●	●	–	●	●
Institution 2	●	●	●	●	●
Institution 3	●	●	●	●	●
Institution 5	●	●	●	●	●
Institution 4	●	●	●	●	●
Institution 9	●	●	●	●	●
Institution 7	–	●	●	●	●
Institution 8	–	●	●	●	●
Institution 6	–	●	●	●	●

10.3.2 Personalized Ranking Tables

The development of an interactive user-driven approach is a central feature of U-Multirank. Users have different views on the relevance of indicators included in a ranking and the tool will recognize this by allowing users to select the individual indicators they feel are relevant. This option is available both for the focused institutional rankings and the field-based rankings.

Personalized ranking implies a two-step process:

- First, users select a limited number of indicators, from one or more dimensions
- In a second step, users can specify the result table by choosing rank groups for each indicator selected (e.g. top level only; at least mid-table, all groups etc.).

The following figure shows how users can select indicators (Fig. 10.2).

The 'green' column refers to the top group only; the 'green and yellow' column refers to at least the middle group and the final column to all groups.

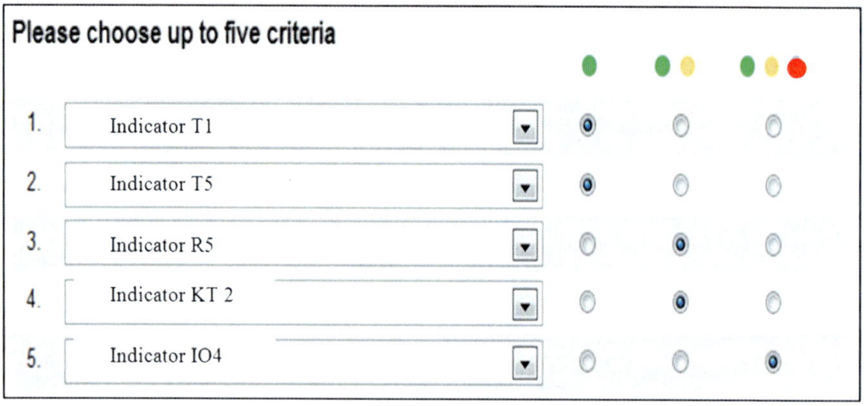

Fig. 10.2 User selection of indicators for personalized ranking tables

The result will be a personalized ranking according to the selection of indicators by the user (Table 10.4).

Table 10.4 Personalized ranking table

	International academic staff	Research publication output	Doctorate productivity	Student internships in local enterprise	CPD courses offered
Institution 4	●	●	●	●	●
Institution 9	●	○	●	○	○
Institution 1	○	○	–	○	○
Institution 2	○	●	○	●	●
Institution 3	○	○	●	–	●
Institution 5	○	●	●	●	●
Institution 8	●	○	○	●	●
Institution 6	●	●	○	○	○
Institution 7	–	○	●	●	–

10.3.3 Institutional Results at a Glance: Sunburst Charts

Not all users will want to read a lengthy table when applying U-Multirank. An intuitive, appealing visual presentation of the main results will introduce users to the performance ranking of higher education institutions. Results at a glance presented in this way may encourage users to drill down to more detailed information.

Graphic presentations may help to convey insights into the institutional results 'at a glance' with the performance of the institution as a whole presented without being aggregated into one composite indicator.

The number of presentation modes should be limited, so that there is a recognizable U-Multirank presentation style and users are not confused by multiple visual styles. Four 'at a glance' presentation options were discussed with stakeholders and there was a clear preference for the 'sunburst' chart similar to the one already used in U-Map. The variations in shading symbolize the five U-Multirank dimensions, with the rays representing the individual indicators. In this chart the grouped performance scores of institutions on each indicator are represented by the length of the corresponding rays: the larger the ray, the better the institution performs on that indicator. As shown in Fig. 10.3, different sunburst charts show different institutional performance profiles.

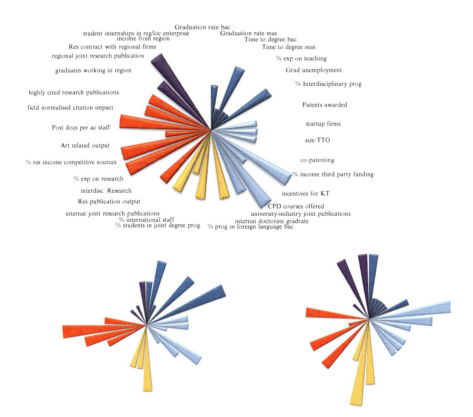

Fig. 10.3 Institutional sunburst chart

10.3.4 Presenting Detailed Results

In addition to the graphic presentation of the results of an institution, detailed information may also be presented in text formats.

An example is a detailed view on the results of a department (the following screenshot shows a sample business administration study program at bachelor level). Here the user finds all indicators available for the institution – compared to the complete sample (the groups) – as well as additional descriptive contextual information (e.g. on the size of the institution/department). This kind of presentation can be made available on the institution, faculty/department (field) and program level (Fig. 10.4).

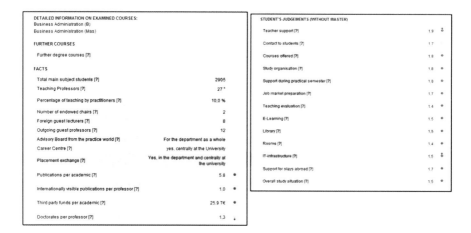

Fig. 10.4 Text format presentation of detailed results (example)

10.4 Contextuality

Rankings do not and cannot provide causal analyses of their results. They are comparisons of performance results and offer information without claiming to be able to explain the differences in performance. Nevertheless, rankings have to take into account that contextual factors are highly relevant when comparing results (Yarbrough et al. 2011). In general two types of context factors can be distinguished:

- Context variables affecting the performance of higher education institutions.
- Context factors that may affect decision-making processes of users of rankings (e.g. students, researchers) although not linked to the performance of institutions.

For individual users rankings reveal that there are differences in reality. For instance: for prospective students intending to choose a university or a study program, low student satisfaction scores regarding the support by teaching staff in a specific university or program is relevant information, although the indicator itself cannot explain the reasons behind this judgment.

Rankings also have to be sensitive to context variables that may lead to methodological biases. An example which has been discussed intensively (cf. Van Raan, 2007) is the use of the publication of journal articles and article-based citations in institutional rankings.

Analytically, relevant context variables can be identified at different levels:

- The institution: context here can refer to the age, size and field structure of the institution.
- The (national) higher education system as a general context for institutions: this includes legal regulations (e.g. concerning access) as well as the existence of legal/official 'classifications' of institutions (e.g. in binary systems, the distinction between universities and other forms of non-university higher education institutions).
- The structure of national higher education and research: the organization of research in different higher education systems is an example. While in most countries research is largely integrated in universities, in some countries like France or Germany non-university research institutions undertake a major part of the national research effort.

A particular issue with regard to the context of higher education refers to the definition of the unit of analysis. The vast majority of rankings in higher education are comparing higher education *institutions*. A few rankings explicitly compare higher education systems, either based on genuine data on higher education systems, e.g. the University Systems Ranking published by the Lisbon Council,[2] or by simply aggregating institutional data to the system level (e.g. the QS National System Strength Ranking). In this latter case global institutional rankings are more or less implicitly used to produce rankings of national higher education systems, thereby creating various contextual problems. Both the Shanghai ranking and the QS rankings for instance are including universities only. The fact that they do not include non-university research institutions, which are particularly important in some countries (e.g. in France, Germany), produces a bias when their results are interpreted as a comparative assessment of the performance or quality of national higher education and research systems.

U-Multirank addresses the issues of contextuality by applying the design principle of comparability (see Chap. 6). In U-Multirank rankings are only created among institutions that have sufficiently similar institutional profiles. Combining U-Map and U-Multirank produces an approach in which comparable institutions are identified before they are compared in one or more rankings.

---

[2] See www.lisboncouncil.net

By identifying comparable institutions, the impact of contextual factors may be assumed to be reduced.

In addition, U-Multirank intends to offer relevant contextual information on institutions and fields. Contextual information does not allow for causal analyses but it offers users the opportunity to create informed judgments of the importance of specific contexts while assessing performances. During the further development of U-Multirank the production of contextual information will be an important topic.

10.5 User-Friendliness

U-Multirank is conceived as a user-driven and stakeholder-oriented instrument. The development of the concept, the definition of the indicators, processes of data collection and discussion on modes of presentation have been based on intensive stakeholder consultation. But in the end a user-driven approach largely depends on the ways the results are presented. In U-Multirank a number of features are included to increase the user-friendliness.

In the same way as there is no one-size-fits-all-approach to rankings in terms of indicators, there is no one-size-fits-all approach to the presentation of the results. The presentation modes should allow for addressing different groups of users differently. According to the Berlin Principles, rankings should 'provide consumers with a clear understanding of all of the factors used to develop a ranking, and offer them a choice in how rankings are displayed' (International Ranking Expert Group, 2006, principle 15). U-Multirank, as with any ranking, will have to strike a balance between the need to reduce the complexity of information on the one hand and offering detailed information that meets the requirements of specific users on the other.

U-Multirank seeks to offer a tailor-made approach to presenting results, serving the information needs of different groups of users and taking into account their level of knowledge about higher education and higher education institutions. Basic access is provided by the various modes of presentation described above (overview tables, personalized rankings and institutional profiles). In addition access to and navigation through the web tool will be made highly user-driven by specific 'entrances' for different groups of users (e.g. students, researchers/academic staff, institutional administrators, employers) offering specific information regarding the results. Such a tailor-made approach implies different kinds and degrees of 'guiding' users through the ranking processes.

Another important aspect of user-friendliness is transparency about the methodology used in rankings. For U-Multirank this will include within the web tool a description of the basic methodological elements (institutional and field-based rankings, grouping approach), a description of underlying data sources (e.g. self-reported institutional data, surveys, bibliometric data, patent data) and a clear definition and explanation of indicators (including an explanation of their relevance and what they are measuring). This description of the methodology can be linked to the presentation of results (e.g. by using hyperlinks) and hence increase users' understanding of the ranking substantially.

In the end the user-friendliness of a ranking tool cannot be assessed *a priori*. Tracking ranking use will be important. How will users choose to navigate through the web tool? What indicators are selected most frequently in personalized rankings? How deeply do users examine the results and where do they stop navigation? Tracking of user behavior will be systematically built into the development of the web tool to allow continuous adaptation to the needs and interests of users.

References

International Ranking Expert Group. (2006). *Berlin principles on ranking of higher education institutions*. Retrieved June 24, 2006, from http://www.che.de/downloads/Berlin_Principles_IREG_534.pdf

van Raan, A. (2007). Challenges in the Ranking of Universities. In J. Sadlak, L. N. C. (Eds.), *The world-class university and ranking: aiming beyond status*. UNESCO-CEPES: Bucharest.

Yarbrough, D. B., Shulha, L. M., Hopson, R. K., & Caruthers, F. A. (2011). *The program evaluation standards: a guide for evaluators and evaluation users* (3rd ed.). Sage: Thousand Oaks, CA.

Chapter 11
Concluding Remarks

Frans A. van Vught and Frank Ziegele

In this book we have addressed the general topic of rankings in higher education and research as well as the development of a new multidimensional ranking tool. We looked at the various issues surrounding the ranking debates, and analyzed current practices and their impact. We have been critical of some of the current ranking practices and methodologies and have developed our own approach. In Part I of this volume we discussed the current practices in general and drew a number of conclusions with respect to a new and better methodology. In Part II we expanded on this new approach, which we call U-Multirank. U-Multirank is intended to address the weaknesses in the existing approaches and to offer a multidimensional and user-driven perspective to ranking. We present U-Multirank as a new ranking tool, completely different from existing global ranking instruments.

This book is the result of almost 2 years of intensive work on all facets of international rankings by a team of researchers who conducted the analyses of current ranking approaches and designed and tested the alternative new multidimensional instrument. Several have also contributed to this volume, in which ranking issues are addressed on three levels:

- We analyzed the 'state of the art' of existing rankings, identifying their features, strengths and weaknesses as well as their influence.
- We drafted a new concept for international rankings, labeled 'U-Multirank'.
- We carried out empirical testing of the new multidimensional concept via a worldwide pilot study.

F.A. van Vught (✉)
University of Twente, Enschede, The Netherlands

F. Ziegele
Centre for Higher Education (CHE), Gütersloh, Germany

This final chapter presents some concluding remarks on ranking in higher education and research in general as well as on the applicability of our new multidimensional approach.

In any ranking the basic normative ideas should be made transparent. We have formulated a set of normative positions for our specific approach to ranking: user-drivenness, multidimensionality and multileveledness, a participative approach.

In the introductory chapter we described our epistemological and conceptual normative ideas regarding ranking. We introduced three basic ideas.

First of all we suggested that in our view there is no such thing as 'an objective ranking' and that the notion of what should be seen as 'good performance' behind any ranking is always related to the subjective assumptions of the ranking producer. These subjective positions about what is and what is not 'good performance' are not always transparent in existing rankings, leading to the risk that the subjectivity is hidden and a false impression is created of a so-called 'objective performance list'.

A hypothetical solution would be to create and accept an 'authority' that would define the 'right' indicators following the idea of an ideal university. However, this proves to be impossible in higher education, since the diversity of university profiles and the diversity of stakeholders' preferences doesn't easily allow consensus about a definitive set of criteria defining the best performance for all stakeholders. The only way to deal with these diversities is to take the normative position of a user-driven approach, accepting the subjective character of a ranking as a design principle and leading to the empowerment of its users This also implies a multilevel approach: some situations in which stakeholders' decisions could be supported by rankings refer to the institutional and some to the field level.

The user-driven approach does not exclude the option that certain 'authorities' would create their own rankings, claiming that their choice of indicators reflect the most relevant aspects of performance in higher education and research. As a matter of fact these 'authoritative rankings' are a special form of the application of the principle of 'user-drivenness', allowing specific organizations, representative bodies, client groups or institutions to present their specific normative positions as convincing and attractive views on what should be seen as relevant and less relevant performance.

Our analysis of the existing global rankings showed that these rankings only cover a small percentage of the total number of higher education institutions worldwide Moreover, they only address a very special higher education institution profile: the 'globally active, comprehensive, research-intensive university', which is presented as the most attractive general 'world brand' because of its research-based performance and reputation in the international context. All other institutional profiles are not addressed in these current rankings, simply because their characteristics are not covered by the indicators applied.

To make up for this deficiency – and as a second normative starting point – we suggest taking a multidimensional approach to ranking. A multidimensional approach allows a large variety of institutional profiles to be included in rankings, thus paying attention to the horizontal diversity of institutional missions and profiles. In addition, the multidimensional approach offers the opportunity to distinguish the various 'functions' of higher education and research institutions and to assess the performances according to these various functions, rather than forcing institutions to all strive towards a dominant profile of research-intensiveness. Finally, the multidimensional approach opens up the possibility to compare sets of institutions with similar missions and profiles, which appears to be more useful than ranking institutional profiles that are very different and can hardly be compared.

A third normative idea behind our views on ranking regards the 'participative approach'. So far a participative approach has hardly been used in global rankings. The idea to involve the users of the rankings in the processes of selecting the indicators and compiling the data is relatively new in the ranking world. We suggest that the application of feedback loops with users leads to a higher level of usefulness for these users, while also creating a better chance of having access to data. Experience shows that stakeholders often have strong feelings about the relevance of indicators, and are eager to interpret the outcomes of rankings in the context of their personal ideas about quality in higher education and research. A participative approach to ranking emphasizes the principle of user sovereignty and stimulates users' reflections on the relative importance of indicators and performances.

We offer our basic normative ideas in order to be as transparent as possible about our views on ranking. These ideas are based on our analyses of the current ranking instruments and their results and impacts. But they remain normative positions; our normative positions.

Quality assurance activities and rankings in higher education and research are related, but not similar.

In our view quality assurance activities and rankings are both transparency tools. Both are information tools designed to communicate information on higher education and research institutions' efforts and performances to external and internal stakeholders. But quality assurance activities first of all aim to provide 'proof of quality' to stakeholders, and their information provision function is secondary to this objective. Rankings (and other transparency tools, like classifications and league tables) are instruments that intend to create transparency about the activities and performances of higher education and research institutions. But, by doing so, these instruments often imply an implicit view on the relevance of the efforts and outcomes of these institutions. As a matter of fact, the choice of indicators, criteria and data presentation modes in transparency tools reflect an, often implicit, definition of quality. This is a main reason why, in our approach, we not only try to be as transparent as possible about our own choices but also emphasize the importance of a user-driven approach: it should be left to the stakeholders/users to decide which indicators, and hence which aspects of quality, should be the focus of a certain ranking.

Quality assurance activities provide 'proof of quality' for two main reasons: accountability and quality enhancement. The accountability function leads to an externally focused perspective on quality assurance, while the enhancement function is mainly internally focused. In both orientations the provision of information of course plays a major role, but this role is largely limited to reassuring stakeholders that the quality is satisfactory (as in accreditation) and/or collegially controlled (as in peer review systems). An active focus on the support of the decision-making processes of stakeholders is usually not found in quality assurance activities.

Rankings intend to bring transparency to the performance of higher education and research institutions and to provide information on their performance to a variety of stakeholders. As such, rankings are decision support instruments that seek to assist stakeholders in forming their own judgments on the basis of relevant information. Rankings address the problems of information deficiency and asymmetry regarding higher education and research resulting from the fact that, in economic terms, the activities of higher education and research institutions are to be seen as 'experience goods' or 'credence goods'.

Quality assurance activities and rankings are nevertheless clearly interrelated. The provision of information is a major aspect of any quality assurance activity and hence also rankings can play an important role in quality assurance. In particular when external actors are to be involved in judging the quality of performance of higher education and research rankings could become a highly useful instrument. In addition, rankings support the decisions of a variety of clients of higher education and research institutions and thus inspire these institutions to communicate their qualities in the best possible ways. Rankings in this sense stimulate the internal quality cultures of higher education and research institutions, and invite them to present their results according to their specific missions and profiles.

Quality assurance and rankings are not to be seen as competitive transparency tools. They have different functions and orientations, but are also clearly interrelated. Both are crucial instruments for the further development of higher education and research worldwide.

Although several methodological flaws exist in their current applications rankings nevertheless appear to be attractive to many stakeholders and have major impacts.

Our overview and analysis of the state of the art in rankings in Part I of this volume showed that an inventory of the methodological problems regarding rankings produces the following list:

- Rankings are not always clear about their specific clients and target groups. They often appear to assume that whatever information is provided should be relevant to all potential clients. Moreover, regularly the implicit assumption appears to be that the availability of indicators also defines the relevance of indicators.
- Most rankings only address institutions for higher education and research as a whole, and appear to ignore the internal diversity within these institutions. Differences in performance between faculties, departments, centers and other units within the institutions are not taken into account, and neither are differences between academic fields.
- Most rankings appear to focus on a very limited part of the activity profiles of higher education and research institutions, in particular on research productivity and research reputation. At the same time these rankings appear to suggest that they address the overall quality of the institutions, implicitly limiting the concept of quality to the dimension for which (bibliometric) data are most easily available.

The other dimensions of the activity profiles (teaching & learning, knowledge transfer, international orientation, regional engagement) are largely ignored.
- Many rankings provide composite overall indicators in which sets of weighted indicators are combined into a single performance measurement. Composite indicators are highly problematic because they lack the conceptual base from which they should be calculated and its designers cannot provide the theoretical and empirical arguments for assigning particular weights to the constituent parts. In addition, the choice for certain indicators and weights imply an implicit definition of the 'ideal model' of a higher education and research institution. Furthermore, composite indicators appear to be far from statistically robust and they tend to patronize users and clients since, by providing fixed combinations and weights, they imply choices about the relevance and appropriateness of certain indicators.
- The many rankings that provide league tables ignore the statistical problems related to the characteristics of methodological scaling and the existence of standard errors in data. League tables have to assume continuous ratio scales and by doing so exaggerate differences between institutions ranked in these tables.
- Most rankings are unable to address the differences in performance that are the result of cultural, language and other contextual factors. This is particularly problematic in the bibliometric assessment of research performance, where the effect of differences in publication cultures is clearly visible. The existing international bibliometric databases are still facing the challenges of publication cultures that are not focused on traditional academic, international, English-publishing journals, and of including research institutions that are not part of university organizations.
- Rankings often are insufficiently transparent about their methodologies, and regularly appear to adapt these methodologies without being explicit about it. The outcomes of rankings are not always replicable because of methodological and/or statistical changes.

Yet, while rankings are often criticized – and usually rightly so – their impact is nevertheless large. Several categories of stakeholders are heavily influenced by ranking results, although they are not always willing to publicly admit so. Institutional leaders react to the outcomes of rankings in their institutional strategies and communication behavior. Students appear to take ranking results into account when making their choices for enrolling into institutions and programs. Policy-makers use ranking outcomes to design and adapt national higher education and research policies (including funding, merging and excellence policies). Employers appear to pay attention to rankings in their recruitment and contracting policies. Journalists report on ranking outcomes to the general public, thus creating an impact on institutional reputations.

Rankings also have system-level effects. They fuel the higher education 'reputation race'. They create public images of assumed quality. They contribute to academic stratification and institutional wealth inequality. And they trigger institutional behavior of 'gaming the results' (see Chap. 5). The various impacts of the outcomes of rankings make it clear that there is sufficient reason to take rankings seriously and to try to improve their conceptual and methodological bases.

Improving the current approaches to ranking is highly needed but offers some major challenges.

As just noted, our analysis of the various higher education and research rankings around the world pointed out a number of shortcomings. It also should be noticed, however, that some ranking organizations are taking initiatives that intend to improve their existing methods and to make them more transparent. In addition, the 'Berlin Principles' designed by the International Ranking Export Group (IREG) and the suggestions by a special expert group (AUBR Expert Group) set up by the DG Research & Innovation of the European Commission show that there is an increasing international awareness regarding the need to strengthen the conceptual and methodological foundations of rankings. Multidimensionality and a clear and targeted user-focus are mentioned as important aspects of the further development of ranking in higher education and research.

As may have become clear in Part II of this volume, these new aspects of ranking are not easy to develop. With respect to multidimensionality the challenge is first of all the availability and international comparability of data. If we move beyond the traditional focus on bibliometric data, rankings largely have to rely on institutional data provision. Multidimensional rankings that want to take the variety of institutional missions and profiles into account cannot be realized without the application of institutional and student surveys. Therefore these rankings have to succeed in convincing higher education and research institutions to invest time and energy in data-collection and reporting. This makes multidimensional rankings vulnerable: if they don't see clear benefits from the ranking outcomes, institutions may not be inclined to get involved in data provision.

Another challenge is the potential risk of a limited attractiveness of multidimensional rankings in comparison with monodimensional league tables and composite indicators, particularly to the general public. Simple league tables are often striking, and are easily taken up by the media. Multidimensional rankings that address a variety of target groups may offer more elaborate information, but cannot be reduced to an overall list of winners and losers. Multidimensional rankings need to invest in presentation modes and communication processes, explaining to clients and stakeholders how the various outcomes can be interpreted. In order to be effective in these communication processes multidimensional ranking producers will have to analyze the decision-making processes of user groups (such as students, parents, institutional leaders, policy-makers, business leaders) and the information needs in these processes. In our view, these needs can be revealed by intensive stakeholder dialogue; what we have called 'a participative approach'.

The user-driven approach to ranking presents another specific challenge. If a ranking is based on the user's selection of institutions and indicators, the ranking result is not a unique performance list such as the ones that normally are the outcome of the existing rankings. In a user-driven approach users can produce their own 'personalized' rankings. Eventually these personalized rankings may become 'search engines' that present information ('hits') based on combinations of search terms (indicators). Such search engines will be based on smart technologies (of indexing and storing links) and on the surfing behavior of large numbers of users, resulting in visually attractive and user-friendly information provision. Ranking information will thus become integrated in new communication tools based on internet and social media. The release of a new ranking outcome will not the publication of an updated list, but the integration of a data update in the ranking database, allowing a variety of users to produce a large number of their own personalized rankings in an interactive way.

We nevertheless still call such a multidimensional, user-driven methodology a 'ranking' since it remains a tool to render vertical diversity transparent. Also multidimensional ranking results show high and low performances and position institutions/programs in the context of the performance of their peers and competitors. But multidimensional ranking results also offer differentiated pictures of strengths and weaknesses of institutions and programs. They show differentiated performance profiles to a variety of users.

The challenges of further developing the methodology of ranking in higher education and research are substantial, but – we feel – must nevertheless be addressed. Rankings do exist in higher education, and will not easily lose their impact. Criticism of rankings is relevant, but not sufficient to create better approaches. New instruments must be designed and tested. U-Multirank is the result of such efforts to design and develop a new approach. While U-Multirank cannot immediately resolve all the methodological problems of the current rankings, it at least addresses a number of these challenges.

U-Multirank is a new ranking tool, based on a coherent set of assumptions and ideas regarding multidimensional and user-driven ranking.

U-Multirank is a transparency instrument offering multiple ranking options to users. It is based on our normative positions regarding ranking: user-drivenness, multidimensionality, multileveledness and a participative approach. U-Multirank recognizes that higher education and research institutions serve multiple purposes and perform a range of different activities at different levels. It is a tool that allows a number of different rankings according to the selection of dimensions and indications by users.

U-Multirank is user-driven: it is *you* (the client/stakeholder/user) who is enabled to rank comparable profiles according to the criteria important to *you*. The pilot project during which we designed and tested U-Multirank has specifically been focused on this multiple ranking concept. Taking this concept seriously, we not only distinguished five different dimensions regarding the functions performed by higher education and research institutions, we also addressed two levels regarding these functions (institutional and field level) and incorporated the user-driven approach of a multitude of potential users. The result is a truly multidimensional ranking tool that allows the comparison of a multiple set of different activity profiles, thus creating the possibility for a large variety of higher education and research institutions to compare themselves to organizations with similar or related profiles. U-Multirank does not limit itself to a single, dominant profile of only one type of higher education institution, i.e. the research-intensive, comprehensive research university. It also allows regionally focused institutions, bachelor degree awarding colleges, polytechnics, art schools, music academies, specialized research centers and many other types of higher educations and research organization to appear in international rankings and to benchmark themselves at an international level with counterpart institutions that may have similar orientations on user-defined dimensions.

U-Multirank intends to serve the needs of a broad variety of users, allowing them to select dimensions and indicators according to their own criteria and preferences. Different users can create their own 'personalized rankings' focusing their own specific rankings at the topics regarding higher education and research that they judge to be most relevant. In addition, U-Multirank offers the option to present 'authoritative rankings', in which a specific selection of dimensions and indicators is pre-defined and selected on the basis of the 'authority' of a certain organization, institution, association or network. Authoritative rankings can be produced and published on behalf of higher education membership organizations, specific associations of higher education institutions, national or international public authorities, client representation organizations, independent foundations, etc. The only condition is that these organizations define (and motivate) their selection of dimensions and indicators.

U-Multirank also has an eye for the empirical fact that higher education and research institutions perform differently in different fields. Faculties, departments, centers and various other units within higher education institutions often have their own view on relevant performance in their specific disciplinary or interdisciplinary fields. U-Multirank offers the option to produce rankings at two different levels of activity, the institutional level and the field level. By doing so, U-Multirank addresses the internal diversity in higher education and research institutions.

In addition, U-Multirank intends to allow the adaptation of indicators to the specific characteristic of fields. An important aspect of the participative approach is the involvement of field experts and stakeholders in the process of defining and selecting indicators for field-based rankings.

'Version 1.0' of U-Multirank shows that a multidimensional, user-driven ranking tool is feasible at a global level.

The U-Multirank pilot project proved that a user-driven, multidimensional ranking tool is feasible at world scale. During the pilot project a broad variety of feasibility aspects was explored and tested. We analyzed the conceptual clarity of the sets of indicators; we tested the availability and consistency of data for these indicators. We studied the feasibility of the data collection instruments. And we explored the potential for up-scaling the pilot application to both a global scale and a broad spectrum of fields.

The pilot test shows that the number of feasible indicators is more limited in some dimensions than in other. In particular in the dimensions 'knowledge exchange' at the field level and 'regional engagement' at both institutional and field levels feasible and applicable indicators appear to be only limitedly available. The future challenge certainly is to design and develop more and generally acceptable indicators in these areas.

Regarding the up-scaling to a global level, the pilot project results are encouraging. There appeared to be a strong expression of worldwide interest to participate in the pilot sample, although in some parts of the world the recruitment of institutions for participation in the pilot project proved to be difficult. We concluded that there is a broad stakeholder interest in the further development and implementation of U-Multirank and we expect that substantial numbers of higher education and research institutions from all over the world will be willing to participate in multidimensional global rankings.

The extension of U-Multirank to a broad variety of disciplinary and interdisciplinary fields may also be expected to be feasible. The set of field indicators applied in the pilot study may be regarded as a solid and useful base for such an extension, although it also should be noted that in order to allow a broader coverage of fields, specific field indicators will have to be developed. As mentioned before, for this the participation and commitment of field experts and stakeholders will be highly important.

U-Multirank offers some innovative ideas to the international debate on and the state of the art of ranking.

The characteristics of U-Multirank, in particular its emphases on multidimensionality and a user-driven approach, appear to already have influenced the international debates on ranking in higher education and research. Various other international rankings have introduced new elements into their own approaches that are rather similar to the basic approach of U-Multirank. The expansion of data collection beyond bibliometric data, the development of field-based rankings and the introduction of user-driven weights in indicator selection processes are examples of recent adaptations in existing ranking methods that might be triggered by our U-Multirank methodology. But a coherent and comprehensive ranking methodology that addresses the broad variety of functions of higher education and research institutions, and that allows both personalized and authoritative rankings is so far only found in U-Multirank. U-Multirank offers a new epistemologically sound and conceptually and methodologically transparent approach to global ranking.

In addition U-Multirank brings some specific new elements to the state of the art of international ranking, potentially leading to substantial progress in ranking methods. A first new element is the two-step approach of combining a mapping and ranking transparency tool. By using U-Map, the horizontal diversity of higher education and research systems is addressed and the various activity profiles of higher education and research institutions are made transparent, allowing the identification of institutions with similar or related activity profiles. By applying U-Multirank to groups of institutions with (partially) similar activity profiles multiple rankings of groups of comparable institutions can be created and specific performance profiles can be shown. A second new element regards the design and implementation of a number of innovative bibliometric indicators, analyzing co-publications (of academic organizations with respectively industrial, international and regional co-authors) as a way to report on the performance in the dimensions 'knowledge transfer', 'international orientation' and 'regional engagement'. A third new element concerns the introduction of a global student satisfaction survey instrument, which when tested proved to be feasible in a global context. Finally, the introduction of field-based rankings offers the option to root the rankings in the academic community and to increase their acceptance as relevant and useful transparency tools.

For the further development and implementation of U-Multirank a number of issues will have to be seriously addressed.

Now that 'Version 1.0' of U-Multirank is available, its further development and international implementation can be taken up. However, in order to make an effective international rollout possible, a number of conditions will have to be fulfilled.

First of all, the further development of applicable and widely acceptable indicators will have to be stimulated. In particular in the dimensions 'regional engagement' further discussions and testing will be needed to allow a growing international consensus on feasible indicators. Similarly, at the field level a debate will have to take place on the relevant indicators for 'knowledge transfer'. In addition, in order to allow the expansion of the number of field-based rankings, field-specific indicators will have to be selected and added to the base set of field-based indicators.

Secondly the availability of international comparative data needs to be improved. So far international databases comprise only limited data at the level of higher education and research institutions. Even regarding the crucial dimension of 'teaching & learning' comparable data on for instance labor market success of graduates appear to be nonexistent. A concerted international effort to improve the data-availability will be crucial for the further development of international transparency tools. The international harmonization of data-collection standards, the integration of national databases into joint international databases and the combination of international data-sets are highly important aspects of such a concerted international effort.

Thirdly, 'user-friendly' and attractive presentation modes of the outcomes of rankings will be needed. Both experienced and 'lay' users should be enabled to make use of performance rankings. The presentation modes should include attractive graphical presentations (like the 'sunburst chart' applied in U-Multirank) and make use of symbols and colors (like in the 'grouping approach') to create clear and coherent impressions at first glance. A web-application should provide clear guidance and explanation, and in particular address the needs of specific user-groups. A differentiated information provision format should be an integrated part of the web tool. The presentation modes should refrain from simplistic and risky methods (like league tables) and be based on sound methodological principles.

Fourth, given the fact that international databases are limited to bibliometric and patent data, data-collection from higher education and research institutions will remain necessary. Data delivery should therefore be sufficiently attractive for these institutions. The costs of collecting and delivering institutional data should be out weighted by their benefits such as the ranking outcomes. On the costs side, 'prefilling' of questionnaires with externally available data and coordination of data collection processes (now often organized as separate tracks) will reduce the workload for the institutions involved. On the benefits side, offering benchmarking opportunities with comparable institutions and tailor-made ranking outcomes applicable in internal planning & control processes may stimulate the willingness to deliver data.

Generally speaking, for institutional data-collection to be successful the organization of the data-collection processes should be clearly focused on the costs/benefits balances of the higher education and research institutions involved.

Finally, a crucial condition for a successful international implementation of U-Multirank will be its institutionalization. The 'authority' of the actor organizing the ranking processes and the 'ownership' of the data are sensitive issues in the world of ranking and should be carefully approached. In our view, U-Multirank should be independently institutionalized, with extensive advisory and communication facilities for experts and stakeholders. There should be no direct decision-making authority for political bodies, governments or interest groups, and there should be a highly transparent governance structure to safeguard the independent character of the ranking outcomes. Funding could come from independent foundations and from sponsoring public and private organizations, as well as from the sales of standardized products and services (such as data visualization, benchmarking support processes, SWOT analyses). Interested parties could be invited to create and publish their specific 'authoritative rankings'.

The future of U-Multirank and of the further development and implementation of multidimensional ranking in general to a large extent depends on how the various issues just mentioned will be addressed. Multidimensional and user-driven rankings in higher education and research have been proven to be feasible. The coming years will show whether they will also be internationally realized.

Index

A
Academic Ranking of World Universities (ARWU), 18, 26, 28, 29, 31, 33, 42–44, 46, 47, 56, 58–59, 61, 65, 66, 68, 78, 137
Accountability, 11–21, 79, 181
Accreditation, 14, 19–21, 33, 100, 101, 113, 132, 181
Activities, 3, 4, 13, 17, 18, 27, 30, 33, 35, 52, 54, 58, 68, 76, 86–89, 94, 98, 101, 106, 109, 112–117, 119–121, 123, 125, 126, 129–132, 136, 139, 145, 148, 181–183, 185–187
AHELO. *See* Assessment of Higher Education Learning Outcomes (AHELO)
Anchoring vignettes, 140
ARWU. *See* Academic Ranking of World Universities (ARWU)
Ashby's Law of Requisite Variety, 11
Aspen Institute, 31
Assessment of Higher Education Learning Outcomes (AHELO), 50–51, 99
AUBR Expert Group, 35, 41, 47, 51, 52, 95, 184
Australian Research Quality Framework (ROF), 52
Authoritative rankings, 94, 180, 186, 187, 189

B
Benchmarking, 18, 27, 29, 32, 52, 77, 98, 122, 188, 189
Berlin principles, 40, 47–48, 78, 79, 87, 95, 176, 184
Bias, 45–47, 52, 58, 59, 61, 78, 79, 118, 122, 123, 168, 175

Bibliometric indicators. *See* Indicators
Bologna process, 49, 99
Business school rankings, 28, 31, 65
Business week, 26, 65

C
Callaert, J., 125, 135
Carnegie classification, 26, 27, 35, 53–54
Carnegie foundation, 26, 53, 54
CHE excellence ranking, 30, 63, 64
CHE ranking, 28–30, 32, 72, 77, 100, 165, 167, 169
Classification, 12–14, 19, 25–37, 52–55, 62, 93, 94, 110, 112, 121, 126, 128, 129, 136, 140, 175, 181
Commission for Employment and Skills (UKCES), 32
Comparability, 19, 33, 34, 37, 47, 53, 79, 87, 92–94, 98, 100, 103, 109, 111, 130, 140, 145, 175, 184
Composite indicators. *See* Indicators
Contextuality, 46, 87, 95, 111, 174–176
Coverage, 46, 86, 107, 127, 128, 130, 132, 140, 164, 187
Credence good, 12, 89, 182

D
D'Hombres, B., 45
Disciplines, 15, 17, 28, 48, 49, 51, 52, 63, 86, 101, 102, 107–110, 113, 115, 118
Diversity
 diversity within, 41–42, 182
 horizontal diversity, 13, 75, 94, 180, 187
 vertical diversity, 13, 74, 94, 185

E
Eccles, J.S., 44
Economist ranking, 26, 65
EHEA. *See* European Higher Education Area (EHEA)
Ehrenberg, R.G., 74, 76
Epping, E., 125, 135
EUMIDA. *See* European University Data Collection project (EUMIDA)
European Higher Education Area (EHEA), 29, 49, 50
European Observatory for Assessment of University-based Research, 51
European University Data Collection project (EUMIDA), 35, 114, 126, 129–131
Experience good, 12, 89, 182

F
Feasibility, 16, 35, 50, 85, 86, 92, 93, 98, 125, 135–138, 140–165, 170, 186
Federkeil, G., 25, 39, 85, 97, 125, 135, 167
Field-based ranking, 5, 6, 12, 28–29, 31, 42, 58–60, 62–67, 79, 93, 97, 99–102, 104, 106, 108, 109, 111, 114–116, 118, 122, 123, 136, 140, 143–145, 148–150, 153–155, 158, 160, 163, 165, 169, 170, 172, 176, 186–188
File, J., 135, 167
Financial times ranking, 26, 28, 31, 65
Focused institutional ranking, 93, 97, 101, 106, 108–110, 114, 115, 117, 118, 122, 142, 146, 151, 152, 155, 156, 161, 162, 169, 172
Forbes ranking, 26, 62–64

G
Gaming the rankings, 35, 71, 76–78
G-Factor ranking, 68
Global rankings, 4–6, 27, 28, 30, 33, 34, 43, 55, 62, 67, 68, 73, 75, 78, 86, 93, 125, 137, 164, 168, 179–181, 187
Google, 68, 127
Grouping, 26, 48, 52, 94–95, 170, 176, 188
Guardian ranking, 26, 44

H
HEEACT rankings, 28, 32, 42–44, 56, 61, 78, 109, 167
Hirsh index, 17
Horizontal diversity. *See* Diversity
Humanities, 30, 41, 46, 56, 59, 85, 87, 107, 110, 113, 115, 127, 128, 148, 165

I
IHEP. *See* Institute for Higher Education Policy (IHEP)
Impact, 3, 12, 16, 19, 30, 34, 42, 46, 47, 49, 51, 52, 56, 58, 59, 61, 63, 65, 67, 68, 71–80, 86, 89–91, 99, 103, 106, 107, 110, 112, 113, 116, 117, 121, 126, 127, 139, 160, 176, 179, 181–183, 185
Indicators. *See also* U-multirank
 bibliometric indicators, 49, 51, 58, 59, 107, 108, 139, 145, 160, 187
 composite indicators, 4, 43, 44, 65, 75, 79, 87, 103, 119, 145, 155, 173, 183, 184
 range of indicators, 18
Input, 3, 5, 6, 21, 48, 89–91, 94, 95, 99, 101, 102, 107–109, 113–115, 117, 129, 130
Institute for Higher Education Policy (IHEP), 27
Institution, 2, 11, 25, 40, 71, 85, 97, 125, 135, 167–169, 180
 types of institutions, 78, 168
Institutional profiles, 27, 53, 86, 94, 95, 136, 168, 169, 175, 176, 180, 181
Integrated Postsecondary Education Data System (IPEDS), 35, 53
Interactive ranking. *See* User-driven ranking
International orientation. *See* U-Multirank, dimension International Orientation
International Ranking Expert Group (IREG), 47, 48, 52, 176
International rankings, 3–5, 17, 34, 52, 53, 61, 66, 78, 79, 92, 137, 165, 167, 179, 186, 187
IPEDS. *See* Integrated Postsecondary Education Data System (IPEDS)
IREG. *See* International Ranking Expert Group (IREG)

J
Jongbloed, B., 97, 125, 135

K
Kaiser, F., 85, 97, 125, 135, 167
Kerr, C., 26
Knowledge transfer. *See* U-Multirank, dimension Knowledge Transfer

L
League table, 1, 2, 4, 11–14, 26–37, 39–48, 55, 60–62, 65, 67–68, 72, 74–79, 86, 87, 89, 91, 94, 169, 170, 181, 183, 184, 188

Index 193

Leiden ranking, 17, 26, 29, 30, 32, 43, 49, 56, 62, 78, 109
Leuven, K.U., 129
Lisbon Council, 175

M
Mapping, 16, 94, 168–169, 187
Matching, 28, 48
Matthew effect, 72, 75–76
Medicine, 46, 58, 59, 72, 165
Methodology, 4–6, 28, 36, 39, 44, 45, 47, 48, 59–61, 65, 79, 80, 113, 130, 176, 179, 185
Mode-2 research, 18, 19, 72
Multidimensionality, 1, 3, 4, 40, 87, 95, 180, 184, 185, 187
Multileveledness, 1, 185

N
National ranking, 26–30, 32, 34, 42, 43, 47, 78
National student survey (NSS), 36
National Survey of Student Engagement (NSSE), 34, 36
Natural sciences. *See* Sciences
New Public Management, 15, 19, 20
NSSE. *See* National Survey of Student Engagement (NSSE)

O
OECD, 34, 43, 50, 106, 112, 121, 129
Oldenburg, H., 14
Outcome, 2, 15, 37, 46, 48–51, 61, 72, 90, 99, 103, 106, 113, 117, 125, 135–166, 181, 183–185, 188, 189
Output, 3, 4, 13, 16, 18, 21, 34, 46, 55, 56, 63, 67, 72, 74, 75, 89, 91, 99, 106–111, 113, 126, 128, 130, 139, 146–149, 165, 170–172

P
Patents, 18, 34, 54, 61, 68, 107, 112, 115, 116, 121, 125, 126, 128–130, 132, 137–140, 151, 153, 155, 176, 188
PATSTAT, 34, 129, 139
Peer review, 14–21, 51, 57, 182
Performance, 5, 13–21, 26, 30, 31, 41–43, 45, 46, 49, 51, 55, 59, 61, 63, 66, 67, 71, 73, 75–79, 85–91, 94, 95, 97–100, 106–108, 112–115, 120, 121, 127, 128, 130–132, 139, 148, 164, 168, 170, 173–176, 180–188

Personalized ranking, 44, 93, 167, 169–173, 176, 177, 184–186
Perspektywy ranking, 28, 32, 43
Popper, K.R., 2
Pre-filling, 55, 188
Prestige, 13, 26, 28, 68, 73, 78
Profile. *See* Institutional profiles

Q
QS National System Strength Ranking, 175
QS World Rankings, 66
Quality, 3, 5, 11–21, 26, 27, 29, 36, 40–43, 45, 50, 53, 55, 56, 61–63, 71, 74, 75, 77, 78, 85, 89, 90, 92, 99, 100, 102, 104, 105, 107, 109–111, 118, 119, 126, 127, 144, 165, 167, 175, 183
Quality assurance, 12, 14–21, 33, 35, 48, 49, 52, 55, 79, 99, 181, 182

R
RAE. *See* Research Assessment Exercise (RAE)
RatER rating, 68
Regional engagement. *See* U-Multirank, dimension Regional Engagement
Relevance, 6, 16, 19, 44, 66, 90, 91, 97, 98, 101, 103, 106, 108, 116, 119, 140, 142–144, 146, 148–154, 156, 158, 160–164, 171, 176, 181–183
Reliability, 20, 36, 55, 78, 92, 98, 100, 109, 120, 140
Reputation, 4, 29, 30, 35, 36, 41, 42, 44, 57–63, 75–78, 117, 119, 180, 182, 183
Reputation race, 13, 28, 41, 43, 74–75, 183
Research. *See* U-Multirank, dimension research
Research Assessment Exercise (RAE), 15–17
Research institute, 47, 126–128
Research university, 4, 12, 13, 26, 55, 66, 75, 78, 87, 106, 168, 186
Response rate, 36
Roessler, I., 135

S
Saisana, M., 45
Salmi, J., 73
Sciences, 4, 15, 18, 30, 31, 42, 45, 46, 49, 56, 58, 59, 61, 62, 68, 75, 85, 87, 106–111, 115, 116, 122, 127, 128, 136, 138, 139, 148, 165
The Scientist's ranking, 67
SCImago ranking, 67

Scopus, 34, 46, 67, 72, 127, 128
Shanghai Jiao Tong Ranking. *See* Academic Ranking of World Universities (ARWU)
Stakeholder involvement, 5, 6, 97–98
Student survey, 36, 100, 131, 133, 138, 144, 145, 184
Studychoice 123, 26, 31, 32, 34, 48–49, 63, 64

T

Teaching and learning. *See* U-Multirank, dimension teaching & learning
THE ranking. *See* Times higher education (THE) ranking
Third mission, 4, 43, 113, 120, 138
Thomson Reuters, 18, 34, 43, 45, 46, 62, 72, 110, 127, 128
Tijssen, R., 125, 135
Times higher education (THE) ranking, 26, 41, 59–60, 137
Transparency, 11–21, 29, 30, 33, 48, 79, 80, 85, 166, 168, 176, 182, 185
Transparency tools, 2, 11–13, 27, 34, 39–41, 46, 48, 52–68, 77, 88, 90, 92, 94, 164, 181, 182, 187, 188
Tuning project, 50

U

U-Map, 26, 27, 54–55, 90, 93, 94, 115, 126, 129–132, 136, 168–169, 173, 175, 187
U-Multirank
dimension International Orientation, 120
dimension Knowledge Transfer, 120
dimension Regional Engagement, 121
dimension research, 112, 113, 131
dimension teaching & learning, 99
indicators, 39, 90, 91, 94, 97, 98, 100, 108, 120, 125, 127, 128, 140, 165, 168, 169, 173, 186

University of Applied Science, 87
User-driven ranking, 1, 6, 12, 168, 170, 185, 186, 189
User-friendliness, 6, 167, 176–177
US News & World Report, 26, 30, 32, 43, 60, 62, 65

V

Validity
concept validity, 78, 98, 140, 142–144, 146, 149–154, 156, 158, 161–163
construct validity, 92, 98, 140, 142–144, 146, 149–154, 156, 158, 161–163
face validity, 78, 98, 140, 142–144, 146, 149–154, 156, 158, 161–163
van Vught, F., 1, 11, 25, 39, 71, 85, 135, 167, 179
Vertical diversity. *See* Diversity
Visualization, 169, 189

W

Wall Street Journal ranking, 65
Washington Accord, 100
Web of Science. *See* Thomson Reuters
Webometrics, 28–30, 32, 42, 68, 78
Westerheijden, D.F., 1, 11, 12, 25, 39, 71, 85, 97
World-class university, 55, 73, 78
Wuhan University ranking, 67

Z

Ziegele, F., 1, 135, 167, 179
Z-score aggregation, 45

Printed by Publishers' Graphics LLC
BT20121014.19.20.11